Winning Reviews

KU-113-751

Other books by the editors

Yehuda Baruch: MANAGING CAREERS – THEORY AND PRACTICE
Sherry E. Sullivan (with Lisa Mainiero): THE OPT-OUT REVOLT: WHY PEOPLE
ARE LEAVING COMPANIES TO CREATE KALEIDOSCOPE CAREERS

Winning Reviews

A Guide for Evaluating Scholarly Writing

Edited by Yehuda Baruch, Sherry E. Sullivan and
Hazlon N. Schepmyer

Selection and editorial matter © Yehuda Baruch, Sherry E. Sullivan and
Hazlon N. Schepmyer 2006
Individual chapters © contributors 2006
Book cover design by Tony Hooper and Aya Baruch

All rights reserved. No reproduction, copy or transmission of this
publication may be made without written permission.

No paragraph of this publication may be reproduced, copied or transmitted
save with written permission or in accordance with the provisions of the
Copyright, Designs and Patents Act 1988, or under the terms of any licence
permitting limited copying issued by the Copyright Licensing Agency, 90
Tottenham Court Road, London W1T 4LP.

Any person who does any unauthorized act in relation to this publication may
be liable to criminal prosecution and civil claims for damages.

The authors have asserted their rights to be identified as the authors of this
work in accordance with the Copyright, Designs and Patents Act 1988.

First published 2006 by
PALGRAVE MACMILLAN
Houndmills, Basingstoke, Hampshire RG21 6XS and
175 Fifth Avenue, New York, N. Y. 10010
Companies and representatives throughout the world

PALGRAVE MACMILLAN is the global academic imprint of the Palgrave
Macmillan division of St. Martin's Press, LLC and of Palgrave Macmillan Ltd.
Macmillan® is a registered trademark in the United States, United Kingdom
and other countries. Palgrave is a registered trademark in the European
Union and other countries.

ISBN-13: 978–1–4039–9223–9 hardback
ISBN-10: 1–4039–9223–1 hardback

This book is printed on paper suitable for recycling and made from fully
managed and sustained forest sources.

A catalogue record for this book is available from the British Library.

Library of Congress Cataloging-in-Publication Data
Baruch, Yehuda.
    Winning reviews : a guide for evaluating schorlarly writing / edited by
Yehuda Baruch, Sherry E. Sullivan and Hazlon N. Schepmyer.
        p. cm.
    Includes bibliographical references and index.
    ISBN: 1–4039–9223–1
    1. Manuscripts–Editing. 2. Academic writing. I. Sullivan, Sherry E., 1966–
II. Schepmyer, Hazlon N., 1976– III. Title.

PN162.B36 2006
808.02–dc22   2005056576

10   9   8   7   6   5   4   3   2   1
15   14   13   12   11   10   09   08   07   06

Printed and bound in Great Britain by
Antony Rowe Ltd, Chippenham and Eastbourne

QM LIBRARY
(MILE END)

To my parents.

Yehuda

To my mother, Eileen M. Sullivan, who embodied beauty, grace, courage, wisdom, and, most of all, unconditional love.

Sherry

To my venerable sages: Fay Schepmyer, Neville Schepmyer, Martin G. Evans and John Fraser.

Hazlon

And to all of the anonymous reviewers, who willingly give their time and energies to help make our system of knowledge building work.

Contents

List of Tables and Figure

Tables

Figure

Foreword

This book addresses a fundamentally important and shared responsibility that is deeply held among management scholars, namely, improving our academic review process. The book's contributors are most impressive scholars. More important, they offer invaluable insight and advice, which are so well contained in the book's chapters, and they provide a forceful and collective voice to what many authors, reviewers, editorial board members and journal editors have felt for many, many years. I believe that this book should be read and discussed by both novice and well-seasoned research scholars alike from not just the organizational sciences but from all the social sciences as well. I hope too that journal editors refer their new reviewers to the chapters contained in this book.

This volume derives directly from three extremely well-received professional development workshops organized by Haze Schepmyer at annual meetings of the Academy of Management. I had the good fortune to participate in two of these sessions. Haze, Yehuda, Sherry and all of the book's contributors provide a great service to management scholars and to all academic social scientists as well. Most important, perhaps, these scholars inform (or remind) us what it means and how to be a gate keeper for one of our most important resources: our collective body of research knowledge. To all of the book's contributors, our profession owes you a great debt of gratitude.

Tom Lee
University of Washington Business School
Seattle, Washington, USA

Preface

Yehuda Baruch, Sherry E. Sullivan and Hazlon (Haze) Schepmyer

Reviewers are the unsung heroes of academe. Their professional service touches the lives and careers of countless of individuals. Their service impacts the author who receives their reviews and uses them to make decisions about how to revise a manuscript and how to conduct future research. Their service impacts the editor who has limited journal space and must make decisions about which articles to accept or reject – about which articles will become part of the knowledge base and which will be relegated to the file drawer. Their service impacts practitioners who use the information from published articles to alter organizational processes and improve the lives of workers. Their service impacts students who read the articles to learn more about complex concepts and ideas. Their service impacts fellow academics who build upon these articles, conduct additional research, write up their findings, and submit their manuscripts for review – starting the reviewing cycle all over again.

Although reviewers clearly perform an activity that is crucial to the creation and development of knowledge, there is little agreement about the process itself. Some consider reviewing to be an art, others see it as a trainable science, and still others view it as a combination of the two. Most recognize the peer review of manuscripts for publication as an important element in promotion and tenure decisions, despite the fact that there is no formal training to prepare and qualify scholars for serving as a reviewer. Moreover, there is neither a shared philosophy on how reviews should be completed nor a common source of guidance for approaching the task. As a result, this important link in the knowledge creation chain is often left to chance. If by luck, a manuscript is reviewed by individuals who have learned, usually by trial and error, how to complete a comprehensive, quality review, then the process works and superior research is revised and published. If by misfortune, the reviews are poorly done, important research may not be published in the appropriate journal or – worse yet – bad science may become part of the knowledge base. Because of the limited intellectual interest and research on the topic, the practice of reviewing may be in danger of hindering the very knowledge-building process that it was intended to strengthen and preserve.

Some efforts have been made to improve the review process, with one such effort serving as the impetus for the writing of this book. Haze Schepmyer organized the Academy of Management professional development workshop titled "Learning the Art and Craft of Reviewing: From Today's Best Reviewers to the Best Reviewers of Tomorrow," to provide doctoral students with the opportunity to discuss the process of reviewing with some of the best reviewers in the Academy. This session highlighted some of the critical concerns challenging reviewers, editors, and authors. It also emphasized the need for a systematic examination of the reviewing process. Soon after that session, Sherry E. Sullivan and Yehuda Baruch joined forces with Schepmyer to develop this book in the hopes of making a valuable contribution to both the literature and the profession.

This is the first book dedicated entirely to the topic of reviewing. It provided a forum in which scholars from around the world could share their own exploration of experiences with and knowledge of the issue of reviewing. The scholars who wrote the chapters for this book come from a variety of perspectives and backgrounds. Many are well-established, highly published experts in their areas of specialization. Most have served as journal editors, associate editors, and consulting editors or as conference program chairs and track chairs. Some have won numerous best paper and best reviewer awards. Others are long time members of several journal editorial boards. All of the authors, however, share the common goal of enhancing the critical – but often overlooked – review process.

Readers of this volume will find that certain suggestions are offered and agreed upon by the majority of the scholars, regardless of their various backgrounds and experiences. In other words, there seems to be some common standards for conducting reviews that cross the boundaries of disciplines (e.g., psychology, organizational behavior, strategy), level of analysis (e.g., micro vs. macro), or research methodology employed (e.g., qualitative vs. quantitative). For instance, a number of the authors agree upon the importance of providing structured reviews and discuss similar strategies for handling the ethical concerns often encountered by reviewers. In contrast, others disagree with commonly held beliefs about reviewing (e.g., the value of developmental reviews), share unique suggestions drawn from a different lens, or offer advice which applies to particular reviewing circumstances. Thus, this volume illustrates both areas of convergence – standards and procedures that scholars agree upon, as well as areas of divergence – suggestions and ideas that scholars disagree upon and which highlight the diversity of opinions and willingness to engage in scholarly debate in our academic community.

This book is divided into four sections: (1) the art and science of reviewing, (2) the practice of reviewing, (3) reviewing different types of works and (4) answering reviews to get published. There are thirteen original chapters in this volume, with one additional chapter that includes three well-received articles previously published in the *Journal of Management Inquiry*.

The first section of the book provides an overview of the purpose of the reviewing process, viewed through the lens of reviewing as an art or as a science. In the first chapter, Robert L. Dipboye critically examines the various roles of reviewers from both the theoretical and practical perspectives. He explores how reviewers should prepare for the task and what pitfalls they should guard against in their efforts to generate a contribution to their subject area. He also outlines specific techniques for improving the quality of reviews. In the second chapter, Richard L. Priem and Abdul A. Rasheed highlight the growing need to perceive reviewing as a service to the academic community. Looking at the peer review process as a selection mechanism, they discuss the two major functions of reviews: evaluation and development. They identify the various professional service roles that reviewers play as well as the responsibilities associated with each of these roles. They offer useful suggestions for creating systems and standards for recognizing and rewarding reviewers' contributions. In the third chapter, Ann Marie Ryan makes a persuasive case for when not to accept the invitation to review. She details issues, including lack of experience, possible conflict of interests and bias, and insufficient resources – especially time – that prevent individuals from completing quality reviews. Ryan offers a realistic view of the specific circumstances that signal when refusing a request to review is in the best interest of all parties involved.

The second section of the book focuses on the practice of reviewing – the actual nuts and bolts of the process. It begins with authors Sherry E. Sullivan, Madeline Crocitto and Shawn M. Carraher tackling the seemingly simple question: "How does one correctly review a manuscript"? They frame their answer around five interconnected issues and summarize these issues in a "reviewer's checklist." This checklist should serve as a valuable guide to individuals in the early stages of their reviewing careers. Likewise, experienced reviewers could use the checklist as a tool for helping to insure the writing of a comprehensive review. In the next chapter, Debra L. Shapiro and Sim B. Sitkin provocatively argue that we *can* and *do* put academic lives in peril whenever reviews are less than completely fair. Drawing on insights from the organizational justice literature, they identify and outline four key process characteristics of doing reviews, emphasizing the importance of providing a timely, constructive, selfless review which is consistent with the published acceptability-criteria. They argue that because the "publish or perish" axiom applies to authors, reviewers must be cognizant that they are faced with the parallel responsibility "review fairly or kill." In the next chapter in this section, Hazlon Schepmyer, I. J. Hetty van Emmerik and Christine Oliver propose that while on the journey from novice to experienced reviewer, individuals should seek out advice from three important groups: peer advisors, step-ahead advisors, and traditional advisors. To illustrate this three-tier mentoring model, the authors cleverly enact the framework. Schepmyer, in the role of peer advisor, offers unique insights for novices stemming from her own experiences as she made the transition from reviewing term papers for her fellow doctoral students to reviewing manuscripts for a scholarly, peer-reviewed journal. Van Emmerik, in the role of the step-ahead advisor, offers tips on how to succeed at the reviewing process. She details her own strategies that have earned her outstanding reviewer awards from several professional organizations. Oliver, in the role of the traditional advisor, explains five core techniques for writing outstanding reviews which are based on her 18 years of reviewing experience, including her six years of experience as editor of the *Administrative Science Quarterly*. Many may be surprised by her contention that reviewer quality is largely independent of the reviewer's status, years of experience, affiliation, and area of expertise. Instead, she argues that quality comes from reviewers adhering to these five core techniques.

The last chapter in this section is composed of three articles from a 2003 issue of the *Journal of Management Inquiry*. These thought-provoking articles focus on the fundamental issues of the fairness and value of the peer review process – a process that is deeply embedded in our system of knowledge development. These articles underscore the fact that through the establishment and implementation of journal policies, editors and reviewers wield considerable power over our discipline's intellectual vitality and future development. To begin, Arthur G. Bedeian, using survey results from 173 authors of top-tier journal articles, identifies major flaws in the review process. These flaws include authors making revisions they felt were wrong in order to satisfy reviewers as well as the poor treatment of authors by editors or reviewers. Based on the results of one of the few empirical studies of the reviewing process, he asks: "What are the repercussions of a system in which authors don't contribute for fear of being victim to the criticism bias"? In direct support of Bedeian's arguments, John B. Miner highlights the inevitable talent loss caused by the cynicism surrounding the publication process. His discussion is rooted in a deep concern about how this process affects the egos of authors and prospective authors – young and old – and subsequently affects the knowledge base. Like Bedeian and Miner, William Starbuck recognizes the weaknesses in the reviewing system, but suggests that we make the best of the situation, using the metaphor of turning lemons into lemonade. He explains stimulating ideas such as his counterintuitive Golden Rule: although "no reviewer is ever wrong," that does not mean authors should always follow reviewers' advice.

The third section of the book focuses on reviewing different types of works, including qualitative and quantitative manuscripts, articles submitted to scholarly practitioner journals, as well as the often misunderstood process of reviewing scholarly books. This section not only summarizes some of the general guidelines for reviewing presented in sections one and two of the book, but also provides a more in-depth examination based on the specific challenges and rewards of reviewing a particular type of work. Cary L. Cooper and John Burgoyne begin this section by providing an insider's guide to the process of reviewing qualitative manuscripts. They define what is meant by qualitative, walk us through the reviewing process, and provide interesting advice on such factors as evaluating qualitative research methods and analyses. Next, S. Gayle Baugh, James G. Hunt and Terri A. Scandura provide a lively discussion of what to look for in a high-quality empirical article. They pose such questions as: Does the article provide a "hook" to encourage people to read it? Is the article interesting enough to keep the often weary and time-pressured scholar's attention? Does the article add value to the literature? They offer specific suggestions on how to evaluate the framing of hypotheses, research design, and statistical analysis of results as well as how to avoid common mistakes including HARKing, or when a reviewer wrongfully encourages an author to hypothesize after results are known. While the first two chapters of this section concentrate on manuscripts submitted to scholarly academic journals, the next chapter by Sheila M. Puffer, James Campbell Quick and Dan McCarthy explores how to review a manuscript specifically written for a scholarly practitioner journal. They offer an insightful explanation of the differences between scholarly practitioner journals and other types of journals, and how these differences impact the review process. They describe the characteristics of effective reviewers and detail the steps in the review process emphasizing such factors as evaluating the executive overview as well as the link between theory and practice. This section closes with Walter Nord's delightful insights on how to review scholarly books. He argues that books are an overlooked source of academic knowledge, contending that a well-crafted book review can help others find an outstanding piece of scholarship that otherwise may have gone unnoticed but is well worth the academic's valuable time. Likewise, a review can also direct readers away from books that are little more than brain candy.

The focus of the last section of this book is slightly different from the previous sections as it examines how authors should respond to reviewers in order to get published. This section serves a boundary-spanning function, linking important players in the knowledge creation chain; it is intended to provide insights to reviewers and authors alike. Shaker A. Zahra and Donald O. Neubaum begin this section by deftly using social exchange theory as a framework to help reviewers and authors improve their chances of a successful revision and conquer the challenges of producing a publishable piece. They outline a list of "Dos and Don'ts" in the revision process and discuss the importance of developing trust among the participants in the knowledge-creation process. In contrast to Zahra and Neubaum who focus on the successful revision, Yehuda Baruch and Yochanan Altman provide eye-opening insights into a hidden and surprising phenomenon: why many authors don't revise and resubmit even though they are invited to do so. The phenomenon of authors not revising and resubmitting is detrimental to the stakeholders in the knowledge-building process (e.g., readers, researchers) because: (a) individuals may lose the opportunity to read potentially valuable scholarship if the manuscript ends up in a file cabinet drawer or (b) it drains resources from the overall system as another set of editors and reviewers must devote time and effort to the manuscript if it is submitted to another journal. Baruch and Altman unravel this mystery, providing suggestions to reviewers on how to encourage authors to revise and resubmit. This section ends with Daniel C. Feldman's enlightening and entertaining discussion of how reviewers and authors should successfully communicate with editors. Feldman, in his role as editor of the *Journal of Management*, sought to increase authors' and reviewers' understanding of the journal submission and review process by offering a series of editorials and workshops on the topic. His chapter is a continuation of that mission and draws not only on his service as an editor and a reviewer, but also from his experience as a successful author of over 100 articles and six books.

In conclusion, this book seeks to demystify the often undervalued and under-examined process of reviewing while also emphasizing the important role reviewers play in the creation of new knowledge. Although we do not suggest that this collaborative effort includes all perspectives on reviewing, as the first volume dedicated to systematically examining the process of reviewing, we think it will help individuals become more skilled reviewers and encourage a greater examination of the importance of reviewing to building knowledge. Additionally, by consolidating the thoughts and expertise of these scholars into one volume, this book should prove to be a valuable resource for those engaging in the reviewing process, whether it be novices completing their first reviews or seasoned reviewers writing their one hundred and first reviews. We hope this book motivates administrators to not only make formal training on reviewing a requirement of their doctoral programs, but to also appropriately reward faculty who provide service to the profession by writing quality reviews. And finally, we expect this book will inspire reviewers, the unsung heroes of the knowledge development process, to continue learning and honing their skills.

Acknowledgements

This book would not be possible without the guidance and support of our editorial, marketing and production teams at Palgrave. We want to especially thank Stephen Rutt, Publishing Director, our copy-editors Azlin Rasheed and Shirley Tan, our editorial manager Jacky Kippenberger. In addition, our thanks to our many wonderful authors, who enthusiastically devoted much time, thought, and effort to writing their respective chapters and who provided feedback to their fellow authors as part of the peer-review process used for this book. We are grateful to Jon Briscoe, William Carden, David Martin, David O'Connell and Fay Schepmyer who shared their expertise by serving as our panel of external reviewers. Our sincere appreciation to our many colleagues in the Academy of Management who encouraged and supported our efforts to produce this book. Special thanks to Aya Baruch for the artwork used on the book jacket.

Notes on Contributors

Co-Editors

Yehuda Baruch (D.Sc., The Technion, Israel) is a professor of Management at University of East Anglia Norwich UK and has been a visiting associate professor at the University of Texas at Arlington, as well as a visiting research fellow at London Business School. He has published over 65 papers in refereed journals on topics including: careers, research methods, technology, and strategic and international human resource management. He is the editor of *Career Development International,* an associate editor of the *Journal of Managerial Psychology,* serves on the editorial board of several journals, including *Journal of Management,* is past chair of the Academy of Management's Careers Division, and author of the book, *Managing Careers: Theory and Practice,* FT-Prentice Hall/Pearson (2004).

Sherry E. Sullivan (Ph.D., The Ohio State University) is a tenured associate professor at Bowling Green State University and was a tenured associate professor at Memphis State University. She is a Fellow of Southern Management Association and has served on the board of the Academy of Management's Women in Management Division, chair of the Career Division, treasurer of Midwest Academy, and chair of the International Division of the U.S. Association of Small Business and Entrepreneurship. She has published over 80 journal articles and is co-author, with Lisa Mainiero, of the book *The Opt-Out Revolt: Why People are Leaving Companies to Create Kaleidoscope Careers* (forthcoming, 2006).

Hazlon (Haze) Schepmyer (Ph.D., Madison University) has taught at the University of Toronto and at York University. She is co-founder and current chair of the Academy of Management's Doctoral Students' Liaison committee as well as a member of the Academy's Mentoring committee. She is a regular presenter at conferences, including: Academy of Management, Canadian Psychological Association, International Human Resource Management, and European Association of Work and Organizational Psychology. Her current research interests are career stage theory, strategic career management, and the professional development of minorities and youths.

Contributing Authors

Yochanan Altman is a professor at London Metropolitan University and visiting professor with the University of Paris (Panthéon-Assas). He has authored more than 70 articles, serves on the boards of five journals and is the past editor of *Journal of Managerial Psychology*, founding editor of the *Journal of Management, Spirituality and Religion*, and international editor for *Human Resource Planning*.

S. Gayle Baugh is an associate professor at the University of West Florida. She was the Academy of Management's Gender and Diversity in Organizations Division chair, secretary of the Careers Division, and president of Southwest Academy. She has served on the board of Southern Management Association and on the editorial board for *Group and Organization Management*.

Arthur G. Bedeian is a Boyd Professor at Louisiana State University. He is a former editor of the *Journal of Management*, a charter member of the Academy of Management's Journals Hall of Fame, a Fellow and past-president of the Academy of Management, and a Fellow of both the Southern Management Association and the International Academy of Management.

John Burgoyne is a professor of Management Learning in the Department of Management Learning, University of Lancaster, of which he is a founding member, and at Henley Management College. He has been a research policy consultant to the UK Government's Council for Excellence in Management and Leadership.

Shawn M. Carraher is the Brewczynski Endowed Chair in Entrepreneurial Studies, director of the Center for Emerging Technology & Entrepreneurial Studies, and head of the Entrepreneurial Studies Program at Cameron University and on the graduate faculties of Tec de Monterrey and Nova Southeastern University. He has authored more than 60 articles, serves on the boards of 14 journals, and was president of the Southwest Academy of Management.

Cary L. Cooper, CBE, is a professor of Organizational Psychology and Health at Lancaster University Management School. He is immediate past president of the British Academy of Management and Fellow of the Academy of Management, Royal Society of Medicine, Royal Society of Health, British Psychological Society, Royal Society of Arts, British Academy of Management and Honorary Fellow of the Faculty of Occupational Medicine of the Royal College of Physicians.

Madeline Crocitto is an associate professor at the State University of New York at Old Westbury. She is on the boards of the Eastern Academy of Management and the Careers Division of the Academy of Management. She has received excellence in reviewing awards from the Careers Division and Management Education and Development Division of the Academy of Management as well as the United States Association of Small Business Enterprise and has served as a reviewer for several journals.

Robert L. Dipboye is a Chair of Psychology at the University of Central Florida. He has served as an associate editor of the *Journal of Applied Psychology* and on the editorial boards of the *Academy of Management Review* and the *Journal of Organizational Behavior*. He is a fellow of the American Psychological Association, SIOP, and the American Psychological Society.

Daniel Feldman is the Synovus Chair of Servant Leadership and Associate Dean for Research at the Terry College of Business. He was the editor-in-chief of the *Journal of Management* and associate editor and consulting editor for *Human Resource Management* and *Journal of Organizational Behavior*. He is the author of six books and over 100 journal articles.

James G. (Jerry) Hunt is a Paul Whitfield Horn Professor of Management and the outgoing director of The Institute for Leadership Research, Texas Tech University. He is a former editor of the *Journal of Management* and *The Leadership Quarterly*, and is a Fellow in the Academy of Management and Southern Management Association. He has more than 200 publications.

Daniel J. McCarthy is the McKim-D'Amore Distinguished Professor of Global Management and Innovation at Northeastern University, a Fellow at the Davis Center for Russian Studies at Harvard University, and the lead corporate director of Clean Harbors, Inc. He has more than 80 publications, including four editions of *Business Policy and Strategy, Business and Management in Russia, The Russian Capitalist Experiment*, and *Corporate Governance in Russia*.

John B. Miner was the Carmichael Chair in Human Resources and faculty director of the Center for Entrepreneurial Leadership at the State University of New York – Buffalo. He has written over 50 books and over 135 articles. He is a former president of the Academy of Management and currently has a private practice in Oregon.

Walter R. Nord is a Distinguished University Professor of Management at the University of South Florida. His co-edited *Handbook of Organization Studies* (with S. Clegg and C. Hardy) received the 1997 George Terry Award. He received the 2002 Distinguished Educator Award from the Academy of Management.

Donald O. Neubaum is a faculty member at Oregon State University. He is on the editoral review board of four journals, including the *Academy of Management Journal, Journal of Management,* and *Entrepreneurship Theory and Practice*. He received the *Academy Of Management Journal*'s Best Reviewer Award in 2004 and the *Journal of Management*'s Best Paper Award in 2000.

Christine Oliver (Ph.D., University of Toronto) is the Henry J. Knowles Chair in Organizational Strategy in the Schulich School of Business at York University. She has served as chair of the Organizational Theory Division of the Administrative Sciences Association of Canada, Representative-at-Large on the Academy of Management Board of Directors, and chair of the Organization and Management Theory Division of the Academy of Management. She is also a past editor of *Administrative Science Quarterly*.

Richard L. Priem is a professor of Management and holds the Robert L. and Sally S. Manegold Chair in Management and Strategic Planning at the University of Wisconsin–Milwaukee. He is a well-published author, an award-winning teacher, and a Fulbright scholar. He currently serves on the editorial boards of the *Academy of Management Journal* and the *Journal of Management*, and has served on the executive committee of the Business Policy & Strategy Division of the Academy of Management.

Sheila M. Puffer is a professor of International Business at Northeastern University and a Fellow at the Davis Center for Russian Studies at Harvard University. She is a past editor of the *Academy of Management Executive*, served on the Academy's Board of Governors, and has authored more than 125 publications, including *The Russian Management Revolution, Business and Management in Russia, Corporate Governance in Russia,* and *International Management.*

James (Jim) Campbell Quick is the John and Judy Goolsby Distinguished Professor, the University of Texas at Arlington. He is a Fellow of the Society for Industrial and Organisational Psychology, American Psychological Association, and American Institute of Stress. He is the founding editor of *Journal of Occupational Health Psychology,* an associate editor of the *Academy of Management Executive,* and the 2002 winner of the Harry and Miriam Levinson Award.

Abdul A. Rasheed is a professor of Strategic Management and International Business at the University of Texas at Arlington. He obtained his Ph.D. from the University of Pittsburgh and his MBA from the Indian Institute of Management, Calcutta. His areas of research interest include strategic decision processes, environmental analysis, outsourcing, franchising, foreign market entry, international comparisons in strategy and governance, corporate disclosure, and corporate restructuring. His research has appeared in journals such as *Academy of Management Review, Strategic Management Journal* and *Journal of Management.*

Ann Marie Ryan is a professor of Organizational Psychology at Michigan State University. She currently serves as editor for *Personnel Psychology* and is a past president of the *Society for Industrial and Organizational Psychology.* She has published widely on the topics of fairness and employee selection and employee attitude surveying.

Terri A. Scandura is a professor at the University of Miami. She is past-president of the Southern Management Association and past chair of the Academy of Management's Research Methods Division. She is an associate editor of *Group & Organizational Management* and the *Journal of Management* as well as a departmental editor of the *Journal of International Business Studies.*

Debra L. Shapiro is a professor at the University of Maryland. She has authored over 60 journal articles and book chapters, is a three-time "Best Paper Award" winner from the Academy of Management (AOM), AOM Board of Governors Representative-at-Large, a past chair of the Academy's Conflict Management Division, and an associate editor of the *Academy of Management Journal.*

Sim B. Sitkin is an associate professor and director, Center on Leadership and Ethics, Fuqua School of Business, Duke University. He has authored/edited over 50 publications, received best paper awards from two AOM divisions and from the International Communication Association. He is currently senior editor of Organization Science, associate editor of Journal of Organizational Behavior, and formerly served on the AOM Board of Governors and as past chair of the Academy's Managerial and Organizational Cognition Division.

William (Bill) Starbuck is the ITT Professor of Creative Management at New York University. He was president of the Academy of Management, editor of *Administrative Science Quarterly* and is a fellow of the Academy of Management, the American Psychological Association, and the Society for Industrial and Organizational Psychology. He has served on the editorial board of 16 journals and has edited four books, including the *Handbook of Organizational Design*.

I. J. Hetty van Emmerik is an associate professor at the Department of Sociology, Utrecht University, The Netherlands. She is associate editor for Europe for the Journal of Managerial Psychology and recently received five Best Reviewer Awards.

Shaker A. Zahra holds the Robert E. Buuck Chair in Entrepreneurship at the University of Minnesota. He has served as a member of 15 editorial review boards, is on the Southern Management Association Board, and is the incoming Program Chair of the Academy of Management's Entrepreneurship Division.

Section 1

The Art and Science of Reviewing

1

Peer Reviews in the Production of Knowledge: Why I Stopped Worrying and Learned to Appreciate the Flaws in the Review Process

Robert L. Dipboye

In this chapter I describe the crucial part that reviewers could play in the generation of knowledge. The competitiveness of the publication process has turned reviewers into watchdogs who see their primary task as screening out the work that is unworthy of publication. A more effective role, however, is for reviewers to define themselves not as mere gatekeepers but as partners with authors and editors in the effort to produce knowledge. In the first part of the chapter I focus on scientific standards as they have been idealized and how reviewers can evaluate manuscripts against these standards. An important point I want to make is that even recommendations to reject should provide important feedback on how researchers can improve the rigor, relevance, and value added of their work. Although reviewers should hold manuscripts to the scientific ideal, they should also realize that it is impossible to maximize rigor, relevance, and value added in any single study. In the next section I will discuss the inherent conflicts among these standards and the tradeoffs that are inevitable in the research process. I will end the chapter on a more hopeful note by considering the implications of an evolutionary perspective for the review process.

The nature of knowledge in scientific disciplines

As scholars in the field of behavioral sciences, a primary objective is to produce and disseminate knowledge about human behavior. Many of us are concerned with more than an accumulation of facts but aspire to a body of knowledge that allows understanding and practical application. A positivistic model guides this endeavor in the behavioral sciences. A reality apart from the observer is assumed. Scientific methods, and the hypothetico-deductive strategy of inquiry are accepted as the legitimate means of generating knowledge. Two caveats are in order here. First, I am in large part ignoring the post-modern challenge to the positivistic approach. The positivistic model still dominates, and shapes the editorial policies and guidelines of the major journals. My comments in this chapter are most relevant to those who review for these journals. A second caveat is that I will for the most part ignore the major deviations of the scientific model as practiced from the scientific ideal.

The role of reviewers in the generation of knowledge

The scholarly communication process consists of roughly three stages: communication within informal networks, including listservs; the initial public dissemination of research through conferences and preprints; and finally, formal publication in "prestigious journals" and books (Gabbay, 2000; Graham, 2000). In the informal phase, ideas can spring from a variety of activities such as thinking, talking to colleagues, reading past research literature, and listening to presentations at conferences. Some evaluation and feedback are likely in all these informal settings, but it is only when manuscripts undergo the scrutiny of a formal review process and are published that they become an official part of the knowledge of a scientific field. The refereed literature in a field serves as the repository for knowledge. As much as those in the academic community may lament the "publish or perish" mentality, the distribution of knowledge made possible by scholarly journals and books is largely responsible for the rapid growth of scientific disciplines in the last 100 years (Halliday, 2001).

Reviewers and editors are the gatekeepers who determine what is published and allowed into the permanent record of the discipline. The authors may display their genius in lectures to students, papers at national meetings, comments on listservs and in informal conversations, and in the practical solutions of real-world problems. Despite these contributions, if the work has not survived the review process and been published in a recognized scholarly venue, that author remains an anonymous member of the community of scholars. This is so because most scholarly areas require some certification of the authenticity of ideas. I once attended a symposium in which an industrial and organizational psychologist who worked for a large corporation asserted that the technical reports and private meetings held by industry groups were superior to the published literature in the field. Although these proprietary venues obviously have value for the small circle allowed access, the information exchanged is unlikely to become a lasting part of the knowledge base. A vibrant scientific discipline is only possible when findings undergo the public scrutiny of reviewers and are made available to the wider community of scholars.

The criteria that reviewers use in the production of knowledge

The primary task of reviewers is to evaluate manuscripts on the basis of scientifically sound criteria. The most common outcome of the review process is rejection, and the reasons include inadequate justification for doing the study, a method that cannot answer the question, variables that fail to match the constructs, a poorly written manuscript, no theory, insufficient definitions of variables, inadequate rationale for the design, lack of relevance to the field, failure to demonstrate the contribution, conclusions that are not aligned with results, and over use of statistical and other technical procedures to the neglect of interpretation (Sackett & Larson, 1990; Daft, 1995). Rather than search for reasons to reject, reviewers should expand their role to assist the author and editor in the generation of knowledge. This expanded role requires that reviewers evaluate and provide feedback on three dimensions that appear to underlie the various factors influencing reviews: rigor, relevance, and value added.

Reviewers should evaluate conceptual and methodological rigor

The role of the reviewer is to decide if the work meets the standards of rigor expected in normal science. Rigor refers to whether the research is designed and conducted in a manner that allows findings and inferences that are trustworthy and accurate. Thus, rigor applies to the hypotheses and research questions that are the focus of the research, the methods used to address these questions and hypotheses, and the conclusions that are drawn from the findings. The reviewer should ask several questions in judging rigor. Are the research questions and hypotheses clear and do they logically follow from theory? Do the conclusions logically follow from the results and the interpretation of these results? Are key terms clearly defined? Are the procedures used in gathering data set forth with sufficient specificity to allow replication? Do research methods allow the objective observation of events so that different scientists can arrive at the same conclusions using the same methods? Are experimental and statistical controls used necessary to testing the hypotheses and addressing the research questions? Are precise measurements used that allow fine distinctions to be made among events and does the author demonstrate their reliability and validity? Are the statistical procedures appropriate to the data and the inferences drawn? Rigor is further defined by whether research methods allow the objective observation of events and different scientists can arrive at the same conclusions using the same methods. Scientific rigor will remain as the primary basis for evaluating research, and the more prestigious journals will continue to have low acceptance rates primarily because of the difficulty of meeting these standards.

Conceptual rigor

The reviewer can judge the rigor of a study first by the manner in which the author frames the research in the introduction of the manuscript. A rigorous study is marked by an argument in which the author builds a logical case for the research. The author roots the research in theory and then derives from this theory the hypotheses and questions that are the focus of the research. Theory can come in the form of loosely stated conceptions as well as in specific statement consisting of propositions, corollaries, and hypotheses. Knowledge is essentially the story that the author tells from the results and the theory provides the structure of the story. There are several ways researchers can fall short on this dimension. Authors can arrive at hypotheses and questions that are non sequiturs and that make little sense in the context of the theory. They can state them so vaguely that they are incapable of falsification. They also may fail to clearly link their hypotheses and research questions to a theory or may present them so that they are linked equally well to many different theories.

Internal validity of the research design and methodology

Research in the behavioral sciences often is concerned with whether one variable causes another. To allow for causal inferences, research is designed to rule out alternative explanations by holding constant, eliminating, manipulating, measuring, randomizing, or matching factors that may pose alternative explanations. A research study lacks internal validity to the extent that the design of the study fails to eliminate important alternative interpretations for the findings and incorrect causal inferences are drawn from the findings.

The gold standard for judging internal validity is the true experiment in which participants are assigned to treatment groups on a random basis. True experiments allow for greater internal validity than nonexperimental research in which random assignment is missing. Quasi-experiments have many of the characteristics of a true experiment but lack random assignment are often superior to nonexperimental research, but are still less rigorous in terms of internal validity than true experiments. While using the true experiment as the standard, reviewers should keep in mind that it is never possible to eliminate all the alternative explanations and that their task is to not only enumerate the potential confounds but also to judge whether potential threats are sufficiently important to warrant consideration. Reviewers should also recognize that many of the issues and phenomena that are of concern to behavioral scientists cannot be studied through experimentation. Knowledge accumulates through the convergence of findings from the use of diverse methodologies. Consequently, the value of any single study must be considered within the context of the general body of research on the topic. If there is already experimental research providing the basis for internally valid inferences, reviewers should show considerable tolerance in the evaluation of nonexperimental or quasi-experimental research that falls short on internal validity but contributes in other ways to the body of knowledge.

Construct validity of measures and manipulations

Whereas internal validity refers to whether the X we manipulated or measured actually caused the changes in Y, construct validity refers to whether the operationalizations of the variables X and Y actually reflect the underlying constructs that the X and Y are intended to reflect. According to Binning and Barrett (1989, p. 479), "Psychological constructs are labels for clusters of covarying behaviors. In this way, a virtually infinite number of behaviors is reduced to a system of fewer labels, which simplifies and economizes the exchange of information and facilitates the process of discovering behavioral regularities." A theory is a set of constructs and the interrelationships assumed to exist among these constructs (Selltiz, Wrightsman, and Cook, 1976, p. 16). In the so-called deductive approach, the researcher starts with a theory, deduces from this theory a specific statement of how variables related to the constructs will be related, and then gathers data to test the hypothesized relationships. Whether the theory is seen as accurate or not depends on whether the statements deduced from the theory are supported by the data. An opposite strategy of research is the so-called

<u>inductive</u> approach. The researcher starts by gathering data and then derives from the observed relationships a theory. However, even in the inductive approach the researcher is likely to have some prior notion of what constructs are important and their possible relationships. Whichever strategy is adopted, the ultimate objective of research in I/O psychology is to arrive at theory that can be used in the description, explanation, and prediction of behavior.

The construct validity of the independent variables in an experiment refers to whether the manipulation of the independent variable actually reflects the underlying construct that it is intended to reflect. Thus, an investigator may intend to examine the effects of anxiety on motivation by manipulating anxiety through verbal abuse of a supervisor. The construct validity of a measure refers to whether the number obtained truly reflects what the user intends to measure. If I intend to measure job satisfaction with a series of questions, do these questions in fact reflect job satisfaction? Whereas the standards used in evaluating internal validity must bend to accommodate nonexperimental and quasi-experimental research, I would advise reviewers to show relative inflexibility in their evaluations of construct validity. There is little reason to tolerate the use of measures or manipulations that are unreliable or inaccurate. Yet, reviewers must again show realism in their judgments. Construct validity can never be judged on the basis of one study but requires consideration of what other studies have found with these manipulations and measures.

Statistical conclusion validity of the analyses

This refers to whether the association between two variables reflects an actual covariation or a chance event. Factors that work against statistical conclusion validity are low statistical power, violated assumptions of statistical tests, fishing and the error rate problem, unreliability of measures, and unreliability of treatment implementation. In judging statistical conclusion validity reviewers should be even less forgiving than they are in judging construct validity. Rigor in analysis should not be equated with complexity or sophistication of the analyses. Highly complex analyses are a virtue only if they are needed to answer the research question. They are a weakness if simpler analyses would suffice.

Reviewers should evaluate relevance

The scientific community is embedded in an ecology that includes stakeholders such as corporations, government, lay public, and benefactors. No matter how rigorous the research, unless the products of scientific inquiry are of value to these constituencies, a science discipline is unlikely to survive, much less succeed. We can build a body of knowledge based on highly rigorous research and a body of innovative and creative insights, but it is possible that the only persons interested in the knowledge are a few scholars who read the journals in which it is published. In contrast to rigor, where the rules are relatively clear, relevance is multi-faceted and requires that we distinguish between instrumental and conceptual relevance (Beyer, 1997; Beyer & Trice, 1982). A study has instrumental relevance if the research results can be applied in specific, direct ways to solve problems. Conceptual relevance involves using research results for general enlightenment; results influence actions but more indirectly and less specifically than in instrumental use. Similarly, Schutz (1970) in a discussion of what it means for a thing, idea, or piece of information to be relevant distinguishes between "topical relevance" which refers to direct use and "interpretative relevance" which allows us to understand and make sense of that which we notice.

It is not surprising that the layperson would consider relevance to be crucial but there is also evidence that researchers consider this important. Thomas and Kilmann, (1994) found in a survey of scholars in the organizational sciences that 91% of respondents felt that organizational sciences should contribute to practice and only 9% endorsed a pure "basic research" goal of producing knowledge of organizational phenomena for its own sake. The biggest failing of the organizational sciences according to this survey was the failure to achieve relevance, with most respondents believing that current research is rigorous enough but not sufficiently relevant (67%). Mitroff and his colleagues believe that the omission of real-world problems from the research cycle is not peculiar to the organizational sciences but is a common pathology in all scientific inquiry that is threatening to destroy society's support for science (Mitroff, Betz, Pondy, & Sagasti, 1974). In their view, all research should begin with real-world problem situations that serve as the basis of broad conceptualizations of the phenomena, formulation of a scientific model (theory), and the derivation of implications or solutions from the scientific model.

Reviewers should examine the relevance of the research in their evaluations of manuscripts, especially in those journals that are outlets for applied research. Yet, this is the most problematic of the bases for recommending acceptance or rejection of a manuscript. Instrumental relevance can only be evaluated in the context of the potential users of the research and their needs (Thomas & Tymon, 1982), but manuscripts often lack a clear statement of either users or their needs. Reviewers tend to bring their own idiosyncratic notion of what constitutes relevance to the review process. What is relevant to one reviewer is irrelevant to others and vice versa. Reviewers are overly influenced by the setting or participants in the research in either a negative or positive direction. Thus, a recommendation to reject or accept may be "just because" the study is a laboratory study or field study, or samples a particular type of person. The common target is laboratory research with students. Reviewers in the applied social sciences frequently lambast such studies as irrelevant, or even in cases where they recommend acceptance, view it as an unfortunate flaw. But studies in real world settings are also criticized on occasion because they involve what is considered a "unique" sample of participants, somehow unrepresentative of the "real world." Reviewers may allow superficial similarities with real world settings to shape their evaluations of relevance. A third sin which I would consider a deadly transgression is to evaluate relevance on the basis of the current fad or fashion in practice. What is relevant today may be irrelevant tomorrow.

My observation of "these sins of relevance" have led me to the conclusion that manuscripts should never be accepted or rejected just because the study is in a real world setting or in a laboratory unless the journals place specific restrictions on the settings of the research they will consider (Dipboye, 1990). Relevance is such an ambiguous concept that it should seldom be the focus of a review. The exception is if the author claims relevance or the journal is concerned with the evaluation of specific techniques or interventions. Louis (1994) provides several criteria that reviewers can use in judging relevance in these situations. The reviewer should ask whether the manuscript has goal relevance, meaning that the research addresses a practical situation and the goals of the practitioner in that situation. For instance, if the manuscript is under review for a management journal, does the author address in the research the administrative situation, the operating dilemmas of the manager, and outcomes (or dependent variables) that are of concern to the user? Another question to ask is whether a practitioner could operationalize the independent variables in an intervention. A third question to ask is whether the research suggests solutions that can be used in a brief amount of time. Additional issues for the reviewer to explore in evaluating instrumental relevance are whether researchers take into account what works and what does not, develop a theory of action that practitioners can use, and then test, validate, and refine these theories in the field (Mathias, 1994, pp. 133–44).

All of these are legitimate bases for evaluating a manuscript that claim relevance, but I must warn reviewers to avoid an overemphasis on pragmatism. Reviewers should be sensitive to the fact that the most useful research is often that which has generality rather than being bound to specific situations. Perhaps for that reason, many of the higher status journals do not emphasize instrumental relevance but focus more on conceptual relevance. When general understanding rather than a specific solution to problems is the intent, reviewers should evaluate the manuscript more on the heuristic value of the manuscript. Rather than focusing on surface similarities or the setting of the research, the reviewer should ask whether the research adds to understanding, increases awareness of present and emerging needs and problems, enables interpretations of complex issues, and provides a language for communication of the issues (Weiss, 1980; Weiss & Bucuvalas, 1980). Conceptually relevant research should provoke the practitioner to engage in sensemaking and to go beyond specific instances represented in the research to a wide variety of instances. Conceptual relevance can never be determined with certainty from one study but requires a program of research using different participants, settings, and responses over time. Most important, conceptual relevance requires that the research generate theory that can be a source of intriguing ideas, diagnoses, and action (Bartunek, Gordon & Weathersby, 1983).

Reviewers should evaluate value added

Research may meet all the standards of scientific rigor and demonstrate relevance but may still fail to meet the third criterion. A study that has added value produces results that substantially advance knowledge. In defining what is meant by added value of the contribution, I should start with what it is not. Research in the behavioral sciences is often driven by the previous literature rather than by theory or problems. As a consequence, researchers peck away at relatively small and trivial issues rather than taking a fresh look at the issue. The same procedures are used again and again and anything that deviates from the accepted procedure is rejected. An important task of the reviewer is to determine where the manuscript under consideration stands relative to the existent literature and whether the contribution justifies publication. Manuscripts that are literature driven are more warranted in the early stages of the research on a topic than in later stages. Once the basic findings and methodology in an area are established, however, a point is reached where reviewers should expect the research to be driven less by the specific studies that have gone before and more by the "big questions."

Several critics of the behavioral sciences have brought attention to what they consider to be the failure of reviewers to distinguish between a contribution to the literature and a contribution that constitutes a substantial advance in knowledge. Staw (1995, p. 86) notes that "Too often topics in the literature take on a life of their own because of the availability of theory or the ease of data collection, regardless of their importance in organizational life. In fact we routinely judge the significance of a research paper by its contribution to the pile of studies already conducted and archived in the journals rather than by its contribution to our understanding of organizations." Sackett and Larson (1990) found that 84% of the published studies they sampled used coupling to generate research questions compared to 13% that used theory and 3% that used real-world problems. Coupling referred to a strategy in which researchers generate research questions from previous work by essentially replicating previous work with slight extensions (e.g., using different subject population, operationalizations or levels of the variables). Campbell, Daft and Hulin (1982, p. 55) decry the frequency with which coupling is used and assert that research driven by theory and real-world problems are more likely to yield important findings.

How then can we judge the value added of a manuscript? One issue is whether it contributes new or unique findings. Sackett and Larson (1990) discuss a study of 429 reviewers from nineteen leading management and social science journals in which it was found that referees do not regard replications of previous work favorably. Fifty two percent stated that a direct replication of an original study would probably be cause for a recommendation to reject. Similarly, Beyer, Chanove, and Fox (1995) observed that authors who claimed expressively novel content were more likely to have their articles accepted for publication in the Academy of Management. An important duty of a reviewer is to consult the meta-analyses in the area of the study. This provides an empirical basis for judging the novelty of a finding and determining whether this constitutes a potentially important contribution. The danger of using meta-analyses is that they capture only the status quo and may discourage asking the important questions. It is perhaps too easy in an area where there is a substantial amount of previous research to conclude that a finding is trivial simply because it is consistent with the meta-analysis or to dismiss the validity of a study that contradicts the meta-analyses. The importance of the findings of a single study relative to the body of research described in a meta-analysis can only be determined by a careful examination of the questions raised and the strategies used in answering these questions. I will include among these strategies falsification, the search for convergence across different methodologies, and strong inference.

From Baconian induction we know that knowledge accrues through a series of studies and never from one and only one study. The conclusions we draw from a single study is probabilistic and contingent on the methods and other circumstances under which the data are collected. The importance of findings that go against meta-analysis results could be dismissed as improbable or flawed. But even if it is a single study, it can be programmatic in the sense of being located within an overall stream of research that provides a context for the contribution. Reviewers need to distinguish simple coupling from research programs designed in a more logical way to substantively contribute to the knowledge base. The research on theories of work motivation could be used as an example. Some research consists of coupling in which a theory is tested using a variable that has not previously been examined. For instance, valence-instrumentality theories of motivation hypothesize that when persons have high expectations that exerting effort on a task will lead to valued outcomes, they will exert higher levels of effort on that task (Vroom, 1964). A large body of research findings has accumulated that supports this basic hypothesis. In light of this substantial, preexisting literature, how might a researcher add value? A coupling strategy would be illustrated by an approach in which researchers see whether the hypothesis is supported in the public sector as well as in the private sector, with objective measures of performance as well as with subjective measures, with women as well as with men, with persons from Asian cultures as well as from western cultures, or with low ability as well as high ability persons. To the extent that the strategy of the author is one of coupling where a variable is chosen without much a priori or conceptual rationale provided, the chances are that the findings of the study will soon be forgotten.

A strategy that is more likely to make a contribution than coupling is that of falsification. If we accept Popper's (1959) assertion that science advances through disconfirmation, an important role of the reviewer is to encourage the author to attempt a disconfirmation or to show how their theory could be refuted. Among the most demanding criteria to impose is whether the underlying theory is capable of falsification. A substantial contribution is most likely when the authors are able to specify what we would find if the theory or hypotheses were false. If the theory can explain anything a researcher finds, then that theory cannot be refuted and is of limited value. This is a high standard for the social sciences where much of the theory is not stated in much detail or formality.

The multimethod-multiconstruct (MMMC) approach is still another strategy that seems more likely to make a substantive contribution than mere coupling. The MMMC approach consists of an attempt to show convergence in findings across different methods. The greatest contributions come from showing that similar findings are obtained from using different methods. If support is found for a theory only when a specific type of methodology is used, the theory is method-bound. This is a huge problem in those behavioral sciences where there is a reliance on self-report measures in field research (Dipboye & Flanagan, 1979). Whatever the measure or manipulation, researchers are likely to keep using what has produced successful results. Major contributions are more likely to come from research in which we test theory using a variety of different measures and manipulations of the same construct. Failure to show convergence provides the basis for rethinking of the theory and is the stimulus for future contributions.

Even more demanding as a strategy than simple disconfirmation is a variant of Popper's disconfirmation that Platt (1964) calls the method of strong inference. According to Platt, rapid advances are made in fields that use a method of inductive inference consisting of the following steps. First, alternative hypotheses are stated for empirical test. Second, crucial experiments are designed and conducted to rule out one or more of the hypotheses. Finally, based on the evidence, further experimentation is conducted to further reduce the alternative explanations. The essential element in this strategy is that it is guided by competing hypotheses as opposed to the typical approach where researchers become attached to a single hypothesis. Rather than declaring one theory the winner and the other the loser, research using a strong inference strategy is more likely to succeed in setting the boundaries for one or the other theory.

So far I have discussed research that makes substantial theoretical advances but similar statements could be made for research that is focused more on application. A study that attempts to show why an intervention works and the conditions under which it succeeds or fails is more valuable than a study that simply confirms or disconfirms the success of the intervention and adds another isolated piece of data on the issue (Brown & Gerhardt, 2002). Similar to theory testing, we need more applied research that attempts to falsify, that evaluates the interventions across different methodologies, and that employs a strong inference strategy.

Whether the research is theoretical or applied, and whatever research strategy is used, the value added of a study is seldom obvious. Reviewers should examine the justification provided by the author of why their research deserves publication and how the findings add value to what is already known. If authors fail to provide a persuasive justification, the reviewer should ask for one. And of course, the reviewers should examine the research in the context of the literature to provide their own assessment of the value added.

Dilemmas in the review process: Why I worry

As important as the peer review process is to the generation of knowledge in the organizational sciences, it is flawed in several respects (Moxley, 1992; Campanario, 1998a, 1998b). Perhaps the most serious charges are that reviewers tend not to agree in their evaluation of the same manuscript (Fiske & Fogg, 1990; Cicchetti, 1991; Peters & Ceci, 1982) and the quality ratings of articles are poor predictors of their later impact (Simonton, 2004, p. 87). Based on these findings, the peer reviewing system would be exceedingly difficult to defend using the same standards that are used in the evaluation of employee selection systems. At the heart of the problem is the impossibility of optimizing, within the same study, all three of the criteria: relevance, rigor, and contribution. Rather, a gain on one of these criteria is usually at the cost of one or both of the other criteria. Consequently, even those manuscripts that are accepted for publication are likely to fall short on some dimensions while excelling on others.

The conflict between rigor and value added

A conflict frequently discussed is that between rigor and contribution. When the primary concern is theory testing, a conceptually tight statement of hypotheses is needed followed by the use of methodologies that provide internal, construct, and statistical conclusion validity. We have come to accept some methods as inherently more rigorous than others partly as the result of the attempt to imitate the physical sciences. The essence of rigor is the ability to exert control over variables through randomization, statistical control, and other proven means.

But according to a sociological perspective on knowledge, methods are legitimated within a paradigm community and are encouraged because they fit the image of rigorous science (Kling & McKim, 1999; Borgman, 1990). Innovations are discouraged not because they are invalid but because they violate what is considered "normal science" and "threaten the internal stability of the profession" (Staw, 1995, p. 93).

The typical reviewer scans a prospective manuscript checking off those aspects which meet the criteria of rigor including, proper control in the form of randomization or statistical control, the use of reliable, validated measures, double-blind procedures, and unbiased sampling. The field of acceptable methodologies is narrowed considerably to the benefit of the accuracy with which we can test hypotheses but at the potential cost to the discovery and innovation associated with making important contributions. Martin (1994) blames the lack of contribution on not so much the rigor of the research as the "scientism" dominating existing work in which researchers in organizational sciences ape the physical sciences in their "emphasis on method and the trappings of science" (pp. 564–5). McCall and Bobko (1990) suggest that "In our zeal to apply the physical science model, elegant statistical procedures, and the power of the computer, we have lost some of our strengths in other methods, notably the more qualitative approaches....We also have a sense that we are not attacking some of the more exciting issues in our field" (p. 412).

Conflict between relevance and value added

There is a tension between judgments of what is relevant and what makes an innovative and important contribution. Just as norms emerge to define what constitutes rigorous science, that which is considered practical and relevant can be dictated by the prevailing fads and fashions. At one time the team concept was not as popular and to talk about selecting for teams or training for teams was considered somewhat impractical. The early team research and programs set the pace and eventually became the norm so that now the team concept is all the rage and likely to be seen as workable. Likewise, methodologies such as structural equation modeling can become fashionable and dominate the literature to the point that they are expected by reviewers even when inappropriate. The focus on the status quo can lead to a devaluation of potential solutions and inattention to problems that loom on the horizon. Abrahamson (1991, 1996) discussed how managers are influenced by rhetoric to adopt practices that the current fads and fashions define as both rational and progressive. The problem is that what is seen as effective and innovative one day may become passé the next and practices that are in or out of fashion seems to have little to do with the research literature on the topic. When topics and practices decline in popularity researchers lose interest and turn to the next fad. Those intrepid researchers who persist in researching what has become passé may find their manuscripts rejected as irrelevant by reviewers.

A second way in which relevance can be at odds with value added is associated with the short-term focus and aversion to the abstract of those concerned with application. Earlier I discussed how a strategy of research more likely to advance knowledge uses falsification, evaluates effects across methodologies, and employs strong inference strategies. All this takes time and effort which may not be possible when relevance is the primary concern. Relevant research is often dictated by identification of a category of potential users, identification of their needs, development of interventions capable of meeting these goals, and then quickly delivering these interventions in the least costly manner. Practical concern often encourages coupling in which researchers seek small, incremental gains and build on previous successes and avoid straying too far from what has been used frequently and shown to work. Making innovative contributions requires bold steps and risk taking. In research concerned exclusively with solving specific problems, practitioner needs, the first step is to see what has the best track record. Establishing the boundaries of what works is secondary to achieving a quick success. Weick (1979, p. 247) suggests that "Whenever people adapt to a particular situation, they lose some of the resources that would enable them to adapt to different situations in the future. They sacrifice future adaptability for current good fit" (p. 247). Research that is impractical, irrelevant, and even silly may be a means to new insights, whereas maintaining a focus on the practical may prevent important advances in application and understanding. When reviewers hold all manuscripts to rigid standards of practicality, they run the risk of preventing important advances in knowledge.

Conflict between rigor and relevance

I defined relevance in terms of usefulness of findings to an external world that is often messy, whereas rigor was defined in terms of controlling for the messiness that characterizes the real world in the interest of testing hypotheses. Ideally rigorous research allows confidence in conclusions as to what "can" happen, whereas relevant research allows confidence as to what is "likely" to happen. The question is whether the two objectives can be achieved in the same study. Some would argue that rigor works against relevance in several ways. The research methods that constitute rigorous research can render the findings irrelevant to real world situations by constraining hypotheses to unidirectional, independent-dependent variables (Cummings, 1978; Lundberg, 1976). The emphasis on psychometric standards of measurement characteristic of rigorous research has led to a focus on what is readily observable and measurable and neglect of those variables that are important but not as subject to rigorous analysis. The treatment of research participants as objects to be manipulated and controlled limits the applicability and generalizability of findings as participants either try to outwit the researcher or passively submit to experimenter demands (Argyris, 1968). The emphasis on statistical significance leads reviewers to concluding practical relevance when the research is trivial in the implications for settings outside of the research setting. The issue that perhaps overrides all of these problems is that in the behavioral sciences practical impact comes from multivariate interventions – packages of variables – delivered in a complex environment, whereas in rigorous research the emphasis is, by necessity, on a few variables studied under sterile circumstances. Consequently rigorous research will often yield findings that appear to have more impact than is actually the case.

Research that captures a specific situation is useful to that specific situation, but its relevance would be highly limited if we cannot generalize the findings. For that reason, research in the behavioral sciences is seldom concerned with events in a specific setting but is instead concerned with developing theory that allows us to generalize across many situations. By contrast, rigorous research requires that we provide tangible indicators of what we hope are the underlying constructs. The typical experiment must out of necessity use specific events to test hypotheses that may have little relation to most real world settings. Likewise, measures are used in field surveys that purport to reflect constructs such as commitment, satisfaction, and the like that are imperfect indicators of the underlying constructs. So on both the independent and dependent variable side of the equation, we use specific events to tap into an abstraction, and it is the abstraction that has the greatest potential usefulness.

There is a contradiction, then, between the specificity required in rigorous research and the abstraction required to develop a theory that is truly useful and can be generalized across specific participants, responses, and settings. Rigor requires meticulous attention to the details of a specific situation in the interest of control. Relevance requires rising above the concrete operationalizations to more abstract conceptions that can be transported across situations.

Why I worry less

These and other conflicts have led some to suggest dramatic changes in the publication system including an abandonment of peer reviewing or a dramatic overhaul. Staw (1995, p. 96) goes so far as to suggest that to increase creativity, journals should function "somewhat akin to presentations at annual meetings of professional societies" by becoming "dispensers of live information." Weick (1995, p. 290) asserts that the anonymity of the process allows reviewers to promote their own interests and rely on idiosyncratic standards without being held to standards of proof. He suggests making reviewers public and holding their evaluations to the same level of scrutiny as the manuscript. Nord (1995) recommends letting the market increasingly determine the worth of our scholarly work essentially doing away with critical review. Current technology has made possible on-line journals that are essentially open to all manuscripts.

I am sympathetic to the calls for radical reform and believe that each of these suggestions ought to be implemented to some extent as a supplement to the current system. We need more forums for exchange of ideas, more accountability for reviewers, and on-line journals that allow the dissemination of most manuscripts that are submitted. But even if we implement these and other reforms, we will still need reviewers for the same reason that we have book critics and movie critics. Just as no one sees all movies or reads all books and must rely on knowledgeable and opinionated gatekeepers to suggest what to see or read, scholars will need reviewers to help them screen out those works that represent flawed work or less important contributions among the huge volume of studies in the behavioral sciences. If the merits of scholarly work were immediately apparent we would not need refereed journals. Scholars would conduct their research and report their findings in written manuscripts that they post on the internet and mail out to as many members of the scholarly community as they can. Works that merit recognition would be quickly recognized without the cost and effort of the journal publication process. In the real world of scholarship, however, there are limits to how much the members of the scholarly community can read and evaluate. Scholars will still need to rely on reviewers to select and screen from among a huge body of those manuscripts that appear in journals.

Peer reviewing is therefore crucial to the production, dissemination, and accumulation of knowledge in all scholarly fields and will continue out of necessity. There are steps that can be taken to improve the reliability and validity of reviewer judgments such as stating the explicit bases for evaluating rigor, relevance, and value added. Editors can develop for reviewers a checklist of things to look for and detailed scales for evaluating each dimension. They can train reviewers in how to use the evaluation system, a rare practice in current journals. They could evaluate reviewers on the quality of their reviews and provide them feedback, an even rarer practice. One could even conceive of a system in which reviewers are provided feedback on the eventual impact of the manuscripts they review. But even with these and other reforms, the flaws we have discussed will persist. Should we give up hope of all progress in the behavioral sciences? An evolutionary perspective on knowledge production provides a more optimistic way of framing these "problems." This approach would suggest that many of the so-called flaws can be more beneficial than may first appear and overly strident attempts to eliminate them may actually hinder the organizational sciences.

Knowledge production as an evolutionary process

The evidence that the reviewing process is vulnerable to invalid and unreliable judgments on the one hand and rigid conformity to the values and norms of the community on the other hand, appears to suggest a hopeless situation. However, the physical and biological sciences have advanced despite these flaws because knowledge production is a process of knowledge accrual that can only be evaluated in terms of the collective enterprise and the stream of research over time. A recurring theme throughout this chapter is that reviewers should evaluate manuscripts in the context of the body of knowledge that has accumulated on the topic. Reviewers should keep in mind the dictum of McGrath, Martin and Kulka (1982, p. 104) that "..... no one study can yield knowledge. Knowledge requires convergence of substantive findings derived from a diversity of methods of study.....We should seek not perfection in the single study, but accumulation over studies, using diverse means."

An evolutionary process consists of three components: variation, selection, and retention. Variations occur that are haphazard, and most fail but a few allow adaptation to external conditions and as a consequence are selected and retained. Evolution also requires a system of selection and rigid retention in which adaptations are held onto even when they no longer are functional. Variation and selective-retention are at odds in this process. Most importantly, evolution does not follow a rational scheme or grand plan. We may, after the fact, reconstruct a goal-oriented and orderly progression, but the true nature of the process is more haphazard. Where the process is more likely to work is where there is a balance between variation in the form of serendipity, chance, and happenstance that allows adaptation to change and orderly selection-retention that maintains the status quo. If we go too far in either direction, the consequences can be catastrophic. In an evolutionary process, moderate rates of mutation are necessary for survival and for evolutionary advantage but selection and retention that maintain useful adaptations are also necessary. A system that swings too far in the direction of either variation or selection-retention risks failure.

Knowledge production can be viewed from a social-evolutionary point of view. As noted by Campbell (1960), creative thought can be described as a product of blind variation and selective retention. From an evolutionary perspective, the evidence that reviewer judgments lack reliability and validity could be seen as contributing randomness to the process and in the grand scheme of things, perhaps this isn't such a bad thing. Simonton (2004) concluded that peer reviews have minimal informational value but positively contribute to scientific creativity. On the otherhand, Pfeffer (1993) has argued that those social sciences that have adhered to specific standards and have limited participation in the review and editorial process to the "elite" institutions, have achieved more power and prestige than those social science disciplines who have not adhered to rigid standards and are more inclusive in the review process. If the publication process swings too far in the direction of variation and away from selective retention, we run the risk of creating an unruly mess that is neither informative nor useful. In contrast, if we go too far in the direction of rigidly enforcing the same standards we run the risk of stifling major advances. According to Simonton (2004), "if peer review were highly reliable, it would most likely exert a stifling influence on the discipline. Scientists would then quickly learn how to ensure the acceptance of their submitted manuscripts, with the result that published articles would become ever more homogeneous, conventional, and unoriginal – in a word, uncreative" (pp. 90–1).

In conclusion, an evolutionary process suggests that we need stability that comes from the application of evaluative standards. To the extent that reviewers can provide valid and reliable evaluations of rigor, relevance, and contribution they provide such stability to the field. But the process will fall far short of perfection and this may be a blessing in disguise. Reviewers should do their best to ferret out the methodological and statistical errors. They should be alert to innovations and contributions even when they fall short on scientific rigor. They should be more appreciative of relevance. However, we will go too far if we attempt to impose exactly the same standards on all reviews. Reviewers will differ in the extent to which they emphasize rigor, relevance, and contribution among themselves and over different manuscripts. Rather than striving for a total elimination of these differences, we should recognize that it is this variety that provides the source of innovation, creativity, and change.

So what can reviewers do?

Although an evolutionary perspective provides some assurance that the flaws in the peer review system may provide the variation needed to produce innovations and advances, this is not to imply that reviewers should take no efforts to improve their reviews. To the contrary, they should attempt to provide the best evaluations they can on rigor, relevance, and value added. In the long term, the system will adjust for the differences among reviewers in their evaluations and their idiosyncratic biases. A greater worry than disagreements among reviewers is the potential harm that the review process can inflict on the motivation of scholars to conduct research and submit their work to the review process. In my opinion, the healthiest situation is one in which there is a large variety of manuscripts submitted for scrutiny and the least healthy is a review process that discourages submissions and stifles creativity. With a rejection rate that is 80% or higher in our most prestigious journals, the reviews that authors receive too often constitute attempts to justify the decision rather than constructive feedback on improvement. In an analysis of reviewer comments, Spencer, Hartnett and Mahoney (1986) found that 40% of reviewer reports contained more than 25% emotional persuasions and unsubstantiated comments suggesting prejudice and emotionality in the review process. Finke (1990, p. 669) suggests that highly original and innovative advances in a given field are rejected due to the referees' whimsical stance and often consider them "uninformed, quixotic or simply irresponsible." Cummings, Frost, and Vakil (1985, p. 479) describe reviewers who were "almost exclusively critical...skeptical and relatively insensitive to the form and tone with which their criticism was communicated." The motivation for the critics was that they had to "find something wrong in a manuscript" so that their review would count.

The danger of a reviewing system that encourages overly critical, self-righteous, biased, and insulting reviews is that too many authors will conclude that the entire system is unfair and will cease the attempt to publish. Simonton (2003, 2004) suggests that genius, creativity, and impact reflect quantity as much as or more than quality. Those who make the greatest contribution are those who keep plugging away in their respective fields and do not give up. I suspect that one reason that some potentially productive scholars give up is that they become discouraged, cynical, and even bitter as the result of their treatment by reviewers. This leads me to the rather radical conclusion that the only standard that should be rigidly imposed on reviewers by editors is to convey their comments on manuscripts in a fair and just manner (see chapter 5 for a more detailed discussion). They should avoid exacting revenge for their own past rejections and avoid emotional attacks on the intentions or intelligence of the author. Moreover, they should actually spend time on the manuscripts they review so as to provide thoughtful and detailed feedback that conveys that care has been taken by the reviewer. It is by maintaining a sense of justice in the publication system that the publication process will be able to generate a valid, relevant, and important body of knowledge. The major task in managing the review process is aptly described by Weick (1995, pp. 292–3) as transforming "a particularistic, private evaluation system incrementally into a more universalistic, public system while retaining the relatively scarce, overworked voluntary participants who think the private channel is working just fine (until they submit work of their own)." The greatest threat to this transformation is not that flawed work will make its way into the journals. The greatest threat is that in an overly zealous attempt to evaluate rigor, relevance, and value added we will destroy the sense of justice that sustains the efforts of reviewers, authors, and editors and holds them together as a community of scholars.

References

Abrahamson, E. (1991). Management fads and fashions: The diffusion and rejection of innovations. *Academy of Management Review, 16(3)*, 586–612.

Abrahamson, E. (1996). Management fashion. *Academy of Management Review, 21(1)*, 254–85.

Argyris, C. (1968). Some unintended consequences of rigorous research. *Psychological Bulletin, 70,* 185–97.

Bartunek, J. M., Gordon, J. R., & Weathersby, R. P. (1983). Developing "complicated" understanding in administrators. *Academy of Management Review, 8,* 273–84.

Beyer, J. M. (1997). Research utilization: Bridging the gap between communities. *Journal of Management Inquiry, 6,* 17–22.

Beyer, J. M., Chanove, R. G., & Fox, W. B. (1995). The review process and the fates of manuscripts submitted to AMJ. *Academy of Management Journal, 38,* 1219–60.

Beyer, J. M. & Trice, H. M. (1982). The utilization process: A conceptual framework and synthesis of empirical findings. *Administrative Science Quarterly, 27,* 591–622.

Binning, J. F. & Barrett, G. V. (1989). Validity of personnel decisions: A conceptual analysis of the inferential and evidential bases. *Journal of Applied Psychology, 74,* 478–94.

Borgman, C. L. (1990). *Scholarly communication and bibliometrics.* Thousand Oaks, CA: Sage.

Brown, K. G. & Gerhardt, M. W. (2002). Formative evaluation: An integrative practice model and case study. *Personnel Psychology, 55,* 951–83.

Campanario, J. M. (1998a). Peer review for journals as it stands today – Part I. *Science Communication, 19,* 181–211.

Campanario, J. M. (1998b). Peer review for journals as it stands today – Part II. *Science Communication, 19,* 277–306.

Campbell, D. T. (1960). Blind variation and selective retention in creative thought as in other knowledge processes. *Psychological Review, 67,* 380–400.

Campbell, J. P., Daft, R. L., & Hulin, C. L. (1982). *What to study: Generating and developing research questions.* Beverly Hills, CA: Sage.

Cicchetti, D. V. (1991). The reliability of peer review for manuscript and grant submissions: A cross–disciplinary investigation. *Behavioral and Brain Sciences, 14,* 119–86.

Cummings, L. (1978). Toward organizational behavior. *Academy of Management Review, 3,* 90–8.

Cummings, L., Frost, P. J., & Vakil, T. F. (1985). The manuscript review process: A view from the inside on coaches, critics, and special cases. In L. L. Cummings & P. J. Frost (eds) *Publishing in the organizational sciences.* Homewood, IL: Irwin, 469–508.

Daft, R. L. (1995). Why I recommended that your manuscript be rejected and what you can do about it. In L. L. Cummings & P. J. Frost (eds) *Publishing in the organizational sciences.* Homewood, IL: Irwin, 164–82.

Dipboye, R. L. & Flanagan, M. F. (1979). Research settings in industrial and organizational psychology: Are findings in the field more generalizable than in the laboratory? *American Psychologist, 34,* 141–50.

Dipboye, R. L. (1990). Laboratory vs. field research in industrial and organizational psychology. In C. L. Cooper & I. T. Robertson (eds) *International review of industrial and organizational psychology.* Vol. 5, 1–34.

Finke, R. A. (1990). Recommendations for contemporary editorial practices. *American Psychologist, 45,* 669–70.

Fiske, D. W. & Fogg, L. (1990). But the reviewers are making different criticisms of my paper! *American Psychologist, 45,* 591–8.

Gabbay, S. (2000) Connecting minds: Computer-mediated communication in scientific work. *Journal of the American Society for Information Science, 51(14),* 1295–305.

Graham, T. (2000) Scholarly communication. *Serials, 13(1),* 3–11.

Halliday, L. L. (2001). Scholarly communication, scholarly publication, and the status of emerging formats. *Information research, 6(4).* Electronic journal available at http://informationr.net/ir/6-4/infres64.html

Kling, R. & McKim, G. (1999) Scholarly communication and the continuum of electronic publishing. *Journal of the American Society for Information Science, 50(10),* 890–906.

Louis, M. R. (1994). Useful knowledge and knowledge use: Toward explicit meanings. In R. H. Kilmann, K. W. Thomas, D. P. Slevin, R. Nath & S. L. Jerrel (eds) *Producing useful knowledge for organizations.* San Francisco: Jossey-Bass, 25–36.

Lundberg, C. (1976). Hypothesis creation in organizational behavior research. *Academy of Management Review, 1,* 5–12.

Martin, H. J. (1994). Making knowledge more useful through the proper development and use of theory. In R. H. Kilmann, K. W. Thomas, D. P. Slevin, R. Nath & S. L. Jerrel (eds) *Producing useful knowledge for organizations.* San Francisco: Jossey-Bass, 564–79.

Mathias, P. F. (1994). "Introducing change in organizations: Moving from general theories of content to specific theories of context." In R. H. Kilmann, K. W. Thomas, D. P. Slevin, R. Nath & S. L. Jerrel (eds) *Producing useful knowledge for organizations.* San Francisco: Jossey-Bass, 133–44.

McCall, M. W. Jr. & Bobko, P. (1990). Research methods in the service of discovery. In M. D. Dunnette & L. M. Hough (eds) *Handbook of industrial and organizational psychology.* Palo Alto, California: Consulting Psychologists Press, Inc., 381–418.

McGrath, J. E., Martin, J., & Kulka, R. A. (1982). *Judgment calls in research.* Beverly Hills, CA: Sage, 103–18.

Mitroff, I. I., Betz, F., Pondy, L. R., & Sagasti, R. (1974). On managing science in the systems age: Two schemas for the study of science as a whole systems phenomenon. *Interfaces, 4,* 46–58.

Moxley, J. (1992). *Publish don't perish: The scholars' guide to academic writing and publishing.* Westport, CT: Greenwood Press.

Nord, W. R. (1995). Looking at ourselves as we look at others: An exploration of the publication system for organization research. In L. L. Cummings & P. J. Frost (eds) *Publishing in the organizational sciences* (2nd ed). Thousand Oaks, CA: Sage Publications, 64–78.

Peters, D. P. & Ceci, S. J. (1982). Peer-review practices of psychological journals: The fate of published articles, submitted again. *The Behavioral and Brain Sciences, 5,* 187–95.

Pfeffer, J. (1993). Barriers to the advance of organizational science: Paradigm development as a dependent variable. *Academy of Management Review, 18(4),* 599–621.

Platt (1964) Strong inference. *Science, 146,* 347–53.

Popper, K. R. (1959). *The logic of scientific discovery.* New York: Harper Torchbooks.

Sackett, P. R. & Larson, J. R. Jr. (1990). Research strategies and tactics in industrial and organizational psychology. In M. D. Dunnette & L. M. Hough (eds) *Handbook of industrial and organizational psychology.* Palo Alto, California: Consulting Psychologists Press, Inc., 419–89.

Schutz, A. (1970). *Reflections on the problem of relevance.* New Haven: Yale University Press.

Sellitz C., Wrightman, L. S. & Cook, S. W. (1976). *Research methods in social relations.* New York: Holt, Rinehart and Winston.

Simonton, D. K. (2003). Scientific creativity as constrained stochastic behavior: The integration of product, person, and process perspectives. *Psychological Bulletin, 129(4),* 475–94.

Simonton, D. K. (2004). *Creativity in Science: Chance, logic, genius, and zeitgeist.* New York, NY: Cambridge University Press.

Spencer, N. J., Hartnett, J. & Mahoney, J. (1986). Problems with reviews in standard editorial practice. *Journal of Social Behavior and Personality, 1(1),* 21–36.

Staw, B. M. (1995). Repairs on the road to relevance and rigor: Some unexplored issues in publishing organizational research. In L. L. Cummings & P. J. Frost (eds) *Publishing in the organizational sciences.* Thousand Oaks: Sage, 85–98.

Thomas, K. W. & Kilmann, R. H. (1994). Where have the organizational sciences gone? A survey of the academy of management membership. In R. H. Kilmann, K. W. Thomas, D. P. Slevin, R. Nath & S. L. Jerrel (eds) *Producing useful knowledge for organizations.* San Francisco: Jossey-Bass, 69–81.

Thomas, K.W. & Tymon, W. G. JR. (1982). Necessary properties of relevant research: Lessons from recent criticisms of the organizational sciences. *Academy of Management Review, 7,* 345–52.

Vroom, V. (1964). *Work and motivation.* New York: John Wiley & Sons.

Weick, K. E. (1979). *The social psychology of organizing.* Reading, MA: Addison Wesley Publishing.

Weick, K. E. (1995). Editing innovation into Administrative Science Quarterly. In L. L. Cummings & P. J. Frost (eds) *Publishing in the organizational sciences* (2nd ed). Thousand Oaks, CA: Sage Publications, 284–96.

Weiss, C. H. (1980). Knowledge creep and decision accretion. *Knowledge: Creation, Diffusion, Utilization, 1,* 381–404.

Weiss, C. H. & Bucuvalas, M. J. (1980). Truth tests and utility tests: Decision-makers' frames of reference for social science research. *American Sociological Review, 45,* 302–13.

2
Reviewing as a Vital Professional Service

Richard L. Priem and Abdul A. Rasheed

Thoughtful, accurate and developmental reviews of academic papers are an important but ultimately limited resource for management and behavioral sciences scholars. Demand for this resource is growing: the *Journal of Management* expects 500 manuscript submissions in 2005 and the *Academy of Management Journal* anticipates up to 800, each represents a substantial increase over previous years. But in the short run the number of qualified and experienced reviewers is relatively rigid – even more so than is the number of journal pages available in which to publish – so the supply of high-quality reviews cannot be ramped up quickly. In short, increasing pressure likely will be placed on the review system as the number of scholars actively participating in social sciences research expands.

Because peer reviews are "public" goods, however, the review situation is analogous to the "Tragedy of the Commons" (Hardin, 1968), wherein finite, publicly held resources – e.g., grazing lands, fisheries, or national parks – will inevitably be overused by rational, utility-maximizing individuals to the ultimate detriment of the collective. Following the logic of the Commons, for example, it is rational at the margins for individuals to graze their cattle on "free" public grazing lands, even if by doing so they reduce the aggregate productivity of the land through overgrazing. Similarly, in our review system, any scholar may submit a manuscript and fully expect to receive a set of top-notch peer reviews, with no private costs to be borne by the scholar. Under this situation, the Commons logic suggests that some scholars likewise may "overgraze" the peer review system.

It is easy to find examples of review misuse; two should suffice. First, Daily, Dalton, and Rajagopalan (2003) edited a special issue of the *Academy of Management Journal* on the subject of "Governance through

Ownership". They sent out 56 manuscripts for peer review during the special issue process. Fourteen of the authors *who had submitted manuscripts to that special issue* declined to review a manuscript for the same special issue. One author who declined had submitted *two* manuscripts. According to Daily et al: "That individuals are willing to reap the full benefits of the peer review system without meeting their professional – and collegial – responsibility to participate in the system causes us to wonder what this behavior portends for the future of the peer review system on which our profession so heavily depends" (2003: 157).

The second example comes from a recent experience by the first author of this chapter. I received the same paper – absolutely identical – for review three times sequentially from three *different* top journals. The first time around I prepared the best review I could, and I believe the two other reviewers did similarly thorough and conscientious jobs. What a disappointment when I later received the same paper from another journal and found that the authors had made *no* changes – not one – based on my comments or those of the other reviewers! For the second review I reused the previous set of comments, briefly mentioning that I had seen this paper before. Alas, I received the paper yet again from a third journal, and yet again the authors had eschewed correcting even the spelling or grammatical errors identified in previous reviews. I declined the third review, giving the authors a chance to see something new from a different reviewer. These authors clearly were "gaming" the peer review system, hurting not only the system but also the authors themselves; after receiving six reviews (one twice), their paper had not improved one whit.

It appears from these examples that free-riding and shirking behaviors may be commonplace in the peer review system. Moreover, authors can engage in these behaviors with relative impunity, in part because of the lack of visibility of reviewing as a service. Of course, the fact that some will misuse the system, combined with the growing demand for reviews, makes it ever more imperative that others participate fully and fairly.

Reviewing: the invisible service

Perhaps it should not be surprising that free-riding and shirking are seen from some scholars when it comes to professional reviewing responsibilities – after all, there is little extrinsic reward for such service. Most universities follow similar evaluation systems for faculty, wherein a faculty member's contributions are evaluated in terms of teaching, research, and service, according to some predetermined weighting system. Oft-asked questions about reviewing are: where does reviewing fit in the scheme of things? Is it a research activity? Or is it service? And how can a faculty member's reviewing contribution be measured and rewarded? As far as we know, these issues seldom have been addressed successfully in most business schools, despite the important role that reviewers play in the development of the scholarly disciplines. This makes reviewing something of an "invisible" service – the need is always there, but the work is seldom seen and applauded. Further, journal editors themselves rarely give feedback to reviewers about either the quality of their reviews or their timeliness. The occasional "our thanks are due to three anonymous reviewers" footnote, and perhaps a listing in fine print in the last issue of some journals, seems to be the only reward for the countless hours a conscientious reviewer spends reading and evaluating journal manuscripts. No wonder some reviewers accord last priority to doing timely reviews, decline most review requests, provide only "slapdash" reviews or, even worse, vent career frustrations through blisteringly negative reviews.

This state of affairs is unlikely to change unless members of the social sciences research community understand the critical role they must play as reviewers: a role so vital that the very development of our fields depends on how seriously and conscientiously it is fulfilled. Some scholars of course will respond fully and enthusiastically to the need for high quality reviews, as they always have done. And many scholars understand fully the many self-development benefits of reviewing often, which include: staying current with emerging trends, building critical thinking skills useful for writing one's own papers, better understanding the editorial process, and so on. Puffer, Quick and McCarthy (chapter 10) describe these and other benefits in more detail. Unless this currently-invisible service becomes a more visible aspect of one's career, however, mere exhortations to be more conscientious or to take the responsibilities of reviewing more seriously are likely to have little effect on others.

Our objective in this chapter is to identify and evaluate the various professional service roles that reviewers play. Building on Dipboye's previous discussion of knowledge production as an evolutionary process, we first briefly examine the characteristics of the peer review process itself as a selection mechanism. We then discuss two major functions of reviews, namely, the evaluative and developmental functions. We examine the responsibilities that come with these roles, and we offer some tentative suggestions for developing systems and standards for recognizing and rewarding reviewer contributions. For furthering reading on how and why to write developmental reviews, see chapters 4 and 5.

"Peer Review" selection systems

The marketplace is the most common system for selection among goods, wherein consumers select from among alternative products or services on offer. But other kinds of selection systems – like the peer review system in management and behavioral sciences scholarship – are fairly widespread and often coexist. Wijnberg & Gemser (2000) explored two selection systems that are common for products in hard-to-value, cultural industries like scholarship: peer selection and expert selection. The Academy of Motion Picture Arts and Sciences is an example of pure peer-based selection, because all members of the Academy have an equal vote in determining which movies are awarded an "Oscar". Movie or restaurant critics, on the other hand, are examples of expert-based selection. In these cases those with acknowledged "expert" skills evaluate possible alternatives on behalf of less knowledgeable consumers, with the goal of increasing the quality of consumers' selections while reducing consumer search time. Each of these cases closely parallels portions of the peer review selection process in social sciences scholarship. Our reviewers' comments most closely represent "peer selection", where peers "vote" on manuscripts. Editorial decisions most closely represent "expert selection", as editors select high quality manuscripts on behalf of consumers. Therefore, Wijnberg & Gemser's (2000) analysis likely offers some insights for our review system, as we explain next.

   Wijnberg & Gemser (2000) analyzed the transformation that occurred in the selection system for works of art following the advent of Impressionism in painting. Before the Impressionist movement, a peer-based system was in place for valuing paintings. An Academy comprised of established artists was the "selector", and new artists' paintings were "selected" as worthwhile and therefore valuable based on the Academy's quality perceptions. Access to the Academy guaranteed an artist's career. The issue for Impressionists was that the established artists were resistant to innovation, and acceptance of new artists and techniques was slow. A different selection system more favorable to Impressionists soon came into place alongside the Academy, based on expert valuations by art critics, art dealers and museum curators. These experts lacked the vested interest in the status quo held by the Academy artists and, therefore, they were more likely to identify and reward innovations such as Impressionism (Wijnberg & Gemser, 2000). Thus, valuation of hard-to-value works of art shifted from artistic peers to experts, in order to encourage and reward innovation. In this case, the experts were not the end-users; instead, they were setting value standards for the ultimate art consumers.

Social sciences scholars should see parallels between the selection systems just described for works of art and our own system for scholarly works. Reviewers and editors, serving as peers and experts, respectively, create value for the scholarly audience by reducing the search effort required to find high-quality research. Because journal reputation is what allows scholarly consumers to limit their search and still believe they are accessing the best research, journals must expend considerable efforts toward building their reputations. Furthermore, we all likely are familiar with the inertia problems associated with "invisible colleges" (Crane, 1972), just as the Impressionists were – reviewers and some editors most often stay within established traditions when accepting articles. Clearly, for our system to work most effectively we must strive to be fair and impartial, and to eliminate any biases against innovative work that challenges the status quo. Such impartiality for reviewers would include not being "stuck on" our own theoretical predilections and, certainly, not asking authors consistently to cite our own works.

Wijnberg and Gemser's (2000) work also leads us to several propositions for prospective authors in our own system. First, some journals can be classified as dominated by reviewers; in those journals, editors make their editorial decisions mostly by counting the "votes" of reviewers. When this sort of strongly peer-based selection is the rule – i.e., in reviewer-dominated journals – Wijnberg and Gemser's (2000) work suggests that mimicry, or at least closely imitating success, may be effective in increasing the likelihood of getting published. Second, some journals can be classified as dominated by the editor; in those journals, editors make their editorial decisions independently after considering the comments of reviewers. When this sort of strongly expert-based selection is the rule – i.e., in editor-dominated journals – innovation is more likely to be rewarded, in part because experts have reputation-driven incentives to identify innovative goods. Third, in some journals, reviewers and editors often have a symbiotic relationship, wherein the legitimacy of one is enhanced by the legitimacy of the other.

The functions of a review

Given these characteristics of the peer review selection process in social sciences scholarship, what are the key functions of the review system? And how are these functions a professional obligation for those who benefit from the system? We address these questions next.

The evaluative function

The primary role of the reviewer is to evaluate a paper. Clearly, there is some degree of subjectivity involved in most evaluations. Other chapters in this volume address the issue of enhancing the quality of reviews, and we therefore will not go into that in this chapter. The more important question for us is: how does one fulfill one's professional role as a reviewer?

One of the roles that most editors want a reviewer to play is similar to the role played by *quality control* inspectors on a production line. The quality control inspector is not expected to create a set of standards, but instead to ensure that the product conforms to quality standards established by the company. Thus, it is the responsibility of the reviewer to understand the criteria established by the editors for what constitutes "quality" for a specific journal. Currently, the problem we face is twofold. On one hand, few journals or journal editors thoroughly communicate a clear set of standards of what is acceptable and what is not for their journals. Therefore, considerable ambiguity is common regarding differences in standards across journals. And many reviewers prefer to follow their set of personal standards and criteria without ever bothering to read the standards and adhere to them even when such standards exist. This often results in conflicting feedback by multiple reviewers, perceptions of unfairness by authors, and a considerable dilemma for editors. Reviewing a manuscript submitted to a second or third tier journal as if it were a submission to the best journal in the area is just as unfair as treating a manuscript from a Tier 1 journal as if it was submitted to a Tier 3 journal. That is, acceptability of a manuscript is only partly a function of the manuscript itself – it is equally a function of the journal as well. This is a distinction that reviewers must bear in mind as part of their professional responsibility.

Individual reviewers imposing idiosyncratic views about what constitutes a theoretical contribution or what is an appropriate methodological approach, without attending to the editorial policies of the journal and its status within the hierarchy of journals, can lead to both Type 1 errors (i.e., rejecting a paper deserving of acceptance) and Type 2 errors (i.e., accepting a paper that should have been rejected). Many of us have taught from time to time topics such as quality control and hypotheses testing. We also teach our students how to tailor products for specific markets. Unfortunately, in the practice of our profession these concepts seem to have made very little impact.

A second important evaluative function in our professional role as reviewers is to help editors act as *gatekeepers*. The gatekeeper role is distinct from the quality control function. Here, the reviewer's role is not one of ensuring that a manuscript's quality conforms to expectations set out by the editorial board, but instead one of judging whether the topics covered in a manuscript belong to the domain of the journal. Our experience is that, when there is any question at all, editors appreciate reviewer viewpoints concerning a manuscript's fit with the journal's domain. Unduly narrow conceptualizations of a domain may lead to truly original ideas being denied the possibility of appearing in a journal, whereas overly loose definitions of the domain can lead to a lack of any domain coherence at all for a journal.

The developmental function

While it is understood that reviewers have to function as quality control inspectors and gatekeepers, the true value added in the reviewing process comes from the developmental role played by reviewers. The policing role described above can lead to good "law and order" in the field, but the goal of the leading journals is not to create a police state. The policing role often is neither intellectually challenging nor emotionally rewarding. Both intrinsic satisfaction and contribution to the field can come from reviewers' roles as collaborators in the production of knowledge. The reviewers play a critical role as contributors: to the discipline, to the journal, to the paper, and finally to the authors of the paper too as professional mentors. In the following paragraphs, we briefly discuss these roles.

Over the past two decades, universities around the world have come to place increasing emphasis on research productivity – measured primarily in terms of number of publications – when making tenure and promotion decisions. Given the very high personal stakes, many younger scholars "play it safe" while submitting manuscripts to leading journals. This risk aversion with regard to theoretical approaches and methodological techniques has the potential to result in ever increasing intellectual isomorphism within our disciplines. The tragedy is that young scholars, who in the early years of their careers are most subject to these isomorphic pressures, are also in the most creative years of their careers. This is where the developmental role of reviewers becomes particularly relevant. Reviewers can facilitate the publication of novel, innovative papers instead of "safe" papers that make, at best, marginal contributions to the discipline. As Dipboye pointed out in chapter 1, once an area is established, reviewers should look out for and encourage research that is driven by "big questions" as opposed to what has been done before. However, the current state of the field is such that the authors bear the entire risk if they don't play it safe. We believe that a vital aspect of the developmental role of the reviewers is to identify and encourage innovation by authors, to in a sense be "risk-sharers" by relieving the authors of some of that burden. Certainly reviewers are in a better position to bear risk, because their individual stakes in terms of career and promotion are much lower.

The most obvious contribution that reviewers can make is to the paper itself. Reviewers are chosen on the basis of their expertise. That is, they are knowledgeable about the specific area covered by the paper. Many reviewers are good at identifying what is wrong with a paper, but the important thing is not to stop after identifying deficiencies. Instead, the reviewer has to make a judgment call as to whether the paper can make a contribution if the deficiencies are corrected. If that answer is yes, a conscientious reviewer would then go on to offer constructive suggestions about how the deficiencies can be addressed. Sometimes, this might require taking a different methodological approach. At other times, one may encourage the authors to look at additional streams of literature or to address alternative explanations for the same phenomenon. The key, though, is to identify what needs to be done rather than solely to point out what is wrong.

We as reviewers also have responsibilities to the authors as fellow researchers in the same discipline. We have come across numerous instances of junior faculty members saying "if only the acceptance letter had come a week earlier, I would have made tenure." This suggests the existence of a double-sided problem in academia. On the one hand, many schools have now reduced tenure decisions to a formula. A publication is often referred to as a "hit", essentially suggesting that we have become increasingly afraid to make bold decisions about granting or denying tenure to individual faculty members. Instead, we seek refuge in a magical number of "hits." On the other hand, it also suggests that an individual faculty member has to pay a very high price if a reviewer does not respond on time to a review request. When a paper sits on a reviewer's desk for months, not only does it not add value to the discipline, it actually loses value due to increasing obsolescence of data and, sometimes, even ideas. But the authors clearly pay the greatest price for these delays. Doing a timely review is our responsibility to the authors and to the profession, irrespective of whether we are recommending an acceptance or rejection. This is an integral component of what Shapiro and Sitkin call a "fair review" (see chapter 5).

Finally, good reviewers are also making a major contribution to the growth and development of the journals. Journals are engaged in competition with each other for legitimacy in the marketplace for ideas. A journal that develops a reputation for fast decisions, openness to novel ideas and methodologies, constructive high quality reviews, and fairness in decisions is likely to attract the best manuscripts. Editors depend on reviewers for each of these.

Professional reviewing obligations for management and behavioral sciences scholars

Given the peer review system characteristics and the reviewer functions we have just described, what are the appropriate professional reviewing obligations of a management scholar? To initiate a dialogue, we provide a few suggestions below. These are developed based on the previous discussions or from the author "bill of rights" suggested by Harrison (2002 – Items 4, 5 & 6 below are adapted from Dave's *AMJ* essay). You may have more obligations to add to our list, or you may disagree with some of ours, but we hope these suggestions serve as a basis for reflection and discussion.

1. **Review often!** Try to follow the old factor analysis 5:1 thumb rule, in two ways. First, maintain a 5:1 ratio for review acceptances versus refusals by saying "yes" to five review requests for every one you decline. Second, maintain another 5:1 ratio for reviews you perform versus your own manuscript submissions by completing five reviews for each paper you submit. If everyone would attempt to live by these ratios, editors would have fewer problems finding willing reviewers, and the chances of a "Tragedy of the Commons" quality shortage would be lessened. These ratios may seem steep, but remember: some of your colleagues are likely free-riding or shirking! In chapter 6, Schepmyer and van Emmerik provide novices with specific strategies for identifying opportunities to review often.

2. **Try to be open-minded to something new!** We don't mean that you as a reviewer should compromise on quality – ever. But if a paper comes that contradicts your cherished theory, or that doesn't

use the precise data analytic method from your dissertation, give it a chance with a thoughtful and open-minded reading anyway.

3. **Let the authors have their voice!** Some review comments are vital "musts", while others are personal preferences. Control your own predilections and, during the review process, try not to stick like a barnacle to every obscure point where you disagree with the authors. Focus instead on what is truly important (see Bedeian, 2004, for a discussion).

4. **Apply the standards of logic and evidence to your review!** Nothing is more annoying than receiving a review filled with "it seems to me that" or "the such and such literature might disagree" or "see Smith's work on that". Who is Smith, anyway? Take the time to make sound arguments and provide specific citations. The authors deserve it, and it gives the most possible help to the editor.

5. **Give reviews your full attention!** If you read the manuscript while watching the Super Bowl, and write your review on the back of a napkin at the coffee shop, you are unlikely to attain sufficiency on Item #4 above (see Harrison, 2002, for a discussion). Quality reviews require care and concentration.

6. **Be on time!** We have all waited, and waited, and waited for the e-mail that will tell us the fate of our work at a particular journal. Oftentimes, this wait is due to just one reviewer dawdling, or placing the priority for one's own work above that for the authors' work. We've all experienced this, so let's not do it to others.

7. **Review often!** Okay, we know we listed this one already, but it is surely the most important for the success of our field. Furthermore, Northcraft (2001) has noted apparent positive correlations between declining to review and the potential reviewers' levels of experience, status, and academic rank. Yet these are the people who are most needed. Thus, especially for those who already have achieved scholarly success: review often!

These items are designed as suggestions for the professional obligations of scholars reviewing under the peer review system "as is". Next, we provide a few suggestions for altering the system itself in order to make reviewing a more extrinsically rewarding experience.

Creating incentives for reviewers

One of the major reasons for lack of consistency and timeliness in reviews is the lack of incentives. Intrinsic satisfaction from doing a job well is important, but when faced with multiple demands on faculty time many elect to focus on activities that are most rewarding, either financially or in terms of visibility. The paradox of anonymity in the blind-review process is that, while it enables a reviewer to have a protective shield from professional repercussions, it also takes away most of the incentives to put forth the required effort. If the editor is the principal and the reviewer is the agent, there is clearly an agency problem here. The two traditional ways to resolve an agency problem are incentive alignment and monitoring (Jensen & Meckling, 1976). In this particular case, there are hardly any incentives, and monitoring is not feasible either. Thus, we have a classic agency problem with no easy resolution in sight. We next consider at least a few possible steps for addressing the problem by increasing incentives for reviewers.

First, the time may have come for us to consider rethinking some aspects of the blind-review process, particularly where we can do so without sacrificing the integrity of the process itself. Some journals currently require authors to nominate potential reviewers. We believe that this practice has the unfortunate potential to negatively impact the integrity of the review process. Even if it does not do so in actuality, the practice still can cause perceptions of unfairness. Therefore, we believe that having authors nominate reviewers brings at least the appearance of less accountability and less integrity to the review process. Instead we suggest, following Bedeian (2004), that once a paper is accepted and subsequently published, journals could publish the names of the reviewers along with the article, subject to agreement by the reviewers. This approach has several advantages. First, the reviews are still blind in the sense that the authors do not know who wrote which review. All they see is the names of the two or three reviewers. In the case of rejections, of course, the names of the reviewers would not be published. Second, this process of recognition could create a small bias for accepting as opposed to the current bias towards rejecting. Would this necessarily lead to more articles being recommended for acceptance than the journal space permits, thus creating a problem for editors? We do not expect this to happen, because most reviewers will not want to be known for recommending acceptance of weak papers, which could negatively affect their reputations. Third, and most importantly, we believe that this could actually lead to an improvement in the quality of the publications themselves, because the publication of their names gives the reviewers a sense of "ownership" of the paper. This would actually motivate reviewers to offer constructive suggestions and to work more closely with the authors to help develop the paper. Fourth, name visibility constitutes a reward for the reviewer because of its reputation effects. Finally, it does not cost the journal anything extra to publish the names of reviewers alongside a paper. Based on these reasons, we believe that recognizing reviewers by publishing their names has the potential to enhance the review process without compromising the integrity of the process itself.

Writing a serious, constructive, and conscientious review is a time consuming task. Sometimes a good review may take several days of work to complete. A good review is a scholarly manuscript in itself, but a manuscript that will not be published. There are several things that an editor can do to reward good reviewers. If an individual is doing several reviews a year for an editor, and these reviews are of good quality, the obvious reward is an invitation to serve on the editorial board. Service on an editorial board can lead to professional recognition externally and financial rewards internally for an individual faculty member. If editors take the effort to make it clear to the ad hoc reviewers that the best among them will eventually be invited to the editorial board, this will provide an incentive to the reviewers to take their job more conscientiously. Unfortunately, many journals seeking to build their reputations may want their editorial boards to be filled with "name brand" scholars who may not have the time or motivation to review a large number of manuscripts. This could lead to de facto two-tier boards, similar to the governance practice that is common among German corporations, wherein bigger name scholars actually perform far fewer reviews than do the lesser known board members who actually do the bulk of the reviewing. Instead, we believe all board members should actively share the reviewing burden.

Every good reviewer cannot be invited to serve on an editorial board, however, because no editor wants to have a huge editorial board. Therefore, other types of incentives can be created for those who are not invited to editorial boards. One possible reward could be recognition of a small number of reviewers with "best reviewer" awards. The *Academy of Management Journal* gives "outstanding reviewer" awards to a few particularly deserving board members each year, and the Academy of Management gives "best reviewer" awards to a small number of good reviewers in each of its divisions. This latter program has been very successful in motivating many to participate in the review process as well as to provide timely reviews of high quality. We see no reason why more journals cannot do the same thing for their ad hoc reviewers.

The suggestions we have discussed so far essentially involve non-financial rewards. However, we believe that they have the potential to translate into financial and professional rewards as well. The evaluation systems currently followed in most universities include very little recognition or reward for time spent reviewing journal articles. We suspect this is primarily because the Dean or Department Chair has no means to ascertain either the level of effort or the quality of the output. Unlike journal articles, reviews are not "rejected"! While invitation to editorial boards would take some time and seniority, the other means of recognition that we discussed above are available to all reviewers, including those who are just starting their careers. Including a faculty member's performance as a reviewer as one of the factors in the annual performance evaluation would provide reviewers with a meaningful incentive. Even for tenure and promotion decisions, we believe it is a good idea to take into consideration a faculty member's contributions as a reviewer, as evidenced by self-reports of the number of reviews performed for different journals and through recognition by editors via letters or awards.

Concluding thoughts

We have argued that the peer review system is vital to progress in the management and behavioral science disciplines, but also that there are several characteristics of the system that may combine to slow progress. First, peer reviews are "public" goods that are subject to the "Tragedy of the Commons" (Hardin, 1968); that is, overuse by rational, utility-maximizing individuals could ultimately overburden the system. This is particularly likely if manuscript submissions continue to grow rapidly. Second, performing peer reviews is essentially an "invisible" service – unmonitored and with few extrinsic rewards. Thus, this service is particularly vulnerable to free-riding and shirking by those who benefit, which only exacerbates the Commons problem. And third, peer review selection systems are typically resistant to innovation, as those who are well-established system members tend to protect against challenges to the status quo. This results in considerable inertia.

These problems are far from insurmountable; the peer review system has served us well to date, and likely will continue to do so in the future. But we all must be aware of the issues with peer review and, specifically, of our professional obligations to help the process "work". In short, for a peer review system like ours to be successful, all participants must review often and refuse seldom. And review frequency should increase, rather than decline, with stature in the field. Reviewers must strive to be open-minded to new ideas and, thereby, overcome the "innovation inertia" so often associated with peer review. Respect for authors, conscientiousness and promptness go without saying.

We listed earlier in this chapter the 7 obligations that we believe all scholars have to the peer review process as it is practiced today. You might think of others, or perhaps you might challenge some of the obligations on our list – that's fine. And we have offered several suggestions for changing the peer review process in order to make service as a peer reviewer at least slightly less "invisible". Again, there may be disagreements. We hope that this chapter may at least spur discussion about professional responsibilities in peer review. Certainly, if all scholars would actively fulfill what they individually see as their professional obligation to peer review, the system likely will hold up well even in the face of increased submissions. Moreover, we believe that those who increase their participation also will be pleasantly surprised that participation in peer review is not entirely an altruistic endeavor – we have found that we receive a substantial net gain from our participation as reviewers.

References

Bedeian, A. G. (2004). Peer review and the social construction of knowledge in the management discipline. *Academy of Management Learning & Education, 3*, 198–216.

Crane, D. (1972). *Invisible colleges: Diffusion of knowledge in scientific communities.* Chicago: University of Chicago Press.

Daily, C. M., Dalton, D. R., & Rajagopalan, N. (2003). Governance through ownership: Centuries of practice, decades of research. *Academy of Management Journal, 46*, 151–8.

Hardin, G. (1968). The tragedy of the commons. *Science, 162*, 1243–8.

Harrison, D. (2002). From the editors: Obligations and obfuscations in the review process. *Academy of Management Journal, 46*, 1079–84.

Jensen, M. C. & Meckling, W. H. (1976). Theory of the firm: Managerial behavior, agency costs and ownership structure. *Journal of Financial Economics, 3*, 305–60.

Northcraft, G. B. (2001). From the editors. *Academy of Management Journal, 44*, 1079–80.

Wijnberg, N. M. & Gemser, G. (2000). Adding value to innovation: Impressionism and the transformation of the selection system in visual arts. *Organization Science, 11*, 323–9.

3

To Review or Not to Review? When You Shouldn't Accept a Request to Review

Ann Marie Ryan*

There are many reasons to accept a request to review a manuscript:

- to serve a profession and to advance the knowledge base in an area.
- to fulfill the norms of reciprocity – because someone reviews your manuscripts voluntarily you should do the same
- to develop one's knowledge of how to best craft manuscripts
- to keep abreast of upcoming developments in an area of interest
- to enhance one's professional reputation as an expert, leading to personal satisfaction and perhaps external rewards

Because of these and other motives, those at early career stages are given the advice to accept invitations to review. Indeed, without a norm of accepting requests to review, the scholarship of the field would be greatly compromised. One <u>should</u> accept requests to review.

However, there are a few instances when it is appropriate to turn down requests to review. The purpose of this brief chapter is to provide some guidance on when **not** to review, with the understanding that these are exceptions, not the norm. The advice contained herein comes from my experiences as a reviewer, having served on editorial boards of several journals, doing ad hoc reviews for another dozen or so journals, and currently serving as editor for *Personnel Psychology*. It also comes from a burgeoning literature on the peer review process (see Weller, 2001 for a book-length summary).

Declining to review an article can have multiple negative consequences, some of greater concern than others. Editors must seek

* The author wishes to thank Dan Ilgen for comments on an earlier draft of this chapter.

another reviewer, and having not gotten their initial choice, may be assigning a less expert or less experienced individual. Authors experience delays in learning decisions on their submissions and may also lose out on valued insights that would have been provided by the expert who declined to review. The individual declining to review can be affected too, as he/she may have gained insights from the author's work and he/she may drop off an editor's radar screen as a desirable reviewer.

However, accepting invitations to review when one lacks expertise or time or is biased also creates negative consequences for editors and authors. Lack of timeliness in returning reviews frustrates editors and authors. Biased or shoddy reviews are at best unhelpful to editors and authors and at worst lead to unfair decisions, author dissatisfaction with a journal, and author withdrawal from further involvement in publication of work.

While decisions to decline to do reviews may seem straightforward, this chapter will highlight the gray areas. There is considerable disagreement as to what is problematic in terms of accepting invitations to review. Further, while there are certain behaviors that the majority of researchers would label as unethical, there are many that are less clearly categorized. Each section of this chapter begins with a few scenarios to provoke thinking about situations where individuals often do not decline to review, but where questions can be raised about the fairness of the resulting review. Because there are no formulaic responses to these scenarios, there is not always a clear answer as to whether to accept or decline the reviewing opportunity. Five potential reasons to decline a request to review are discussed: lack of expertise, conflict of interest, bias, reviewing a paper a second time, and insufficient time.

Lack of expertise

For each of these scenarios, would you review or decline the request?

You are asked to review a paper that is in an area related to your research focus, but not exactly what you do. You keep current with the literature in this area although you have never published or even conducted a study in this domain yourself.

You are asked to review a paper that focuses on some constructs you have studied, but uses statistical analytic techniques with which you are completely unfamiliar.

You are a neophyte to a particular research area, having published one paper with a senior colleague on the topic. You are eager to learn more and are asked to review a paper on this area.

You accepted a request to review a paper because based on the title and abstract it seemed like it was a work you knew something about. The review is due tomorrow, and, in reading the paper, you feel there is a lot you don't understand – your expertise in this area is not as deep as you thought.

A clear and compelling reason not to do a review is because one lacks the expertise to evaluate a manuscript. Presumably, if editors are assigning manuscripts to reviewers based on their expertise, this should not occur. However, it is quite possible that an editor's lack of knowledge of the nuances of a research domain (particularly for a journal that covers a variety of subdisciplines) may lead him/her to have an incorrect understanding of a reviewer's expertise. One should never feel uncomfortable turning down a request to review because it exceeds one's expertise, and it serves as an opportunity to better educate the editor regarding one's true forté.

However, there is disagreement as to what constitutes an expert. I would argue that reviewers should avoid adopting a definition of expert that is too narrow. One need not be an expert in *all* aspects of a manuscript to be able to review the manuscript competently. The issue is whether one's expertise allows one to comment cogently on the *central* features of the paper. For example, reviewers will often note in comments to the editor that they are not an expert in a particular statistical technique or are unfamiliar with a measure used or theory discussed. Such comments help the editor in recognizing what aspects of the manuscript might need further scrutiny (from other reviewers with such expertise) and/or further elaboration by the author (as many readers of the journal may also have similar levels of unfamiliarity). The review provided in this instance still has much value for the areas the reviewer was able to evaluate. While some have gone so far as to argue for "compartmentalized reviews," where a content and a method expert each review only portions of a paper (Shugan, 2003), most editors will seek perspectives on the manuscript as a whole but ensure that all aspects of the paper are covered across reviewers. For example, if a manuscript integrates different domains, editors often choose reviewers from each domain without expectation that each will also be able to comment effectively on the other areas. The obligation of the reviewer is to determine what the limits of his/her expertise are and to alert the editor to those limits – it is the editor's job to ensure that an adequate overall review of the paper was performed by the team of reviewers.

Further, limiting reviewing only to those with agreed-upon expert status (e.g., fellows, those with a certain number of publications on a topic) is both impractical and potentially harmful to innovation. "Outsider" perspectives can be of great value in challenging assumptions and in recognizing new and creative approaches to issues; editors may choose a reviewer precisely because he/she is not entrenched in an area.

Editors may also expect board members to "stretch" more than ad hoc reviewers. For example, the board members of *Personnel Psychology* are chosen not just for their content expertise but also because of their skill in providing high quality, developmental feedback. One can provide a useful review of a manuscript outside a narrowly defined expertise area if one is well-trained in methodological issues and broadly read in the fundamental theories of an area.

Some have argued that a lack of expertise among reviewers is a more prevalent problem than acknowledged. Bedeian (2004) reviewed literature on whether the peer review process truly involves "peers" in terms of those having the requisite technical expertise to be equally knowledgeable in the field as the author. For example, taken to the extreme, one could argue that more junior researchers should never review the work of senior researchers. Currently, most journals in the management arena operate from a broad definition of what is a peer and espouse the view that there are legitimate professional reasons not to have only the most senior and seasoned experts as reviewers (e.g., allowing new thinking in an area, new PhDs are often methodologically more up-to-date than senior colleagues). Nevertheless, reviewers need to have a sufficient track record to have demonstrated the expertise they claim.

Bedeian (2003) surveyed authors of two leading journals and found that almost 55% said they had been asked to review manuscripts they were not competent to critique and more than a third of these stated that had submitted a review in those cases. These figures are hard to interpret without further information: Did the reviewers alert the editor to the limits of their expertise? Did the editors have other reviewers that provided the missing expertise? It is also possible (though I think less likely) that individuals are being self-effacing about their competence. Regardless, the data suggest that reviewers may need to be more vigilant about overstepping their competence boundaries.

The scenarios presented at the start of this section illustrate cases where reviewers may be tempted to agree to do a review for ego-fulfilling or developmental reasons or a desire to be of assistance to an editor, but where there may be some deficits in expertise. Each of these represent "gray areas" where a reviewer might very well be able to deliver a useful review (depending in part on the general qualities of the manuscript itself), but also where a lack of expertise may mean that an author is not provided with the highest quality review. In none of these scenarios would an automatic decline of the reviewing opportunity be called for, but rather a thoughtful consideration undertaken of whether one can provide valuable input to the editor's decision. If one truly cannot, then declining is essential. At a minimum, each of these cases indicates a need for reviewers to alert the editor to their limitations, and the editor will weight the review accordingly.

Conflict of interest

For each of these scenarios, would you review or decline the request?

You are reading the method section of a paper and notice that the authors state they have chosen a particular measure over another because of its superior psychometric properties. The measure they did not choose is one you developed and are currently marketing through a test publishing firm.

You are reading a paper that you find to be conceptually underdeveloped but you are excited to find that the authors employed a statistical package that you developed that has not yet garnered widespread use.

You have read a paper you were asked to review and find that it completely contradicts something you recently published.

You are asked to review a paper and immediately recognize it as the work of an "intellectual rival." You suspect that she served as a reviewer for two recent rejections of your work.

You read a manuscript you were asked to review and find it mediocre at best. However, the authors cite your own work a lot and in very laudatory terms.

In reading a paper you were asked to review, you feel that there are 3 or 4 articles you have written that have been overlooked by the authors, but seem relevant to you. You feel they should be cited.

As you sit down to review a paper you think you recognize it as the work of a former colleague. You have not been in contact for several years but remember him fondly.

As you sit down to review a paper, you realize that you attended a conference where this same work was presented and now know who the authors are. You've interacted with several of the authors socially a number of times at various professional venues.

While ethical guidelines vary across professions, a common ethical principle revolves around conflicts of interest. The International Committee of Medical Journal Editors (1993) stated that a conflict of interest occurs when participants in the peer review process have ties to activities that could inappropriately influence their judgment. In a subsequent statement (ICMJE, 1997), the same committee indicated four causes of conflict: financial interests, personal relationships, academic competition and intellectual passion. (See Flanagin, 2000; Morgan, Harmon & Gliner, 2001; and Relman, 1990 for other categorizations of reviewer conflicts of interest). Some authors label only the first as a conflict of interest and treat the latter three as reviewer biases – I will focus on each of these here, and discuss other forms of reviewer bias in a subsequent section.

Financial interest

There has been a growing recognition in the scientific community of the need for clear and full disclosure of any potential interests that might affect the conduct or interpretation of one's research. Many journals request that authors sign a declaration at the time of submission regarding any conflicts of interest (e.g., whether the source of funding for the research might gain from the findings, personal financial stakes). Of note, most journals are concerned with appropriate disclosure of *potential* conflicts so that readers may judge the work in context, rather than blanket policies regarding refusal to consider work where the authors might have a conflict. The same should hold true of reviewers. Any potential conflicts due to financial interests should be appropriately disclosed to the journal editor.

A disclosure does not necessitate a need to decline the review – it is left to the judgment of the editor as to whether the potential conflict is sufficiently problematic so as to prevent a fair review. This may not be an easy decision for an editor, challenged with finding competent reviewers, to make. Finding an expert in the development of personality tests, for example, might necessitate reviewers that have developed personality tests themselves and have financial interests in those tests. Individuals who work for organizations that market online surveying tools may be the most appropriate reviewers in terms of expertise for articles on web-based surveying, although they have financial interests in the area of research. Too high a bar for "no conflict" would result in anyone who practices or consults in an area not being able to review work in that area! Potential financial gain or harm from the publication of a manuscript that is indirect should be disclosed, but it may not undermine the quality of a review. Editors can exercise reasonable judgment as to when such conflict is truly problematic.

Personal relationships

Morgan et al (2001) noted that is commonly considered a conflict to review a paper from a close colleague. The definition of close colleague may be fuzzy, but would include former advisors or major professors, former and current students, individuals within one's department, and any coauthors or collaborators in previous and ongoing research. In general, one should decline to review the work of those with whom you have such close relationships. However, the boundaries really vary across disciplines. For example, in some of the narrow niche neuroscience areas, those with the expertise to evaluate whether a particular technique with a particular animal model was applied correctly may have been trained in only a small handful of labs. Statistical methods papers may end up in the hands of a small cadre of reviewers who possess the expertise to judge the mathematics behind a new technique. Once again, the key is to disclose existing relationships to the editor.

Given that many journals have double-blind review processes (the reviewers do not know who the authors are and vice versa), sometimes one does not recognize a conflict till after the fact. For example, one can review a paper one week and then attend a conference the next where the author's identity (e.g., a former student) and one's conflict becomes apparent. Also, editors may not be able to keep in their heads all the ties and connections that various reviewers have. For example, while I familiarize myself with who tends to collaborate with whom among my editorial board members, I do not have total recall of all their vitae and collaborators, nor do I have awareness of all their former students' names. Indeed, when serving as a program chair for a conference, I once unknowingly assigned a reviewer to read a paper written by his spouse – he wasn't even aware of the conflict till after he read the paper and mentioned to her that someone had done some research highly similar to hers and she pointed out that it was her study! (In that case, he recused himself).

The dilemma of a prior relationship that is not close but that might bias review is brought out in a case in the ethics casebook for I-O psychology (Lowman, 1998). In the case presented the reviewer had knowledge of the work from meeting an individual at a conference and going out to dinner. The issues raised in the casebook surround whether the reviewer was able to maintain objectivity because of a prior positive impression of the author. Of note, the case interpretation does not conclude that the reviewer should have declined to do the review, but that she should have identified to the editor the prior relationship so that the editor might consider that information. Similarly, the last 2 scenarios above would not be considered conflicts of interest by most editors. Indeed, in many research niches it is near impossible to find reviewers that have not had some personal interaction with an author.

Competition and passion

Academic competition can be heralded as the result of a healthy and vibrant area of research and the means by which knowledge is most quickly advanced, or it can be seen as the byproduct of egotism and jealousy. To state one should unequivocally turn down reviews of academic competitors can be viewed as equivalent to not reviewing the work of peers in a research niche. Clearly, the issue is not whether one can review the work of others who are pursuing like research, but whether the academic competition is of such a level and nature so as to bias one's judgment as a reviewer. For example, Parrish (2000) details a case of scientific misconduct before the U.S. Public Health Service where an individual waited several months before declining to review a paper so that he might pursue the same studies himself and delay the publication of a competitive manuscript. In my opinion, one should decline reviews when one views someone as "the competition" rather than as a kindred researcher; however, this judgment may be more indicative of reviewer personality than the true state of affairs.

Godlee (2000) notes that the most difficult conflict to guard against would be intellectual passion, because it would be detrimental to choose reviewers who care nothing about a topic. The key to seeing intellectual passion as a competing interest is when a reviewer is faced with a work that refutes what he/she strongly espouses. In such cases, letting the editor know that your review may be colored by strong beliefs allows the editor to give it appropriate weight.

Dealing with conflicts of interest

While many journals now ask authors to indicate any conflicts of interest at the time of submission, such disclosures are typically focused on financial interests. Further, while reviewers may be asked to self-police with regard to conflicts (e.g., *Personnel Psychology* guidelines urge reviewers to contact the editor if they think they will have a problem reviewing a manuscript), journals do not typically specifically request conflict of interest information for each and every manuscript reviewed. The peer review process thus relies on the integrity of reviewers in terms of revealing conflicts of interest.

Flanagin (2000) notes that journals vary in how they treat conflicts of interest, with some having a blanket policy of assigning manuscripts to other reviewers if a reviewer feels he/she has a conflict of interest. Others suggest that reviewers provide reviews if they feel they can be objective as long as they disclose the conflict to the editor. The question arises as to whether rejected authors then have a right to know about a reviewer's potential conflicts. Flanagin notes that it is important that the editor treat such disclosure as confidential just as is done with author disclosures. If the potential conflict is deemed a real conflict, the reviewer should not do the review, or the completed review not be considered.

In the scenarios at the start of this section, a reviewer could accept each of these invitations and be proceeding in an ethical and professional manner. In each case, however, two actions should occur. First, the editor should be alerted to the potential conflict so that he/she can determine whether it would be problematic to consider the review. Second, the reviewer should spend extra time reviewing his/her review to assess any biases in evaluation (In general, reviewers should spend more time rereading their reviews!). If one feels one cannot be objective, then declining is essential. Asking a trusted colleague to look at a review (not the paper) in terms of "tone" and objectivity may also help. It may be unrealistic to expect complete lack of conflicts of interest. Morgan et al (2001) noted that conflicts of interest are "inevitable and not inherently bad, but not disclosing them and not managing actual conflicts are problems." (p. 1478).

Bias

For each of these scenarios, would you review or decline the request?

You are asked to review a paper and, based on the specific topic and design of the study believe it was written by a prominent researcher in your field. While you found a lot of flaws in the work, you feel that this researcher could certainly address them.

You are reading a paper that seems to advocate for positions in contrast to your own on certain social and legal issues (e.g., affirmative action, parental leave, corporate responsibility, consumer rights). While the research presented is not flawed in its execution, you feel that the ideological tenor of the paper is overboard.

The paper you just reviewed had no glaring methodological flaws and was well-written and well-reasoned. However, in the end, the authors found no support for any of their hypotheses. You feel such work should not take up journal space that could go to more compelling findings.

Studies using student samples role-playing managers always seem problematic to you in terms of generalizability. The latest paper you received to review employs this same design.

Godlee (2000) distinguishes bias from a direct conflict of interest by defining bias as recommendations regarding a manuscript influenced by factors other than quality or relevance to the readership. Personal biases due to liking, friendship, or strong rivalry were included under conflicts of interest. Other biases that have been discussed in the literature include publication bias (against studies without statistically significant results), methodological biases (in favor or against studies employing certain designs or techniques), ideological biases (in favor or against certain viewpoints), and name recognition biases (in favor of established authors) (Hojat, Gonnella & Caelleigh, 2003; Weller, 2001). This section briefly highlights how each of these should be considered in decisions to review.

Publication bias has been the focus of much research (e.g., Martinko, Campbell & Douglas, 2000; Olson et al, 2002), with the general conclusion being that reviewers do have such a bias, but also that many studies that produce null results do so because they are flawed in some aspect (e.g., presence of confounds, unmeasured variables). Thus, a reviewer need not feel that bias is present whenever he/she recommends rejection of a manuscript that has no statistically significant findings. Obviously, reviewers should be assessing a manuscript's contribution on the basis of more than statistical significance, and reviewer guidelines should emphasize this. (There is a large body of literature on why one should not report statistical significance and instead focus on effect sizes and confidence intervals, but I address this chapter to current common practice.) A reviewer who truly feels that he/she would *never* publish a study that had no statistically significant results probably should alert the editor to that strong bias, and not be asked to review manuscripts where he/she would be biased.

Methodological biases are often discussed in the literature as well, such as a preference for field versus lab studies, a preference for certain analytic approaches, etc... Once again, many of these preferences are based on knowledge of the clear limitations of other approaches. For example, the "bias" in favor of multi-source data over single source data arises from concerns about how common method variance influences findings. Determining whether one is biased in reviewing or whether one has made an expert determination that a certain methodological approach lacks merit can be a gray area. Reviewers will often point out to authors that "no one does this anymore" or "the more appropriate approach would be..." – such is the job of reviewers and would not be reflective of bias but of good research standards. The key question here would be whether a reviewer will automatically reject work that uses a method or paradigm he/she dislikes, even if it is not considered flawed by professional consensus, or will automatically give a more positive review to work that uses a technique or paradigm that he/she favors. If a rationale is provided, the editor, authors, and other reviewers can make a judgment regarding one's position.

Ideological biases can also impact reviews. Weller (2001) summarized 6 studies of reviewer ideological biases and concluded that reviewers do indeed tend to favor manuscripts that agree with their viewpoint and this is backed by a large body of literature on attitudes and persuasion (e.g., Gross, Holtz, & Miller, 1995; Tormala & Petty, 2004). When a manuscript is clearly ideological in tone, just as when a manuscript clearly takes a very strong stance on a research issue, editors should attempt to seek a balance of reviewer perspectives. Further, if a paper is considered too ideological in tone, it is often because the authors did not provide sufficient rationale and citation to support their assertions – pointing out such a limitation is the job of a reviewer, not a bias. Editors can also spot reviews whose tone suggests the reviewer is ideologically biased, and discount the review accordingly.

Name recognition bias occurs when a well-known author's work is viewed more favorably. Weller (2001) summarized 9 studies of reviewer ability to guess the identity of authors and concluded that on average, referees could identify 38.1% of authors, with many of those (45.6% or 17.4% of the total) identified because of self-citation. In summarizing 10 studies that looked at bias due to knowing author identity, Weller concluded that the results are equivocal regarding whether a bias in favor of well-published authors does exist.

Note that reviewers may recognize who authored a work in blind-review circumstances, due to the use of a particular set of stimulus materials as in previous research, to a certain narrow topic focus, or to heavy self-citation. Recognizing an author is not in and of itself a biasing factor. Well-published authors are more likely to be detected because their writing style, research methods, and theoretical focus are established. An ethical concern arises when the recognition leads to a biased evaluation of the paper. Along the same lines, Bedeian (chapter 7) found in his study that some authors will cite heavily a particular individual's work in hopes of biasing the editor's choice of reviewers. His research also reveals authors' perceptions of a criticism bias among editors and reviewers.

Dealing with bias

So, how does a reviewer decide if he/she is biased versus offering an expert-based opinion? One way of judging is by examining how one is presenting concerns about the manuscript – are they offered in terms of testable hypotheses? Is there evidence to support your viewpoint? Would others agree with the standards you are using in evaluation?

Walter and Bloch (2001) note that reviewer biases may manifest themselves in more subtle and perhaps unconscious ways than in the content of the review – for example, lengthy delays in returning reviews. Campbell (1987) notes that while producing a biased review consciously is certainly unethical, things are seldom so clear cut and reviewers can unknowingly "mix personal bias with professional judgment." (p. 78).

As an editor, assessing reviewer bias can be difficult. Clearly an overly critical review stands out as problematic and the review can be appropriately discounted in decision-making. More subtle biases may go undetected by an editor less well-versed in the particular research niche (e.g., is it now standard practice in this area to do X or is that the reviewer's own predilection?). Two of the very few emails I have received from authors suggesting a reviewer was biased against a particular methodology or viewpoint occurred when I had purposely picked reviewers who were in the same "camp" as the author! This does not negate the existence of reviewer bias; however, it suggests that "bias" also serves well as an external attribution for rejection.

The scenarios at the start of this section all represent cases where a reviewer, recognizing his/her bias, could provide a useful and competent review. Once again, alerting the editor to one's views is particularly important, as is reviewing the tenor of the review to ensure that critical comments are well explained and justified.

Reviewing a second time around

For each of these scenarios, would you review or decline the request?

You receive a paper to review and notice it is identical to one you reviewed for another journal recently. You had put considerable time into that review and it is apparent that the authors did not adopt a single suggestion of yours before submitting the paper to this journal.

As you begin to read a manuscript you agreed to review, you realize that it seems vaguely familiar. After reading further, you recognize it as having some similarity to a paper you reviewed for another journal several months ago, although it has been changed substantially.

A dilemma that comes up far more often than one might guess is when a reviewer receives a request to review a paper that he/she has already reviewed for another journal – perhaps in a very different version, perhaps not. In the ethics casebook for I-O psychology (Lowman, 1998), a case of an editor recusing herself from acting on a paper she had reviewed for another journal notes that to maintain the credibility and integrity of the review process, avoiding the appearance of impropriety is important. At *Personnel Psychology*, we urge reviewers to inform us of papers one has reviewed previously and we typically reassign the manuscript.

Certainly, one can review a revision of a paper and have a much more positive impression than one's initial view. Certainly, one can note the same flaws that existed in a previous version are still highly problematic. Thus, reviewers often feel that they are giving an objective review of a paper regardless of having reviewed it before. However, reviewers also tend to base current comments on their previous review without attending to the new manuscript and what has been changed. Bedeian (2004) notes that "it is impossible for the same reader to re-read a text from a previous viewpoint, as each experience of reading will have been modified by all previous readings." (p. 201). While one can take this to mean that it is okay to rereview a manuscript because one is always having a different interpretation in rereading, it also suggests that previous readings will influence the current review. The policy of a third reviewer on resubmissions was instituted at *Personnel Psychology* some time ago in recognition of this fact, and to gain a "fresh evaluation" of resubmitted papers.

Both of the scenarios at the start of this section elicit very different opinions among seasoned reviewers and editors as to whether one should decline to review. Many scholars would argue they could give a fair and valuable review in these instances. While my own predilection as editor is to seek another reviewer, I suspect that this is not the majority opinion. Reviewers can rightly argue that authors do not deserve "clean shots" if there has been no attempt to address concerns pointed out in previous reviews for another journal. Some reviewers feel that declining to review a paper one has seen before is actually shirking one's gate keeping responsibility as poor quality work should not be published, and not doing the review creates unneeded work for another reviewer. Many reviewers would also argue that authors need to get the message that one does not just shop around for a home for a paper, but that true scholarship involves laboring to communicate one's ideas and to address criticisms. Reviewers are rightly peeved when they have devoted time to critiquing another's work and that effort is completely ignored. And as Priem communicated in the previous chapter, this kind of experience also leaves reviewers feeling very disappointed when it happens in real-life. Well-published individuals do not ignore reviewer comments that they disagree with but work to craft manuscripts to better justify decisions and to communicate viewpoints. Also, there are probably instances one can point to where the same reviewer saw a much improved manuscript on the second time around and viewed it more favorably; there also can be cases where a reviewer's initial review was favorable but it was not considered strongly by the editor.

Thus, reviewing a paper for a second journal is something where there are clear differences of opinion as to appropriateness. While I have stated my own view is that it is most often best to decline, as long as there are shortages of competent reviewers and authors who totally disregard prior reviews, opinions as to what to do in this instance will vary.

Insufficient time

For each of these scenarios, would you review or decline the request?

You are asked to do a review by the top journal in your area. This is the first time that you've been asked by this journal. However, the requested turnaround time is 3 weeks and you have a grant proposal due, final exams to create and grade for several classes, and a long-planned vacation scheduled within those 3 weeks.

You are one of the more prolific researchers in your field. You maintain your productivity by managing your time well and turning down requests to do things that have no direct value to your research program (e.g., service committees, speaking engagements, and unrelated consulting work). This philosophy includes turning down requests to review.

You are asked to do a review for a journal that has asked you to do 4 other reviews within the last year. You are not a member of the editorial board of this journal.

You do not have time to do the review within the time frame allowed but it is a resubmission of a work and you were a reviewer last time.

One last reason to turn down a request to review is when one truly does not have the ability to do the review in a timely fashion. In my role as an editor, nothing peeves me more than a reviewer who keeps promising to have a review done "next week" without producing anything. While we all overestimate our ability to accomplish things in short periods of time, there is a point at which delays are unconscionable. One hurts one's credibility more by being a chronically late reviewer or by doing only a very cursory review than by occasionally refusing a request to review when overloaded.

With the advent of electronic manuscript management, expectations regarding how quickly a decision can be made on a manuscript have risen. Thus, weighing commitments appropriately helps. Our editorial board members will email when they are planning an extended vacation, a busy period, or a maternity leave with a request not to do reviews during that time. Similarly, a polite refusal of a request to review with an indication of a willingness to review in the future does not hurt one's professional reputation, if it is a rare occurrence.

That said, the peer review process functions because individuals are willing to give of their time to reviewing. If everyone made reviewing a low priority, the peer review system would collapse. Before deciding that reviewing is the activity that cannot be done, be sure to take a good look at what else is draining one's time. Reviewing has value to oneself and the profession (see chapters 2, 4, 6 and 10 in this volume), so first remove other work activities that do not provide as much value. In the first scenario, informing the editor of an alternative date by which you could complete the review and letting him/her decide regarding reassigning would be highly appropriate. In my view, the second scenario is the most straightforward in the chapter – continuously declining is neglecting one's professional duty.

One question that inevitably gets asked by good reviewers is whether one can turn down reviewing if one is asked "too often" (the third scenario). This is particularly an issue when an individual feels he/she is doing as many ad hoc reviews a year for a journal as are editorial board members but without the "credit." Deciding to decline a review in that instance relates to how to best manage an editor's expectations and to convey one's desire for greater recognition for the workload.

When asked to review a revision of a work where you provided an earlier review, there is an unspoken obligation to do the review. If this comes at a particularly bad time for you, negotiate a reasonable turnaround with the editor. There may be cases where reviewing a revision of a manuscript is impossible or highly inappropriate (e.g., a major illness, a newly arisen, clear conflict of interest, recognition that one is too biased to give the revision a fair read). However, these are likely rare events.

Who declines reviews?

In reading through the literature on who should decline reviews, there is very little factual analysis of who does indeed decline reviews. While there was an occasional reference to more experienced authors being more likely to decline reviewing requests (Bedeian, 2004), this is also not interpretable without some context (e.g., are these individuals doing more reviewing overall?, are these authors more likely to experience conflicts of interest because of greater numbers of ties to others?, are they more likely to be on multiple editorial boards and hence more likely to be receiving the same manuscript twice?). It would be useful to better understand whether there are trends in the reasons for declines over time – are more people experiencing/acknowledging conflicts of interest? Is seeing the same paper twice a more common phenomenon and if so what is the cause (e.g., too small a circle of individuals on multiple editorial boards)? Are more people declining because of feeling overloaded? Is a major determinant of declining a lack of resources (knowledge, time, energy) on the part of reviewers?

We also could benefit from further investigation/case examples of when reviewers did not decline but should have. I have come across a few cases where I had to discount a review entirely because the reviewer likely should not have reviewed the paper. For example, in one case the comments to the author began "I am not an expert in this topic" and continued throughout with an apologetic tone – suggesting the reviewer had judged him/herself unfit to review the paper. In another, a reviewer submitted the same exact review as he had at another journal for the manuscript without reading the version submitted, which had been substantially changed from the original – the authors were rightly bothered by the fact that the reviewer had clearly not even read their submission! As noted earlier, I wish reviewers would decline when they are too busy to do a review and I wait months to receive a few cursory sentences that are of no value to me or to the author. (Those reviewers do not get invitations again).

One final note is that delays in declining a request are likely to occur. It is easy to state one should decline "promptly;" however, many of the scenarios discussed in this chapter indicate cases where the need to refuse to review may not be apparent until one is reading the manuscript, presumably closer to the due date of the review. Such delays in those cases are inevitable and authors need to understand that delays due to reassignments of manuscripts are to enhance the fairness of the process. However, as noted earlier, prolonged delays may be an indicator themselves of bias or conflict and should be acted upon by editors.

The role of the editor

This chapter has focused on the reviewer with passing reference to what an editor should do. It is important to note that editors play a role in promoting or deterring inappropriate reviewing. Editors who rely on clerical help or automated software to do all of the picking of reviewers are shirking their responsibilities in judging expertise and potential for bias or conflict. Editors who do not communicate policies regarding accepting and declining reviews – both explicitly in reviewer guidelines and implicitly through pressuring individuals to accept requests – do a disservice that stretches beyond their own journal to the integrity of the peer review process as a whole.

There are fine lines for an editor here. If a reviewer emails "I am really busy and cannot get to this in the timeline provided," is it really applying pressure to just ask him/her to give an alternative date rather than just seeking another reviewer? My experience is that reviewers who are conscientious and competent professionals will not just throw together a hasty review for the sake of meeting a deadline, but that they will give me a good review at a target date that they can meet. Another example is the email that says "I recognize the author" or "I have a really strong view on this topic." In most journals, reviewers are not voters in an evaluation, as mentioned in chapters 2 and 5, but consultants that provide input to the individual who must make the decision, the editor. The question is whether the editor is attentive to the caveats that reviewers provide.

Given this, what should editors do to promote good practice in accepting and declining reviews?

- Provide guidance to reviewers on when to decline (e.g., in written guidelines).
- Probe reviewers when in doubt about their expertise or the existence of conflicts before assigning papers to review.
- Know your reviewers and their connections. In addition to examining reviewer vitae, I "Google" authors and reviewers if I am uncertain about a previous collaboration. Indeed, automated manuscript processing software should allow reviewers to indicate authors whose work they should not review (e.g., former students and close collaborators) and that can be automatically flagged so that papers are not assigned that would be conflicts of interest.
- Use your discretion. If a review comes in that should not have been done, discount it.

- Give reviewers feedback if they do provide reviews where you think they should have declined.
- Promote responsible reviewing through training of students and mentoring of junior colleagues.
- Establish a checklist of factors for reviewers to consider when accepting papers to review or when submitting reviews (e.g., I have no conflict of interest).

For additional discussion of the editor's role, see chapters 4 and 7. For more information about communicating with editors, see chapter 14.

Conclusion

Poor decisions regarding when to review and when not to are of no small consequence – they make the peer review process less fair, less efficient, and generally more frustrating for authors and editors. With electronic manuscript management systems, the ease of clicking the "I accept" or "I decline" link without thinking makes it easy to take the decision lightly, without considering one's professional and ethical obligations. (As an aside, in recently switching from a system where our board members were automatically sent manuscripts to review and only asked to return them when they could not do a review to systems where board members must accept or decline each paper, the number of declines has risen dramatically.) It is difficult to email an editor when one is already late with a review to inform him/her that the manuscript that has sat on your desk all this time is one you really should not review. However, it is essential that thoughtful decisions are made by reviewers so as to maintain the integrity of the process.

For the scenarios presented in this chapter, the course of action was sometimes murky and differences of opinion are likely to exist regarding what to do. In terms of general recommendations regarding accepting or declining reviewing opportunities:

- Skim the paper when it is first received to determine if there are any conflicts that may be problematic, rather than waiting to look it over later.
- Inform the editor of any doubts or concerns regarding whether you should accept an opportunity.
- If, after doing the review, concerns become obvious, tell the editor.
- Set a wide boundary for acceptance. One should be accepting whenever possible.

Sometimes the shortage of qualified reviewers in an area makes it challenging for an editor to find someone who doesn't collaborate with the author, hasn't seen the manuscript before, and has the time to do a review. Not infrequently have I gone through 5 or 6 potential reviewers before finding someone who is competent and willing to do the review and the need for reassigning appears to be steadily increasing. One could argue that the peer review process would collapse from lack of reviewers if all the criteria noted in this chapter were considered fully. Thus, there is a need to caution against too strict an application of these guidelines. However, in the best interest of authors, it would be better to have some delay in getting a manuscript processed than to use reviewers who really should be recusing themselves. Reviews have tremendous impact on the careers of colleagues; knowing when to say no is important to ensuring a fair peer review system. Chapter 5 is devoted to exploring systematically the definition, characteristics and value of a "fair review".

References

Bedeian, A. G. (2003). The manuscript review process: The proper roles of authors, referees, and editors. *Journal of Management Inquiry, 12*, 331–8.

Bedeian, A. G. (2004). Peer review and the social construction of knowledge in the management discipline. *Academy of Management Learning and Education, 3*, 198–216.

Campbell, D. J. (1987). Ethical issues in the research publication process. In S. L. Payne & B. H. Charnov (eds) *Ethical dilemmas for academic professionals*. Springfield: Charles C. Thomas Publishers, 69–88.

Flanagin, A. (2000). Conflict of interest. In A. Hudson Jones & F. McLellan (eds) *Ethical issues in biomedical publication*. The Johns Hopkins University Press: Baltimore, 137–65.

Godlee, F. (2000). The ethics of peer review. In A. Hudson Jones & F. McLellan (eds) *Ethical issues in biomedical publication*. The Johns Hopkins University Press: Baltimore, 59–84.

Gross, S., Holtz, R., & Miller, N. (1995). Attitude certainty. In R. E. Petty & J. A. Krosnick (eds) *Attitude strength: Antecedents and consequences*, 215–45. Mahwah, NJ: Erlbaum.

Hojat, M., Gonnella, J. S. & Caelleigh, A. S. (2003). Impartial judgment by the "gatekeepers" of science: Fallibility and accountability in the peer review process. *Advances in Health Science Education, 8*, 75–96.

International Committee of Medical Journal Editors (ICMJE) (1993). Position statement: Conflict of interest. *Medical Journal of Australia, 159*, 57.

International Committee of Medical Journal Editors (ICMJE) (1997). Uniform requirements for manuscripts submitted to biomedical journals. *Annals of Internal Medicine, 126*, 36–47.

Lowman, R. L. (1998). *The ethical practice of psychology in organizations.* American Psychological Association: Washington, DC.

Martinko, M. J., Campbell, C. R., & Douglas, S. C. (2000). Bias in the social science publication process: Are there exceptions? *Journal of Social Behavior and Personality, 15,* 1–18.

Morgan, G. A., Harmon, R. J., & Gliner, J. A. (2001). Ethical issues related to publishing and reviewing. *Journal of the American Academy of Child and Adolescent Psychiatry, 40,* 1476–8.

Olson, C. M., Pennie, D., Cook, D., Dickersin, K., Flangin, A., Hogan, J. W., Zhu, Q., Reiling, J., & Pace, B. (2002). Publication bias in editorial decision making. *JAMA: Journal of the American Medical Association, 287,* 2825–8.

Parrish, D. M. (2000). When ethics fails: Legal and administrative causes of action and remedies. In A. Hudson Jones & F. McLellan (eds) *Ethical issues in biomedical publication.* Baltimore: The Johns Hopkins University Press, 197–222.

Relman, A. S. (1990). The value of peer review. In Editorial Policy Committee, Council of Biology Editors (eds) *Ethics and policy in scientific publication.* Council of Biology Editors, Bethesda, MD, 272–7.

Shugan, S. M. (2003). Compartmentalized reviews and other initiatives: Should marketing scientists review manuscripts in consumer behavior? *Marketing Science, 22,* 151.

Tormala, Z. L. & Petty, R. E. (2004). Resisting persuasion and attitude certainty: A meta-cognitive analysis. In E. S. Knowles (ed.) *Resistance and persuasion,* 65–82. Mahwah, NJ: Erlbaum.

Walter, G. & Bloch, S. (2001). Publishing ethics in psychiatry. *Australian and New Zealand Journal of Psychiatry, 35,* 28–35.

Weller, A. C. (2001). *Editorial peer review: Its strengths and weaknesses.* NJ: American Society for Information Science and Technology.

Section 2

The Practice of Reviewing

4
The Fundamentals of Reviewing

Sherry E. Sullivan, Madeline Crocitto and Shawn M. Carraher

What is an essential but overlooked component of knowledge creation? During their Ph.D. training, future researchers are taught about theory development, statistical analysis, and ethics in conducting research so that they can make high-quality contributions to the creation of knowledge. One frequently neglected aspect of knowledge development in Ph.D. coursework or faculty development at professional conferences (e.g., junior faculty consortia) is the review process. Just how does one correctly review a manuscript?

Reviewing is an important responsibility in our profession (see Priem & Rasheed, chapter 2). Reviewers assist in the process of knowledge development by helping fellow scholars shape and improve theoretical and empirical research and assist in the refinement of research ideas. They offer authors fresh perspectives, often suggesting articles or literatures which the authors are unaware of but that greatly enhance their research. Reviewers may suggest new ways to examine or test hypotheses, catch mistakes in how the research was conducted, or suggest new methods to check for potential problems (e.g., use of the Scarpello and Carraher, 1997 test for common method variance). In addition, reviewers may provide constructive feedback about structuring the article to increase its readability, thereby permitting the authors to reach a much larger audience.

Similarly, reviewers are direct actors in the advancement of knowledge by preventing poor science from being published. Reviewers are charged with the dual responsibility of providing constructive, developmental feedback to authors, while at the same time, preventing substandard research from reaching a wider audience. Reviewers have the obligation of ensuring that manuscripts with fatal flaws or those which offer no new contributions to our knowledge base are not published.

Given the importance of the reviewer to the knowledge creation process, as stressed in chapter 1 and throughout each chapter in section 2, the purpose of this chapter is to offer practical guidance on how to write a high-quality review. Moreover, because of the dual demands place on individuals by the review process – providing constructive, respectful feedback while preventing unsound science from being published – it is important that we critically examine the review process and offer concrete recommendations about how to construct more meaningful reviews. To that end, this chapter specifically discusses: (1) the basics of how to structure a review; (2) the importance of showing respect to editors, track chairs, and readers; (3) the value of the developmental review; (4) the reviewer's role in the revise and resubmit process; and (5) the importance of providing a realistic review of the manuscript.

The basics of structuring a review

Often, the most difficult step for the reviewer is writing the first part of the review. Reviewers can create trust and demonstrate an understanding of the submission by beginning the review with a brief, one paragraph summary of the manuscript's content. Writing a summary of the manuscript shows that the reviewer has made a sincere attempt to understand the author's thinking (Lee, 1995). If authors don't believe that the reviewers took the process seriously, they may disregard the reviewers' comments regardless of the quality or usefulness of their recommendations. If the authors, however, believe the reviewer is earnest, yet the reviewer's summary does not capture the intent of the manuscript, the authors are alerted to problems of readability and the need for further clarification and revision.

To write such a summary, a reviewer usually must read the manuscript several times. In general, it is advised that the reviewer read the manuscript when it first is assigned. Then the reviewer can check for his/her understanding of the major ideas of the manuscript and determine whether he/she will need to read additional articles on the topic in order to critically evaluate the manuscript's contribution to knowledge. Reading the manuscript early on allows for any questions or problems with the manuscript (e.g., self-identification of the authors within the article) to be addressed to the editor/conference track chair early in the review process.

Sometimes, reviewers are concerned that they lack the expertise to assess a manuscript. It is common for editors/track chairs to assign papers to those who don't normally publish in a particular topical area in order to determine whether the typical scholar can understand the manuscript and if the topic has broad appeal. For example, over half of the first authors of published articles in the *Academy of Management Review* or *Academy of Management Journal* stated they were given papers to review outside their knowledge areas (Bedeian, chapter 7). Reviewers should have faith in the assignments made by editors/track chairs but, as Ryan disclosed in chapter 3, editors don't always know everything about their reviewers' familiarity with a given literature. However, even if reviewers aren't experts on a topic, they can still contribute to the process by critiquing the methodology used, the logic of the propositions and hypotheses, the adequacy of conceptual development, and the readability of the manuscript.

After summarizing the paper, the most positive aspects of the manuscript should be detailed. Often reviewers jump right in, outlining their criticisms without recognizing what the authors have successfully done (Bedeian, chapter 7). Beginning this part of the review with positive remarks acknowledges the time and effort that the authors have devoted to the manuscript. Strengths should be clearly identified, noting such positives as:

- the submission is well-written, flowing easily from one section to the other;
- the arguments are logically presented;
- the literature review is comprehensive;
- the research design and analysis are appropriate;
- the data are sufficient;
- the idea or approach is original; and
- the discussion is cogent and includes implications for future research and practice.

After giving the authors credit for their efforts, the negatives of the manuscript should be clearly and specifically enumerated. Reviewers should avoid vague or unsubstantiated comments, (e.g. "The discussion needs more development."). Instead reviewers should devote themselves to identifying specific problems, suggesting specific means to address these problems, and providing complete references for suggested readings. If the reviewer refers to specific paragraphs and page numbers (e.g., page 15, last paragraph), the authors can more readily find the context of the reviewer's comment and pinpoint areas which need further clarification or explanation. It is often difficult for authors to find minor errors such as missing punctuation, typos, awkward sentences, and the like. The reviewer provides a real service to improving the manuscript's quality by pointing out such errors, especially if the journal doesn't employ a copyeditor.

After providing the authors with details about the problems with the manuscript and how these problems might be fixed, the reviewer should indicate the viability of the manuscript. It is very important that reviewers not send mixed messages to authors by providing them only with positive feedback while recommending to the editor that the paper be rejected. Not only does that put the editor in the awkward position of explaining to authors why a manuscript is being rejected despite the reviewers' glowing comments, but it is unfair to the authors. Often reviewers, fearing that their criticisms will come across as harsh, discouraging or demeaning, fail to provide the negative but constructive feedback that may help authors to improve the current manuscript or the authors' overall research abilities. There are ways to phrase even negative comments so that the sincere intent of the reviewer to provide useful feedback is evident (see also Feldman, chapter 14). The reviewer may also wish to include comments for the editor's/track chair's eyes only, including possible ethical problems with the manuscript (see Shapiro & Sitkin, chapter 5 and Baugh, Hunt & Scandura, chapter 9) as well as suggestions of alternative outlets for a manuscript that has merit but lacks fit to the journal in question. In sum, the goal of a reviewer is to provide authors with valuable, well-organized feedback that with help them revise their manuscript and/or improve their skills as researchers. A well-written review should be structured so as to contain the following elements:

1. the opening summary paragraph;
2. detailing of the positives of the manuscript;
3. outlining of the negatives of the manuscript, noting any fatal flaws;
4. suggesting specific recommendations for revising the manuscript; and
5. closing the review with an overall comment about the viability of the manuscript and thanking the authors for the opportunity to review their work.[1]

By following this structure, the reviewer will most likely cover issues that constitute constructive feedback to the authors.[2] This format should lead logically to the reviewer's decision to recommend to the editor/track chair that the manuscript be accepted, rejected or offered a revise and resubmit.

Respect the editors, track chairs and potential readers

To complete quality reviews, individuals need to devote sufficient time to the reviewing process. One survey of 39 *Academy of Management Review* and 34 *Academy of Management Journal* reviewers reported that it took anywhere from two to over twelve hours to complete a review (Jauch & Wall, 1989). Recognizing that reviewers normally spend less time reviewing a conference paper than journal submissions – which may include an extensive revise and resubmit process – individuals should schedule adequate time once making a commitment to review. Editors and track chairs are severely inconvenienced when an individual who promises to review backs out at the last minute. Likewise, reviewers who miss deadlines can literally slow down the production of a conference program or proceedings and throw journals off schedule. Reviewers who cannot meet deadlines due to an emergency should contact the editor/track chair so a replacement can be found immediately.

To help editors/track chairs make decisions about submissions, emphasis should be placed on the content and quality of the review, not the length of it. Although a few lines of comments are insufficient, reviewers should edit their comments into clear, focused points. Reviewers should number the concerns presented so that it is easier for the editor to draft a letter of response to the authors (Lee, 1995). Likewise, individuals should ensure that their reviews are free of spelling and grammar errors.[3]

On the whole, reviewers must schedule adequate time to complete the review, deliver reviews by deadlines, and provide specific and detailed comments so that the editor/track chair can make timely and informed decisions about the acceptance, rejection, or revision possibilities of the manuscript. As top-journal editors Ryan and Zedeck emphasized in chapters 3 and 6, respectively, reviewers must remember that not only may the jobs of the authors literally be on the line, but the reputation of the journal/conference and the valuable time of readers must also be maintained.

Provide developmental feedback

Reviewers are not only helping editors/track chairs make decisions about which submissions to accept, but they are also contributing to the continual development of authors as scholars and writers. Therefore, it is important that reviewers show respect for the authors by helping to create a process that the authors can have faith in and perceive as fair. To create such a climate, reviewers need to offer recommendations which demonstrate a conscientious effort to help the authors advance knowledge while remaining open to new ideas suggested by authors (Singh, 2003). A survey of 173 first authors who had published in the *Academy of Management Journal* and *Academy of Management Review* found that when the authors believed that the reviewers were competent and agreeable to new ideas, that the authors were then more likely to use the reviewers' comments to enhance the manuscript (Bedeian, chapter 7). Thus, it is important to both the field and to the authors that reviewers use a developmental focus when evaluating manuscripts.

What is a developmental review? Daniel Feldman (2004a), editor of the *Journal of Management* (July 2002 to December 2005) detailed two major components of a developmental review: (1) the identification of the strengths and weaknesses of the paper, noting which are major and minor points and priorities; and (2) offering specific recommendations about how to correct the problems, including ideas about variables, theoretical constructs, and examples to strengthen the paper. These specific recommendations should be framed in what Lee (1995) terms "actionable" advice and go beyond amorphous or impossible suggestions. Examples of specific, actionable suggestions include:

- asking for a clearer statements of purpose;
- reducing the pages allocated to a certain section of the manuscript (e.g., literature review) to prevent wordiness;
- suggesting how to better use or analyze existing data;
- proposing ways to clearly recognize limitations of the study; and
- offering specific rephrasing of hypotheses and ideas as well as changes to increase readability and clarity (Feldman, 2004a).

By providing developmental feedback, reviewers are contributing to the advancement of the field by promoting the completion and publication of high quality research.

Another essential aspect of the developmental review process is demonstrating true respect for the authors. Authors often complain about the lack of respect displayed in reviewers' rude and often condescending comments (Feldman, 2005). For example, we asked some well-known authors what was the worst comment they had ever received from a reviewer. Here are some of the actual comments:

"LOSER!"

"Your choice of careers was regretful."

"I hope the author doesn't resubmit this because you'd have to beat me to make me read it again."

"When I was a high school English teacher my 10th graders wrote better papers than this one."

"If ignorance was water this paper would be a sea."

"Academics don't want papers that they can apply."

"In the future, you should have someone for whom English is their first language read your paper before you submit."(The authors were both born and reared in the US.)[4]

Why would otherwise sane, logical, and collegial academics make these types of comments in a review of another colleague's work? One potential reason may be the depersonalization of the review process. The double-blind review process, where neither the authors nor reviewers know the others' identity, is used to reduce potential bias. However, it may have the unintended side-effect of reducing the respect reviewers display for authors. In this instance, the reviewing process may mimic Milgram's (1963) famous experiments,[5] in which hapless "learners" were supposedly electronically shocked by "teachers" for giving the wrong answers. Like the "teacher" in Milgram's experiments, the reviewer may not view the author as an individual – and thus may not recognize the pain inflicted when a particularly sharp comment or zap is made. As he/she continues through the manuscript, the reviewer administers a zap for each mistake or omission detected, potentially increasing the intensity of the negative comments with each actual or perceived error in the manuscript. This unproductive criticism – which may escalate to the point of resembling a personal attack – often continues just like the zapping of the students in Milgram's experiments. Such negativity may overwhelm the merits of the manuscript and demoralize the depersonalized victim, in this case, the author. The reviewing process may generate more severe depersonalization than shown in some of Milgram's experimental conditions because all parties in the reviewing process are genuine individuals and real outcomes (e.g., tenure, promotion, reputation) are at stake. Moreover, unlike in some variations of Milgram's study, no actors are simulating the learner's pain in an effort to lessen the zapping by the teacher.

In addition to the problems of depersonalization, sometimes as reviewers engage in the delicate balancing of providing developmental, constructive feedback while enforcing high scientific standards, they lose their balance. They falsely believe that they are acting in the best interest of science by ridiculing the efforts of authors (e.g., "I'm sorry a tree died so you could write this paper."). Because bad impressions and experiences linger longer than positive ones (Price, 1996), this type of unproductive feedback creates a "lose–lose" situation for all involved. For those authors asked to revise and resubmit a manuscript, the overly negative comments of reviewers may reduce the effectiveness of the process by creating a confrontational or insulting relationship between the authors and reviewers. In some cases, the author may decide not to make the suggested revision and perhaps be subjected to additional nasty criticisms. Although their manuscript may be eventually accepted for publication, the unproductive exchange between reviewers and authors may taint the authors' impression of the journal or create a cynical attitude about the fairness of the process. The reputation of the journal or conference may be tarnished as the author recounts this negative experience to other colleagues.

Instead of zapping authors or ridiculing their work, reviewers should strive to ask meaningful questions and offer suggestions in a productive manner in order to create an atmosphere of trust. When treated with respect, authors are more likely to be open to changes and offer comprehensive responses, thus generating true intellectual dialogue (Singh, 2003) and improving the quality of the published manuscript. Reviewers may assist in the knowledge development process even if the manuscript is to be rejected by the editor/track chair by providing authors with feedback on how to improve future research. Often it is forgotten that the review process can be a powerful learning experience that can help authors improve subsequent research efforts. In addition to providing a means by which authors can learn and grow as professionals, the reviewing process may also encourage authors to remain in the field and motivate them to continue to conduct research, even if their current manuscript is rejected. Concerns have been raised that the often negative nature of the review process may cause a loss of talent (Miner, 2003). Some colleagues even lament about how tenured faculty become deadwood, perhaps to avoid the rejection of the publication process. Reviewers may fail to realize the real impact their feedback has on the future research of authors. Unkind or caustic reviews may influence whether authors even continue with their research or submit manuscripts to certain outlets. Discouraged authors may focus their abilities on nonresearch activities, thus ending their contributions to the advancement of knowledge. The withdrawal of talented authors from the knowledge creation process may have a ripple effect in terms of slowing the enhancement of certain streams of research. Withdrawing from the publication process erodes the authors' competencies and self-esteem and may produce other negative outcomes including decreased marketability, higher job dissatisfaction, or reduced teaching effectiveness as their knowledge of the field stagnates. In his exploration of the review process as a professional problem (chapter 7), Miner articulates the impact of these ripples at the discipline-level and their broader, dire implications/consequences for the field.

In sum, reviewers must be ever mindful of the impact their comments have on authors. Reviews should thus focus on providing developmental, respectful reviews so that knowledge is advanced and authors benefit from the process.

Managing the revise and resubmit process

Although there is often a lengthy revise and resubmit (R&R) process for journals, there is no such process for conferences. For conferences, which are more likely to attract less developed works, the reviewer may provide a less extensive review than for a journal submission. In contrast, the R&R process for a journal submission may occur over the course of many months and a number of revisions. The R&R process can be especially difficult for authors and reviewers alike when there are disagreements about manuscript quality or contribution to the field.

There are three major guidelines to consider when completing reviews during an R&R process. First, reviewers should not view the R&R process as a series of hurdles for the authors to jump over. It is unfair to the authors, as well as the other reviewers and editor, to ask for corrections and changes and then dismiss these revisions by repeatedly asking for more and different changes. For example, one colleague was told by a reviewer that her theoretical paper was not convincing without data. When the article was then resubmitted with data, the reviewer admonished the author stating that the manuscript tried to do too much by including an analysis of the data. It is the responsibility of the reviewer to recommend specific changes and to accept changes when the authors correctly address the concerns raised. Furthermore, if the authors can adequately explain why it would be inappropriate to make the recommendation changes, the reviewer should be open to an alternative perspective and not add more obstacles for the authors to overcome.

Second, reviewers need to consider the comments of other reviewers and the editor's instructions when evaluating whether the authors have successfully revised the manuscript. Sometimes reviewers offer conflicting advice and the editor may have clarified to the authors and reviewers how this conflict should be revolved (e.g., respond more to the comments of reviewer 2 rather than reviewer 3 regarding issue X). Authors may not make changes in response to all reviewer requests, instead explaining why certain sections of the manuscript should remain unchanged. Reviewers should consider the soundness of the authors' arguments in the context of the remarks of other reviewers and the editor (Feldman, 2004b). Reviewers must remember that the final accept or reject decision is in the editor's hands.

Third, the reviewer should offer suggestions, not mandates. The reviewer represents the potential audience for the research. He/she can best serve the process by raising questions that potential readers would likely ask (Starbuck, 2003). The reviewer, however, should not let his/her biases or agenda shape the article; instead the reviewer should be open to alternative points of view and other research paradigms. Unfortunately, reviewers are not always open to different opinions. Over one-fourth of the authors surveyed by Bedeian (chapter 7) reported that they made changes in their manuscripts even though they did not agree with the recommended revisions. Reviewers should guard against inflexibility and remove themselves from the process if their biases are interfering with their ability to provide constructive feedback. Most important, Baruch and Altman explain in chapter 13 that, should a revision be merited, a key task of reviewers is to increase the chances of authors choosing to accept the invitation to revise and resubmit.

Provide a realistic review

In an effort to be kind, sometimes reviewers are overly positive in their reviews, giving authors false hope. If the manuscript suffers from a fatal flaw, it is actually kinder to note that flaw and recommend that the editor/track chair reject the manuscript than to waste the author's time, especially with a possibly lengthy R&R process. The reviewer should clearly detail the nature of the flaw and explain how this flaw can be avoided in future research. When possible, the reviewer should suggest references such as Daniel Feldman's "The Devil is in the Details: Converting Good Research into Publishable Articles" (2004c) and this book, that can help authors further develop their research and publishing skills.

Even if there is no one fatal flaw, a manuscript may have so many significant flaws or mistakes that it is simply not acceptable for publication (see section 3 in this book for more specific guidelines on reviewing different types of manuscripts). Some significant flaws include:

- the idea is underdeveloped and may be more appropriate for a conference "work in progress" session but not a journal publication;
- the manuscript simply repeats what is already known, uses outdated sources, and contributes nothing new to the knowledge base;
- the authors misuse statistics, overreach from the data, fail to report vital information such as reliability and validity measures, and employ the wrong statistics to test the hypotheses;
- the manuscript is too similar to earlier publications of the same authors;[6] and
- the data cannot answer the questions or hypotheses posed or poor methodology has been used.

If the manuscript does not have a serious flaw but is not a good match for the journal to which it was submitted, the reviewer should suggest alternative outlets to the editor. Similarly, for conference papers, reviewers can advise authors about specific outlets and other sources of publishing information (e.g., Cabell's Directory, the Emerald Library). Individuals new to the field may be unfamiliar with the goals and criteria of a specific journal or conference and may be unaware of other outlets that may be a better match for the manuscript in question.

All in all, reviewers shouldn't hesitate to point out mistakes, errors or issues worthy of revisions. It is the reviewer's obligation to the academic community as well as to the journal/conference to help the editor/track chair make difficult decisions. Although typos and even some statistical errors can often be easily corrected, it is not an easy decision to question a colleague's judgment or the veracity of their work. Regrettably, there are cases of blatant plagiarism or stealing of another's work. Thirty-three percent of the 3427 scientists surveyed by

Martinson, Anderson and de Vries (2005) admitted to committing scientific misconduct (e.g., falsifying data, not giving credit to another for their work, publishing same data more than once) in the last three years. It is the reviewer's responsibility to bring issues of potential scientific misconduct to the editor. Reviewers must take the review process seriously, as the manner in which reviews are accomplished demonstrates the values of our profession and organizations (Lee, 1995). There are some manuscripts that should be stopped before they are further developed – those manuscripts that just repeat previously published works, don't add value, aren't of interest to the academic community, or are advertisements for academic programs disguised as research. If a manuscript has no real hope of publication, reviewers should be objective and provide feedback which can help improve the authors' future research endeavors.

Conclusion

Although it is important to be respectful and polite to authors, reviewers must remember their simultaneous duties. They should help authors develop as researchers and writers while maintaining high standards, so that knowledge is advanced. Reviewers must be watchful so that only original, quality contributions are accepted for publication. Table 4.1 provides a checklist of points that can be used to help reviewers balance their duty to authors with their duty to science.

Table 4.1   Reviewer's Checklist

1. Have I scheduled sufficient time to complete a high quality review? (If not, have I immediately contacted the editor or conference track chair?)

2. Have I read the paper over several times and read relevant articles needed to understand the manuscript?

3. Have I written a clear, one paragraph summary of the article, illustrating my understanding of the author's work?

4. Have I noted both positives as well as negatives of the manuscript?

5. Have I offered constructive criticism, avoiding remarks that may be seen as ridiculing or chastising the author?

6. Have I offered specific, actionable suggestions for revision, including complete cites of recommended readings? In other words, is my review developmental?

7. Have I recognized any potential serious problems with the manuscript such as fatal flaws or lack of originality?

Reviewing is perhaps one of the most under-rated, under-appreciated and misunderstood functions in academic life (Armstrong, 1997). Despite recommendations that reviewer training is needed, in most graduate programs, new faculty orientation programs, and academic conferences, little or no information is available about how to conduct quality reviews (Crocitto & Sullivan, 2003; Miner, 2003). It is hoped that this chapter encourages individuals to examine seriously the reviewing process and how their reviews impact authors, editors/track chairs, and readers, as well as the advancement of knowledge in our field.

Notes

1 It is important that individuals carefully read any guidelines for reviewers provided by the editor or track chair. For instance, some editors prefer that reviewers do not include in their comments to authors a statement about such issues as whether the manuscript should be accepted or rejected or if it needs major or minor revisions.

2 Individuals new to the review process should find Schepmyer, van Emmerik and Oliver's chapter titled "Advice for the Novice Reviewer," especially helpful.

3 One of our colleagues recounted an experience with a top-tier journal in which the reviewer grilled him extensively about his grammar and spelling. The review, however, was littered with typos and errors, creating a bad impression of the journal and the editor's monitoring of the review process.

4 Our thanks to the individuals who shared their comments. The Academy of Management and other organizations have done a good job of promoting an atmosphere where such disparaging comments are discouraged. Although these comments may be less likely to occur today than in the past, they still do happen. We have found through our own experiences as writers, track chairs and editors as well as through discussions with fellow track chairs and editors, that some reviewers still belittle authors. Daniel Feldman, a former editor of the Journal of Management, recommends a solution for the frustrated reviewer tempted to take his/her frustration out on authors. He suggests that if a reviewer needs to vent, that he/she go ahead and vent, but to direct these comments about the manuscript to the editor rather than to the authors (Feldman, chapter 14). See also Feldman's (2005) article which details additional ways in which reviewers can demonstrate respect for authors.

5 Thanks to Lisa Mainiero for her suggestion to illustrate the potential for depersonalization in the reviewing process with Milgram's famous research.

6 Occasionally, authors step over the line and try to publish the same article in slightly different formats in two (or more) different outlets. A submitted manuscript should be appreciably distinguishable from the author's prior work whether it be the utilization of different data sets or new analyses of previously examined data sets. Authors writing multiple manuscripts from the same project or database or who have variations of the same paper

should advise the editor of this (Feldman, 2003). Reviewers should alert the editor if they have concerns about the originality of the manuscript. If reviewers have doubts about the originality of a manuscript, checking sources such as ABI Inform for keywords or even the names of specific authors if self-citing is overly evident, may help detect potential problems. Reviewers who think a manuscript is too similar to previous published articles can ask the authors to specifically indicate the value added of this work compare to previous publications or cited "in press" publications.

References

Armstrong, J. S. (1997). Peer review for journals: Evidence on quality control, fairness, and innovation. *Science and Engineering Ethics, 3*, 63–84.

Crocitto, M. & Sullivan, S. E. (2003). How to complete outstanding reviews. Presentation at the *Academy of Management Meeting*, Seattle.

Feldman, D. C. (2005). Writing and reviewing as sadomasochistic rituals. *Journal of Management, 31(3)*, 325–30.

Feldman, D. C. (2004a). Being a developmental reviewer: Easier said than done. *Journal of Management, 30(2)*, 161–4.

Feldman, D. C. (2004b). What are we talking about when we talk about theory? *Journal of Management, 30(5)*, 565–7.

Feldman, D. C. (2004c). The devil is in the details: Converting good research into publishable articles. *Journal of Management, 30(1)*, 1–6.

Feldman, D. C. (2003). When is a new submission "new"? *Journal of Management, 29(2)*, 139–40.

Jauch, R. L. Wall, J. L. (1989). What they do when they get your manuscript: A survey of Academy of Management reviewer practices. *Academy of Management Journal, 32(1)*, 157–73.

Lee, A. S. (1995). Reviewing a manuscript for publication. *Journal of Operations Management, 13*, 87–92.

Martinson, B. C., Anderson, M. S., & de Vries, R. (2005). Scientists behaving badly. *Nature, 435*, 737–8.

Milgram, S. (1963). Behavioral study of obedience. *Journal of Abnormal and Social Psychology, 67*, 371–8.

Miner, J. B. (2003). Commentary on Arthur Bedeian's "The manuscript review process: The proper roles of authors, referees, and editors." *Journal of Management Inquiry, 12(4)*, 339–43.

Price, L. J. (1996). Understanding the negativity effect: The role of processing focus. *Marketing Letters, 7(1)*, 53–63.

Scarpello, V. & Carraher, S. (1997). Pay satisfaction and pay fairness: Are they the same construct? *South West Academy of Management, 39*, 69–73.

Singh, J. (2003). A reviewer's gold. *Journal of the Academy of Marketing Science. 31(3)*, 331–6.

Starbuck, W. H. (2003). Turning lemons into lemonade: Where is the value in peer reviews? *Journal of Management Inquiry, 12(4)*, 344–51.

5
Fairness as a Key Criterion in Reviewing

Debra L. Shapiro and Sim B. Sitkin

"Publish or perish" is an axiom that is well understood by academics, especially those on the "tenure-track" who have yet to receive tenure at their employing institution. This is because the pre-tenure academics face the severest possible form of academic peril – job loss – if at the time of their tenure-evaluation they have an insufficient publishing record. Importantly, however, the pressure to publish is felt by tenured academics too, since valued resources other than job security (e.g., reduced teaching loads, increase in salary, future promotions, "summer money," opportunities for sabbaticals, allocation of doctoral students) are often tied to continued "productivity" (i.e., publishing) throughout the academic career. In summary, the stakes attached to publishing or not publishing are serious; indeed, they are life-altering. As a result, whenever we are asked to review other academics' papers, we ought to recognize that *"publish or perish"* is <u>not</u> hyperbole; and by extension, as reviewers we have a similar choice – to *"review fairly or kill."* The latter words are severe; we use them to highlight that *as reviewers we <u>can</u> and <u>do</u> put academic lives in peril whenever our reviews are less than completely fair.*

Reviewing fairly rests on the underlying notion that a reviewer has significant influence, even control, over key resources that affect other people and thus there exists a professional obligation to attempt to carry out this role as fairly as possible. In addition, because the purpose of reviewing is to enhance the quality of published research by screening out inadequate quality and also by enhancing the quality of what will ultimately be published, the reviewer has a dual responsibility to be fair to the author or reviewed research *and* the potential future reader of that research. Authors who perceive their work to have been fairly reviewed – whether the assessment is positive or negative – are more likely to be able to undertake positive changes in their manuscripts when compared with those who feel that their work has been unfairly handled. Thus, it is not only out of concern for the feelings of the author but also out of concern for the ultimate quality of the published work that reviewer fairness is important.

In addressing these issues, we structure this chapter in two parts: first, we discuss the roles implied by the idea of fair reviewing, and then we identify what the key process-characteristics are of doing fair reviews.

Reviewing fairly – a role perspective

In this chapter we will argue that fair reviewing rests on the implications of two distinct justice-based roles that reviewers simultaneously occupy. There are some fairness challenges associated with each of these roles, but the most difficult ones arise because these roles to some extent conflict with each other.

Reviewing as a gatekeeping role

Perhaps the most dominant role attributed to scholarly reviewers is "Gatekeeper." In this role the reviewer's primary job is to ensure that poor science does not get published. Doctoral students are trained to find fundamental flaws in even the most esteemed of publications – and they learn those lessons well. Many studies, for example, utilize statistical techniques under conditions that violate the assumptions of those tests. While many statistical tests are actually quite robust and these violations are more technically than practically important in judging the validity of a study, nonetheless some reviewers adopt the undifferentiated critical perspective of the doctoral student and find virtually no research meritorious. Some reviewers seem to never make positive recommendations about any paper they review.

Errors of commission can occur when seriously flawed papers are published because reviewers have not done their jobs diligently. Such lapses in attention to fairness take place when a reviewer is unwilling to challenge a high powered author (when this is known), does not take the time to explain to an editor what the problem is as the reviewer sees it, is lazy about thoroughly reading and thinking about a paper, or does not acknowledge when a paper falls too far outside the reviewer's domain of expertise.

Reviewers who do take seriously their gatekeeper role serve a very valuable function as their identification of flaws and their reasoning may be helpful in assuring quality standards are upheld. Yet, this role raises difficult fairness questions when a reviewer truly believes that a particular methodology is fundamentally inadequate (e.g., many reviewers appear to believe this about qualitative methods), or that a particular theory is fatally flawed or passé, or that theoretical work is overpublished and thus should be rejected out of hand. Such reviewers (and the editors who utilize them) need to examine when balance or acceptance creates an erosion of standards (which they should oppose in their role as gatekeeper) and when it involves encouraging different approaches all with high (if differing) standards. Using Ryan's terminology (chapter 3), serious reviewers must assess their biases.

Reviewing as a developmental role

In selecting associate editors, an editor of a top management journal observed that the most difficult attribute to find was individuals who could recognize, cultivate and bring to completion papers worth publishing. In a field in which fewer than 10% of all submissions are published, it is easy to reject everything since you will be right nearly all the time. But a more fundamental understanding of how fuzzy the boundaries are between degrees of quality (Starbuck, 2005) suggests that significant scientific value results when reviewers help authors – without rejecting their submissions – to maximize the potential contribution of their work. This involves mentoring and coaching skills as much as it does critical analysis and expertise.

We discuss the developmental role at greater length below when we explore the processes associated with fair reviewing. But some of the justice-related dilemmas inherent in this role include: How much time ought reviewers devote to the work of others versus their own?; How many original creative insights ought reviewers keep to themselves versus share with authors when such insights promise to enable a paper to get developed into a seminal piece?; Are reviewers behaving unethically if they are abusive in their criticism – especially (but not only) when the journal for which they are reviewing sets as its operating norms the use of civil and constructive discourse standards, as most of our journals have now done? In short, is there a professional obligation to be helpful, and *not only* to foreswear attacking behavior?

We believe there is such a (two-pronged) obligation and that this view has increasingly become the norm in our field. Additionally, we believe that those who choose *not* to adhere to such expectations should simply not review regardless of their substantive expertise. The developmental role is in part the role of educator – not only of students or younger scholars, but also – of peers.

"Reviewing fairly" means doing what?

Next, we argue that reviews lacking in fairness are those that are late, insensitive, inconsistent with previously-stated criteria for paper-acceptability, and/or self-serving. We discuss the latter review-characteristics, each in turn. We conclude by noting how actions that have been identified as exemplifying "organizational justice" (see Colquitt & Greenberg, 2005, for a recent review of this literature) are consistent with actions by reviewers when they <u>avoid</u> each of these characteristics; or put more positively, when reviewers send reviews that are: (1) timely, (2) interpersonally-sensitive, (3) consistent with criteria for paper-acceptability that have been publicized or stated by journal editors and/or by reviewers in previous communications, and (4) selfless. Importantly, we define "selfless" in a way that highlights that reviewers ought to be fair (i.e., act responsibly) to *many* stakeholders, including (but not limited to) those who submit papers for journal review.

Providing a timely, not late, review

The passage of time is consequential for all of us, assuming we wish to maximize the meaning, contribution, and joy we can create during our time on Earth. The passage of time feels especially consequential, however, for those who hear the "tenure-clock" ticking – that is, for the not-yet-tenured academics for whom this clock is, with rare exception, institutionally set for the first six years of the post-doctorate career. This clock ticks continually, whether a reviewer is quick, on time, or late in delivering a requested review. Because journal editors cannot write their review or decision for a submitted manuscript until they receive <u>all</u> of the reviews that they have requested for this purpose, *it takes only one late review* to delay the review process and to negate the timely efforts of other reviewers.

The latter description suggests that journal reviewers have an immense responsibility in helping academics early in their career to be enabled to receive timely feedback that, in turn, will allow feedback-receivers to strengthen their initially-submitted work into publication-acceptable form. However, *the responsibility of providing timely reviews is not only for journal reviewers*; indeed, this responsibility begins as faculty members for our doctoral students whose initial "clock" is probably the four or five years that many hope to constitute the length of their doctoral program. The latter goal is surely more difficult to achieve when faculty members take months (rather than days or just a couple weeks) to provide verbal- or written-feedback regarding dissertation-drafts or working paper-drafts they have received – a scenario that, sadly, is *not* hypothetical for many doctoral students.

Academics striving to produce publishable work in top-ranked journal outlets include doctoral students as well as faculty members at all career-stages; no one can get published in journal-outlets independent of a review process. Therefore, the review process must be one that minimizes the impediments to the speed with which academics aim to publish their value-adding insights. This is why many top-ranked journals request reviewers to return reviews within four-to-six-weeks after receiving a manuscript. Despite this request, it is very rare when it is met (by all reviewers of a given manuscript), hence probably the reason why it is more the exception than the rule for authors to receive reviews within six or eight weeks after submitting a manuscript to a journal. What accounts for the difficulty in obtaining timely reviews? First, many individuals (including editorial board members) turn down reviewing requests for various reasons (and sometimes do so after a long time lapse), thus increasing the length of time required to identify reviewers; see chapter 3 for instances when it may be appropriate to decline a review. Second, while editors *request* reviewers to be timely with their reviews; they cannot enforce this. A related reason it is difficult to enforce timely reviews is because reviewers are *volunteers* for whom reviewing is a "service to the profession." Third, while such service is admirable and respected (especially when it is in the form of editorial board membership), it is the status of having been chosen as a reviewer or a board member rather than reviewing diligently that is generally recognized. In addition, Priem and Rasheed described in their chapter that the invisible nature of this service prevents it from being a priority on an individual's list of things to do. Even then, reviewing receives far less weight than the number of top-tier publications they themselves can report on their annual performance-record. Because most journal reviewers are themselves attempting to get published, hence "jugglers" of the roles of reviewer and reviewee, the latter juggling act can sometimes create a conflict of interest, a point to which we elaborate in the next section. For example, one of us had to reject a paper recently because only one individual in a highly specialized area was willing to do a review – a large number of highly qualified reviewers were simply unwilling to take the time to review.

In summary, the first characteristic needed if a review process is to be fair is timeliness. Providing timely reviews is important for academics at all career stages, including doctoral students. But perhaps the greatest need for timely reviews is felt by the academics who are seeking tenure (typically accompanied by promotion to Associate Professor) or who are seeking other promotions (e.g., to Full Professor or to Distinguished Professorships); with timely reviews these academics will be far more enabled to speedily strengthen their work so it gets published before the "clock" preceding their evaluation-time expires.

Providing a constructive, not destructive, review

The second characteristic needed if a review process is to be fair is *interpersonal respectfulness*. The term widely used today is "developmental" to describe such an approach to reviewing – where developmental refers both to the reviewer responsibility for enhancing the work and also to building the insights and abilities of the author for future high quality research. Interpersonal respect is important not only to ensure that the reviewer is developmental (and thus building rather than tearing down capability), but also to increase the chances that the author can actually hear and act on the constructive criticism being offered. The proverb *"It's not what you say but how you say it"* succinctly expresses the fact that criticism is generally more easily heard, hence more developmental in effect, when it is communicated constructively rather than destructively. Reviews that are more rather than less constructive tend to exclude evaluative remarks that impugn an author's level of effort, ability, or intention. As an example, phrases such as "your literature review was lazy," "your methods were inept," and "your choosing to omit the work of So-and-So is irresponsible" would never be part of a constructive review. Instead, constructive reviews would tell authors the publications and/or scholar-names whose work ought to be included in order to logically strengthen their literature review. If the submitted manuscript is a qualitative or quantitative empirical paper, then constructive reviews would also tell authors how to better represent their method, clarify their reporting of results, and analytically strengthen their data-related interpretation. In short, unlike destructive reviews, constructive reviews provide authors with potential solutions to identified problem-areas, and they communicate these in a way that leaves authors feeling <u>able</u> to act upon the suggested solutions. (When a problem's solution is not readily known to a reviewer, ideally the reviewer will suggest reading-sources where the solution may be found.) A constructive review accepts what the author is trying to achieve and helps the author see more clearly key obstacles to successful contribution and potential paths through those obstacles. Constructive reviews help – not only the authors receiving these, but – the scholarly literature to which authors strive to contribute; this is because people are generally more motivated to put forth effort, hence more likely to achieve high levels of performance, when they have (rather than lack) self-esteem and self-efficacy (Gist & Mitchell, 1992; Tierney & Farmer, 2002). See Sullivan, Crocitto and Carrher's chapter for a thorough discussion of how to write developmental, actionable reviews and see Schepmyer, van Emmerik and Oliver's chapter for more detail on preparing constructive reviews.

Importantly, many of the premier management and psychology journals explicitly require their reviewers to express criticism in constructive, or developmental, ways. Indeed, some journals (e.g., Academy of Management Review) grade reviewers on this dimension (as well as others) in order to identify which reviewers are most constructive, hence most desirable.

Providing a review that is consistent, not discrepant, with acceptability-criteria

The third characteristic needed if a review process is to be fair is *procedural consistency*. Journals have mission statements that tell potential manuscript-submitters what the paper-qualities are that the journal seeks to publish. At Organization Science, for example, the mission says; "*Organization Science* ... editors are especially interested in manuscripts that break new ground rather than ones that make incremental contributions." The substantive concerns communicated in reviews ought to be consistent with the journal's stated mission; after all, the purpose of reviews ought to help ensure, among other things, that the journal's standards for publication are met. When a reviewer's concern is inconsistent with a journal's stated mission, procedural inconsistency – hence an "unfair review" – is experienced. Reviewers should not confuse upholding standards with imposing biases. The reviewer's job does indeed involve ensuring that published research does meet quality standards, but when this is used as a mask for exercising personal bias (e.g., against qualitative methodologies or against non-empirical papers), it is inconsistent with responsible reviewing. This occurs, for example, when authors receive reviews stating that the journal does not publish studies utilizing "Method X" (their study's method) when the latter method is not identified as unacceptable in the journal's mission statement.

The substance of reviews received by journal-submitters implicitly, if not explicitly, communicate criteria for paper-acceptability. When reviewers raise new concerns after a revised paper addresses all of their previously-raised concerns, this inconsistency also tends to generate cries of an unfair review. In summary, a fair review process is more likely to be experienced when the concerns expressed by reviewers are consistent with the standards of publishability communicated by the journal's mission statement and by the substance of reviews previously received by journal-submitters.

Providing a selfless, not self-serving, review

The third characteristic needed if a review process is to be fair is *"selflessness."* To provide clarity on what we mean by this, let us begin by noting what it is not: Selflessness is not exemplified by reviewers whose behavior seems motivated by a desire for self-aggrandizement or biased gatekeeping. More specifically, selflessness is *lacking* when reviewers require that their own publications be cited when doing so is not essential for the conceptual foundation of the paper they are reviewing; when reviewers tend to negatively evaluate authors who have (rather than haven't) criticized their past theories and/or methods; when reviewers negatively evaluate authors who conceptually or methodologically challenge, rather than support, the reviewers' own conceptual- or methodological-perspectives; and finally, when an author's identity is either known or inferred, when reviewers tend to reject or accept papers of authors they personally dislike or like, respectively. In contrast, selflessness is present when reviewers' actions indicate that they are motivated to serve the needs of all the stakeholders in the review process – not just their own scholarly reputations or the needs of the journal-submitter.

Until now, our focus has been nearly exclusively on the author of a submitted manuscript; yet, the review process involves many constituents, including: (1) the Editorial Team (Editor and Associate-Editors) and editorial board members of the manuscript-receiving journal, (2) the journal's readers, (3) the journal's future potential manuscript-submitters (e.g., graduate students or other scholars), and (4) scholars whose work is cited, or wrongly omitted, in the submitted manuscript.

"Would each of these constituents judge a reviewer's review to be fair?" may thus be the most accurate "fairness litmus test" of a journal review. Scholars whose work is relevant to the submitted manuscript will probably judge a review to be more fair when it includes accurate

(rather than inaccurate) description of cited publications and when it includes (rather than excludes) scholarly publications that directly relate to the submitted manuscript's text.

Because journals' readers (especially paying ones) and future potential manuscript-submitters typically expect a journal's quality to match its mission, these constituency-groups will probably judge a review to be more fair when its substance is consistent (rather than inconsistent) with the journals' mission. The latter forecast is likely, also, for the members of the journals' Editorial Board and Editorial Team; additionally, however, the journals' reviewers will probably assess fairness by how consistent an outcome decision is with the "votes" of the reviewers. Although journal editors have veto power, typically this is exercised when a set of reviews is mixed in their action-recommendations. When Editors' decisions are discrepant with a consistent pattern of reviewers' recommendations, the fairness of the review process is more likely to be questioned by the reviewers who see that their consistently-advised action has been ignored. Yet the editorial role in the reviewing process is critical and should be much more than mere vote-counting or providing post-hoc justifications for reviews. Editors are in their positions because they have been seen as having good, balanced judgment based on a knowledge of the field, and especially when reviewers do not do their job well or have differing ideas, an editor needs to be proactive to ensure research quality standards and clear and consistent author guidance are simultaneously achieved. Balancing editorial prerogative with reviewer influence is thus part of the fairness challenge raised by the review process.

Summary and conclusion: let us review fairly, not kill

In summary, in this chapter we have articulated the need for reviewers to review fairly if they wish to avoid killing the careers of academics aiming to publish, not perish. Specifically, we have identified fair reviews to be those that are: *(1) timely* (e.g., not late), *(2) interpersonally-respectful* (e.g., constructively critical), *(3) procedurally consistent* with the transparent criteria for paper-acceptability publicized or stated by journal editors and/or by reviewers in previous communications, and *(4) selfless*. By selfless, we have emphasized that this means being guided by the interests of *all* of the stakeholders in the review process (not only the needs of the reviewer or the manuscript-submitter), hence being open to well-reasoned arguments whose conclusion may differ from reviewers' own practices or previously-published views.

Borrowing language from the organizational justice literature (see Colquitt & Greenberg, 2005, for a recent review), these four characteristics enhance the likelihood that all stakeholders in the review process will perceive fairness: with regard to the *outcomes* (in terms of editors' final decisions, reviewers' judgments, and the timeliness of these); with regard to the *interpersonal treatment* received during the reviewing process (in terms of the extent to which all constituents feel they have been treated with dignity and respect); and with regard to the *procedural criteria* guiding the reviewing process (in terms of the transparency of this, its consistent application, and the lack of reviewer bias). Said more succinctly, the four characteristics of the review process that we have identified in this chapter as antecedents to a fair review experience will probably enhance the likelihood that *distributive justice, interactional justice,* and *procedural justice* will be perceived by all of the journals' stakeholders (see Shapiro & Brett, 2005, for a review of the organizational justice literature).

It is because all three types of justice are essential for the review process to be as fair as possible that it is time-consuming to provide such reviews. Ironically, this helps to explain why speediness is rarely associated with the review process and, as a result, why providing fair reviews is easier said than done. Nevertheless, we hope our chapter will help sensitize all constituents of the review process to the fact that their needs are among many that must be served if the reviewing process is to be truly fair. As such, being selfless in the way reviews are provided and received is essential for ensuring the continual (volunteer) mentoring that the review process enables management scholars to enjoy.

References

Academy of Management Journal Guidelines for Reviewers
<http://aom.pace.edu/amjnew/reviewer_guidelines.html>
Colquitt, J. A. & Greenberg, J. (eds) (2005). *Handbook of organizational justice.* NJ: Lawrence Erlbaum, Inc.
Gist, M. E. & Mitchell, T. R. (1992). Self-efficacy: A theoretical analysis of its determinants and malleability. *Academy of Management Review, 17(2),* 183–211.
Shapiro, D. L. & Brett, J. M. (2005). What is the role of control in organizational justice? In J. Greenberg & J. Colquitt (eds) *Handbook of organizational justice,* 155–77. NJ: Lawrence Erlbaum, Inc.
Starbuck, W. (2005). How much better are the most prestigious journals? The statistics of academic publication. *Organization Science,* in press.
Tierney, P. & Farmer. S. M. (2002). Creative self-efficacy: Its potential antecedents and relationship to creative performance. *Academy of Management Journal, 45(6),* 1137–48.

6

Advice for the Novice Reviewer

*Hazlon (Haze) Schepmyer, I. J. Hetty van Emmerik and
Christine Oliver*

Introduction[1]

There is only one way to become an experienced reviewer and that is
to start as a novice. In this chapter, we highlight and elaborate on
several specific issues which are particularly important for making the
journey from the novice to the experienced reviewer. In other words,
while some of the topics below were explored by Sullivan, Crocitto and
Carraher in chapter 4 and others will be addressed by Puffer, Quick and
McCarthy in chapter 10, our focus here is on the newcomer's approach
to/perspective on the task of reviewing. We adopt the Ensher, Thomas
and Murphy (2001) mentoring model as a framework to propose that,
along the way, the novice reviewer can learn from traditional, step-
ahead and peer mentors. Following a brief description of these terms,
advice from each type of advisor is offered to demonstrate their different, but interrelated, perspectives. Finally, we conclude with a
summary and a list of "must-read" articles for the novice reviewer.

The novice reviewer and guidance from three types of advisors

Ensher et al (2001) studied mentoring-protégé relationships in an organizational setting but, here, we use their three-tier model as a presentation device to show the different advice relationships that are possible
between novice and more experienced reviewers. In their work, a distinction is made between: (i) **peer mentors**, who hold comparable
positions to the protégé in terms of experience; (ii) **step-ahead
mentors**, who are more experienced but only one level ahead of the
protégé in the hierarchy and (iii) **traditional mentors**, who perform
the classic "venerable sage" role for the protégé.

Regardless of career stage, individuals can reap several unique advantages for career and professional development by having qualitatively different mentors; a growing body of research supports the usefulness of these advice models (de Janasz & Sullivan, 2004; Seibert, Kraimer & Liden, 2001; van Emmerik, 2004). Such advice relationships appear to be a win-win intervention with many benefits. As Ensher et al (2001) mentioned, a positive advice relationship can enhance the self-esteem and increase the knowledge, skills, and abilities of both persons involved. Moreover, advisors can serve to socialize the novice reviewer to the norms of the profession. Accordingly, in the next three sections, we offer (i) advice from a peer advisor, a reviewer with fewer than five years' experience; (ii) advice from a step-ahead advisor, a reviewer with five years' experience and five best reviewer awards, and (iii) advice from a traditional advisor, a reviewer with over 18 years' experience.

Advice from a peer advisor – Hazlon (Haze) Schepmyer

Ensher et al (2001) described the peer-protégé relationship as one that involves partners taking turns at giving and receiving similar types of guidance and support. Peer advice relationships are unique because they offer a degree of mutuality that enables both parties to experience being the giver and the receiver.

As a reviewer with fewer than five years' experience, my first piece of advice is to seek out opportunities to gain experience. For example, attend professional development workshops on reviewing; these are usually offered in the pre-conference part of most association's annual meetings. It is in these settings that you can participate in small-group discussions with experienced reviewers as well as receive guidance and support from other novices who may also have little or no experience. My first few years of reviewing coincided with my doctoral studies and, before graduating, I had reviewed papers for other students in my cohort, for my supervisor as his research assistant, for Academy of Management program chairs, for a track chair in the Southwest Academy of Management and, most recently, for a special issue of Career Development International at the request of the guest editors.

My second piece of advice is to ask others for help, regardless of their career stages, and ask them about recommended readings. By taking this advice, I invited the editors of the top ten management journals (as identified by ISI's impact factor rating for 2004) to share with me their observations about reviewing for the purposes of this chapter. Of the ten contacted, two replied. In addition, I approached several of the top reviewers from various Academy of Management divisions and seven agreed to contribute their insights. Specifically, I asked each editor and top reviewer to tell me which three pieces of advice and which three readings they would recommend to a novice reviewer.[2] The end-result is the following collection of tips on how to approach the reviewing process and a list of "must-read" books and articles for understanding the art and craft of reviewing and for honing one's reviewing skills; the list appears in Appendix A. These quick-reference lists highlight themes which are captured and further developed throughout this section of the book.

There are many perspectives among the words of wisdom below that should reflect and appeal to the variety of readers. Clearly, not all advice will resonate with everyone but, ideally, something in this section will help each of you become a better reviewer, writer and scholar. Several themes emerged so the advice is arranged under the following headings: preparation, writing focus, content assessment, clarity and editing, tone, time-management. Ben Arbaugh offered an important tip that did not fit into any of the categories but reiterates my opening point: "Don't let inexperience keep you from reviewing – reviewing is how you get experience. Besides, in most settings, editors, conference organizers and program chairs have mechanisms in place to accommodate novice reviewers".

Preparation

In order to prepare before doing the actual reviewing, Manuela Brusoni suggests the following: "Read the entire article to get a general idea of the paper. During the first reading, make first–impression notes on the article and look in your personal bibliography on the same topic, look for other literature and compare the paper with some key issues emerging from this quick overview. In some instances, the content may be country-specific from the governance, environmental, legislative standpoints. Therefore, take note of these possible points of view in order to transfer them into the final review". Ben Arbaugh suggests: "If at all possible, try to review on topics you're presently doing research in or reading about".

Writing focus

- It is important to discuss the relative focus in one's review on substance versus style – while one can make comments on clarity of writing, it is not the job of the reviewer to concentrate heavily on style/wording issues in making a judgment. (AMR)

- Although there is not always much time for writing, it is essential to allow sufficient time for "absorbing" the article. This entails leaving a few days between the first read of the article and the writing phase. Recap the main key issues in the literature and, at the same time, focus on the guidance notes and suggestions of the specific editor, in order to match the most appropriate hints in the literature with the individual journal needs. (MB)

Content assessment

- Look for theory and make sure the authors told the story – i.e., explained the "why?" behind their hypotheses. It is not enough that past research found A lead to B, so therefore we expect C to occur. We need to say "why" C should occur. (MF)
- Make sure the contribution is clear. How does the manuscript add to our base of knowledge, and why is it important for us to read? Also, are the implications – both for scholarly researchers and practitioners – addressed? (MF)
- Check to see whether the author(s) can satisfactorily answer the question "Why is this interesting?" in the first 3–4 pages of the paper. (BA)
- Search for the gem of an idea or contribution in an article, even if it's roughly polished. Don't get bogged down in too many execution details, because they can usually be fixed in a revision. (AY)
- Make sure that there is no fatal flaw in the theoretical argument or research design (e.g., the logic is faulty or the data are inappropriate to test the theory). These can't be fixed, so if there is a fundamental problem, it is usually important to point that out and not go any further. (AY)
- When writing, try to keep separate the assessment from the judgment and, in the introduction, deal with comparing the paper against the editor's guidelines and doing a step-by-step assessment of: (i) the problem setting (*questions the paper is trying to answer are built on the past research/literature, questions are stated clearly, questions are challenging and they focus on key themes – not too many issues addressed*), (ii) the methodology (*well-structured, rigorous*) and (iii) the conclusions (*logical, consequential, meaningful*). (MB)
- Focus on evaluating completeness and internal consistency across the paper. Then, make personal comments, first of all saying what is

good about the paper, secondly addressing possible weaknesses, lack of clarity and areas for improvement. (MB)

Finally, as Joe Magee emphasizes, it is important to ask yourself some questions about the elements of the paper such as: Is the theory adequate and logically coherent? (i.e., Is there true theory or just a literature review? Are the topics too broad and disconnected?); Are the hypotheses clear? (i.e., At the end of a theoretical article, do you know ideas that could be tested from the theory? At the end of the introduction in an empirical article, do you know what ideas are about to be tested?); Is there "overhypothesizing" – can all the ideas be captured in a smaller number of hypotheses?

Clarity and editing

- Some of the key issues for new reviewers are to: (i) make certain they don't state a decision in their comments to the author, (ii) number their comments, (iii) provide constructive suggestions along with any criticisms and (iv) proofread reviews! (AMR)
- Be clear, precise, detailed (as needed) and focused. If there is a problem, what is the issue and how can it be done differently and better? (SZ)
- Be specific in pointing out a problem with the paper; give examples of where the issue occurred in the text and how the author(s) might improve it. (AMR)
- Give specific suggestions, along with relevant references, to help the author further develop the paper. Nothing is less helpful than vague, general comments. Note that doing this may mean doing a short literature review yourself, especially if the article is not exactly in your own line of research. (AY)

Time management

- Meet the deadline for returning the review – results of the review process impact authors' lives! (SZ)
- Wait a few days and re-read both your review and the paper as a last check for clarity of argumentation, robustness and acceptability. This final step often provides an opportunity to add some last synthetic and global comments or to adopt an "external" perspective on your writing. Then, take stock of the experience. After submitting the review, recap your experience about the paper(s) and summarize: (i) personal learning, (ii) what surprised you as very interesting, (iii) what you can draw from the level of the discussion

on specific topics, (iv) which areas are possibly incomplete or where might there be a bias in the current research or debate. Finally, share these reflections with colleagues who also act as reviewers or are members of editorial boards. Doing so can help improve our ability as writers and publishers and, if necessary, can lead to changes in your review. (MB)

Tone

- Be constructive and helpful. (SZ)
- Be tactful and constructive in your feedback. If you were to sit down with the author of the manuscript, how would you convey the feedback? Make sure you get your points across, but do so in a way that isn't perceived as an attack on the author. (MF)
- Keep a neutral, positive tone and point out what you liked as well as what you didn't like. Write the review once with what you believe is a positive tone. Then, edit it to make it more positive in tone. (JM)
- My best reviews happen when I assume that I am an AUTHOR on the paper, giving advice to my co-author(s) who have given me the current draft. If I were to "own up" to the paper, what would I do to take it to the next level? In short, avoid critique, and focus on taking action to improve the paper. This often results in a new outline, a review of what I considered to be the key arguments, a re-evaluation of the theory/literature/analysis, a list of suggestions for getting beyond areas where I got stuck and new figures. (BL)[3]

Advice from a step-ahead advisor – I. J. Hetty van Emmerik

We mentioned above that a step-ahead mentor refers to an individual occupying a position one level higher in the organizational hierarchy (Ensher et al, 2001). In the reviewing context, a step-ahead advisor would be someone who has gained several years' experience but can easily recall how it feels to be in the protégés' shoes. Adopting this older sibling role, I will provide four tips on how to begin and succeed at reviewing rather than focus on the art of writing an excellent review, which is addressed in other sections of the chapter.

Ask for examples. A very obvious, but sound, piece of advice when you start reviewing is to ask for examples. As further evidence for one of Schepmyer's points, conferences often offer specific workshops on reviewing where you can collect sample reviews. For instance, the Academy of Management Journal organizes workshops on reviewing and, prior to the workshop, each participant receives a manuscript to review. During the workshop, the participants are offered the reviews of the same manuscript from the journal's editors. Sample reviews are also posted on various websites to give the reviewer an idea of what is expected. For example, the British Medical Journal (BMJ) offers an exercise on its website (www.bmj.com) which states: "Below are three reviews of manuscripts recently published in the BMJ. Having read the presentation on what editors want from reviewers, we would like you to read these three reviews and note their strengths and weaknesses. This exercise should take approximately 15 minutes. Having noted the strengths and weaknesses of each review, read our critique of each review from the editorial perspective". Finally, it is also a good idea to ask people to provide you with copies of their reviews. At the 2002 Southern Management Association (SMA) meeting in Atlanta, I approached Sherry Sullivan, who was just named one of the best reviewers, and asked her for a copy of her review even though it was my first time at the SMA conference and I had hardly any experience as a reviewer for conference papers. Fortunately, in addition to getting copies of her reviews, which were extremely helpful, a friendship started that continues today.

Ask what the editor/organizer expects from you. Because the main objective of reviewing is to improve the quality of submissions, it is important to be familiar with the criteria set by the editor or organizer. This is especially true for the novice reviewer. At the 2004 SMA meeting in San Antonio, and in chapter 14 of this book, Daniel Feldman offered evidence of this potential mismatch by pointing out that reviewers are sometimes driven to "kill the paper", whereas editors want to fill their journals. Along these same lines, Priem and Rasheed pointed out in chapter 2 that reviewers may focus on finding flaws but editors are more focused on developing promising papers. It may also be very helpful to know about the typical rejection rates. Most journal editors and conference organizers provide a standardized review form in order to make the criteria clear and to let the reviewer score the manuscript on these criteria. Sometimes, to gain insight into how the paper fits relative to all of those received by each reviewer, editors also provide space for an overall assessment, for general comments and/or for the ranking of the reviewed papers.

Ask for advice. Many will agree that the most frustrating and time-consuming issue for a reviewer is when you don't know what to do with some part of the manuscript. For example, the authors use multi-level techniques and you have never heard about applying these methods to this specific research design. Certainly, you can do some research on your own, but you can also ask the authors to elaborate on why they used such techniques. And, of course, you can ask the editor what to do. Most typically, reviewers add a "for your eyes only" section to their reviews which is meant to be read by only the editor or organizer of the conference. Caution: it has to be emphasized that keeping a separate communication with the editor is really different from the review.

Ask for follow-up. Particularly when you are reviewing for a journal, it is a good idea to ask for follow-up or feedback on your review. Sometimes this is provided automatically and, together with a letter to thank you for serving as a reviewer, you will also receive the complete correspondence with the authors. In addition, journals frequently have a policy ensuring that each manuscript is allocated to a novice reviewer and to a more experienced reviewer. Thus, you are able to compare your review with the comments and judgments by another reviewer. Furthermore, editors often evaluate the reviews they receive and this is another source of valuable information about the quality of your own review (see chapter 10 for more information about completing evaluation forms and requesting feedback from editors).

In conclusion, good reviewing will inevitably mean investing a lot of time and effort; Moher and Jadad (2003) estimate that a novice reviewer will take, on average, 8–12 hours to review a manuscript and to produce a review. Clearly, more thorough reviewers will devote even more time to the process. Most will agree with Jauch and Wall (1989) who found that reviewing is a demanding, difficult, and time-consuming task, and it is crucial to read manuscripts carefully and often double- or triple-check parts. However, there are important ways one can benefit from reviewing. Helping colleagues always gives us a good feeling and, as seen in my examples above, learning from experienced reviewers may also result in a chance to know more about your colleagues and to become friends. In terms of being a step-ahead reviewer, this means that reviewing is an opportunity to develop skills and a sense of empowerment in helping colleagues (Ensher et al, 2001). When you receive a review from a conscientious reviewer, you will know that someone really put in a lot of effort to improve your work. Moreover, looking at the manuscript, one easily asks "How would I have done it?", and this may provide a fresh look on one's own writings. Finally, most reviewers will agree that it is really exciting to see a paper you reviewed make it to publication and to see how your contribution as a reviewer improved the final manuscript. That's why we do it.

Advice from a traditional advisor – Christine Oliver

Legend in academe has it that a novice reviewer once wrote the following review of a journal manuscript: "Your paper is both interesting and important. Unfortunately, the part that is important isn't interesting and the part that is interesting isn't important." As manuscript reviews go, this review effort isn't without merit. The reviewer got the criteria right. The question is: "What's missing?"

In my six years as editor of *Administrative Science Quarterly*, perhaps what struck me most repeatedly was the extremely high quality of the reviews that we received and the fact that review quality was largely independent of the reviewer's status, years of experience, affiliation, and area of expertise. What was common to all these high-quality reviews, however, was a set of fairly consistent characteristics that, in the final analysis, were all directed toward treating the manuscript, whatever its flaws, as if it had promise as a contribution to the literature, and providing an extensive set of concrete suggestions to the author for fulfilling that promise. For the novice (or seasoned) reviewer, writing a review that gives authors the highest likelihood of developing their work into an excellent paper is the best measure of review quality and it depends on five core techniques of writing reviews.

Give constructive feedback. First, as Shapiro and Sitkin suggested in their discussion of writing fair reviews, the content of reviews must always be constructive. What does that mean? While reviewers should never indicate in the content of their review their advice for the disposition of the manuscript (e.g., "this manuscript should be rejected"; "this manuscript is highly promising and should be published with minor revisions"), reviewers should write their review as if it were going to be the basis for revising the paper for eventual publication in the journal to which it has been sent. By doing so, the reviewer is able to offer comments that are most likely to be helpful in improving the manuscript's quality. This means that part of the burden of manuscript improvement falls necessarily, if somewhat unfairly, to the reviewer. A constructive reviewer never indicates, for example, that "the arguments in this paper are weak." Rather, the reviewer accompanies his or her concern about the need to strengthen the paper's arguments with suggestions for how this might be achieved e.g., "You might develop the argument at the top of page two of your paper by linking it to such-and-such theory and suggesting that your phenomenon of interest is more likely to occur under such-and-such conditions." It is important to note that, if framed appropriately, honest negatives are also better than not being straightforward. A constructive review is one that is direct and rarely identifies a flaw without suggesting a direction or revision, if possible, that might help to correct the flaw.

Take the paper's arguments seriously. A second characteristic of good reviews is the penetration of their insights. Top reviewers are able to drill down to the key problems in the paper and explain clearly how these problems undermine the paper's persuasiveness and value. These insights, at the risk of stating the obvious, depend on a very thorough reading of the manuscript. Good reviewers take seriously, and are seen to take seriously, the paper's content and to engage seriously with the paper's arguments, an outcome that is only achievable by a thorough reading (rather than an aggressive skim) of the paper. It is only a comprehensive reading of a paper that enables a reviewer to understand the full range of errors in the paper's theory or methodology and to root out inconsistencies between the theory and the research design or between the different arguments provided throughout the paper. This does not necessarily mean doing readings beyond the paper to educate oneself about the topic but, in chapter 1, Dipboye mentioned that consulting a meta-analysis might be useful. A paper's clarity and its ability to communicate its arguments and purpose to a relatively broad audience is one of the characteristics of a good paper. However, full familiarity with the manuscript itself is the only way to ensure an insightful review.

Provide an overview of the paper. Third, a high-quality review gives the author both an overview of the paper's main problems (and suggested areas of improvement) and then more detail about where the paper needs to improve, normally provided in the order of the appearance of these problems in the manuscript. High-quality reviews possess no single format or structural template, nor should they. Some reviewers number their points while others use headings such as "The Paper's Theory", "Hypotheses", "Research Design", "Discussion Section". All good reviewers, however, first give a summary of what they see as the paper's fundamental problems and then offer detailed suggestions for improvement, often referring to specific sentences or arguments in the paper, and indicating how the selected text would need to change to improve the manuscript.

Offer suggestions to improve the paper. A fourth aspect of writing good reviews is to ground one's remarks in what one feels the reviewer would need to do to enhance the paper's theoretical contribution to the literature. Advice about improving the flow and clarity of the paper should be oriented toward making the paper's contribution more clearly understood. Advice about changing the paper's theoretical arguments should be accompanied by a rationale for how such changes would enhance the paper's theoretical contribution. Suggestions for correcting flawed logic in arguments and hypotheses should succeed in making the novelty and value of the paper more obvious and compelling. If a piece of advice cannot be justified as an improvement to the paper's contribution (e.g., "please cite a paper I wrote in 1972"), it should be jettisoned from the review.

Adopt a constructive tone. Fifth, while it may seem less substantive as a facet of good reviewing, the tone of the review is, in fact, critical to its quality for four reasons. The author is unable to "hear" suggestions for improvement if s/he is filtering them through a barrage of belittlement and implicit accusation. Accordingly, the author will find it harder to write an effective revision of the paper. Second, the least valuable papers are those that are never written. When the tone of a review is negative, an author (particularly a more junior one) is often sufficiently discouraged to abandon his or her ideas altogether. Third, authors find it harder to build effectively on negative comments ("this paper is poorly written and its arguments are totally without merit") than on positive comments ("the paper's writing needs to be improved in the arguments leading up to the first three hypotheses"). Fourth, all papers possess value; it is simply the degree of value that varies. Whatever a reviewer may think of a paper's contribution, it normally represents what the author believed to be a good effort, and as such should be treated respectfully. Therefore, a reviewer should avoid using demeaning language in his or her review and remove all inadvertent tendencies to exhibit suppressed outrage (e.g., "you have clearly failed to show..."; "these arguments are extremely poor"; "I do not understand how the author could say..."; "why did you not review the literature on...?"). Seasoned reviewers who write the best reviews not only treat authors with respect; they typically open their reviews with a few positive comments about the paper's strengths before moving to the main review of the paper.

In my experience, novice reviewers typically provide very high-quality reviews because they are commonly recent Ph.D. graduates and therefore especially current on the literature and thorough in their feedback to the author. Novice reviewers who have been mentored by caring advisors (an anonymous reviewer for this chapter explained how s/he helped doctoral students by encouraging them to write reviews and then showing them how to improve) or those who have been given the opportunity to critique articles during their graduate training often write the best reviews. However, any novice reviewer possesses the potential to write an excellent review provided that his or her area of expertise is an appropriate match for the paper. If a reviewer is struggling with understanding the paper's strengths and weaknesses, s/he should return the paper unreviewed as soon as possible, with a note to the editor explaining that the paper is not a good fit with the reviewer's areas of specialization. Most journals also welcome correspondence from novice reviewers who wish to volunteer as a reviewer. The novice reviewer's name will then be added to the journal's database for future reference. The important point is to be very specific about the topics, theories and methods you consider to be your areas of expertise, and to feel free to correspond with an editor at any point before or during the review process if you have any questions or concerns.

Most reviewers, whether novice or seasoned, do not write poor reviews because they misunderstand the criteria for judging a paper's quality. Reviewers are typically able to gauge whether a paper is "interesting" or "important." What is less obvious is how reviews should be written to provide optimal assistance to an author, regardless of whether the author's paper is likely to be published in the targeted journal. By consistently writing reviews that are oriented toward optimizing a paper's contribution, chances are that we can raise the bar on what constitutes both interesting and important academic work across the entire field of management.

Concluding comments

In this collection of advice for the novice reviewer, we have outlined a multitude of ways in which one can benefit from having an advice relationship with traditional or step-ahead advisors (more experienced) or with peer advisors (equally or slightly more experienced). Obtaining answers to review problems through an advice relationship allows a solution to be orchestrated in an effective and timely manner (Cross, Borgatti, & Parker, 2001). More broadly, using a variety of sources for information, ranging from colleagues to the concrete samples and guidelines of renowned journals, clearly improves review quality. Regardless of one's level of experience, it is possible to write an excellent review. The rewards of reviewing are both personal and professional: reviewers learn more about a topic through the experience and at the same time contribute to the professional quality of the broader scholarly community.

Notes

1 This chapter evolved from a professional development workshop organized by the first author and held regularly at the Academy of Management's annual conference on behalf of The Academy's Mentoring and Doctoral Students' Liaison committees. During the workshop, doctoral students who are new to the art and craft of reviewing are given opportunities to: (i) hear from top-management journal editors and editorial board members who serve as panelists in the workshop; (ii) participate in small, round-table discussions with some of the best reviewers in the association, as nominated by the division chairs and (iii) meet with other doctoral students who are new to reviewing or who may also have limited experience with reviewing.

2 Many thanks (in alphabetical order) to the following editors and distinguished reviewers for their insights: Ben Arbaugh, MED (2003); Manuela Brusoni, HCM (2004); Monica Forret, CAR (2003); Peter Gray, OCIS (2004), Benyamin Lichtenstein, ODC (2004); Joe Magee, MOC (2003); Ann Marie Ryan, editor, Personnel Psychology; Anne York, BPS (2004) and Sheldon Zedeck, editor, Journal of Applied Psychology. Contributors' initials appear in parentheses after their point(s).

3 An anonymous reviewer of this chapter cautions reviewers to be clear that their job is to help the author maximize his or her contribution because it is ultimately the author's paper. The job of the reviewer is not to turn the manuscript into the paper he or she wishes was submitted.

References

Cross, R., Borgatti, S. P. & Parker, A. (2001). Beyond answers: Dimensions of the advice network. *Social Networks, 23(3)*, 215–35.

De Janasz, S. C. & Sullivan, S. E. (2004). Multiple mentoring in academe: Developing the professorial network. *Journal of Vocational Behavior, 64*, 263–83.

Ensher, E. A., Thomas, C. & Murphy, A. E. (2001). Comparison of traditional, step-ahead and peer mentoring on protégés' support, satisfaction and perceptions of career success: A social exchange perspective. *Journal of Business and Psychology, 15*, 419–38.

Jauch, L. R. & Wall, J. L. (1989). What they do when they get your manuscript: A survey of Academy of Management reviewer practices. *Academy of Management Journal, 32*, 157–73.

Moher, D. & Jadad, A. R. (2003). How to peer review a manuscript. In F. Godlee & T. Jefferson (eds), *Peer Review in Health Sciences*, 183–90. London: BMJ Books.

Seibert, S. E., Kraimer, M. L. & Liden, R. C. (2001). A social capital theory of career success. *Academy of Management Journal, 44(2)*, 219–37.
Van Emmerik, I. J. H. (2004). The more you can get the better: Mentoring constellations and intrinsic career success. *Career Development International, 9(6)*, 578–94.

Appendix A: "Must-Reads" for the Novice Reviewer

ASQ Forum (1995): Sutton and Staw, What theory is not. Weick, What theory is not, theorizing is. Dimaggio, Comments on What theory is not. *Administrative Science Quarterly, 40(3)*, 371–97.
Bakanic, V., McPhail, C. & Simon, R. (1987). The manuscript review and decision-making process. *American Sociological Review, 52*, 631–42.
Bem, D. J. (2002). Writing the empirical journal article. In J. M. Darley, M. P. Zanna & H. L. Roediger III (eds) (2002). *The compleat academic: A career guide*. Washington, DC: American Psychological Association.
Beyer, J. M., Chanove, R. G. & Fox, W. B. (1995). The review process and the fates of manuscripts. *Academy of Management Journal, 38*, 1219–60.
Campion, M. (2002). Article review checklist: A criterion checklist for reviewing research articles in applied psychology. *Personnel Psychology, 46*, 705–18.
Cummings, L. L. & Frost, P. J. (eds) (1995). *Publishing in the Organizational Sciences*. Thousand Oaks, CA: Sage.
Daft, R. L. (1995). Why I recommended that your manuscript be rejected and what you can do about it. In L. L. Cummings & P. J. Frost (eds), *Publishing in the Organizational Sciences* (2nd ed.), 164–82. Thousand Oaks, CA: Sage.
Davis, M. S. (1971). That's interesting! Toward a phenomenology of sociology and a sociology of phenomenology. *Philosophy of the Social Sciences, 1*, 309–44.
Feldman, D. C. (2004). "Being a developmental reviewer: Easier said than done". *Journal of Management, 30(2)*, 161–4.
Gilliland, S. W. & Cortina, J. M. (1997). Reviewer and editor decision making in the journal review process. *Personnel Psychology, 50*, 427–52.
Jauch, L. R. & Wall, J. L. (1989). What they do when they get your manuscript: A survey of Academy of Management reviewer practices. *Academy of Management Journal, 32*, 157–73.
Lee, A. S. (1995). Reviewing a manuscript for publication. *Journal of Operations Management, 13(1)*, 87–92.
Lee, T. W. (1999). *Using Qualitative Methods in Organizational Research*, Thousand Oaks, CA: Sage.
Meyer, A. (1996). Balls, strikes and collisions on the base path: Ruminations of a veteran reviewer. In P. Frost & S. Taylor (eds) *Rhythms of academic life: Personal accounts of careers in academe*, Thousand Oaks, CA: Sage.
Prentice, D. A. & Miller, D. T. (1992). When small effects are impressive. *Psychological Bulletin, 112*, 160–4.
Romanelli, E. (1996). Becoming a reviewer: Lessons somewhat painfully learned. In P. Frost & S. Taylor (eds) *Rhythms of academic life: Personal Accounts of careers in academe*, Thousand Oaks, CA: Sage.

Rousseau, D. M. (1995). Publishing from a reviewer's perspective. In L. L. Cummings & P. J. Frost (eds), *Publishing in the organizational sciences* (2nd ed.), 151–63. Thousand Oaks, CA: Sage.

Schwab, D. P. (1995). Reviewing empirically based manuscripts: Perspectives on Process, in L. L. Cummings and P. J. Frost (eds) *Publishing in the organizational Sciences, 10,* 171–81. Homewood, Illinois: Irwin.

7

The Effectiveness of the Reviewing Process

The Manuscript Review Process: The Proper Roles of Authors, Referees, and Editors

Arthur G. Bedeian*

Abstract

Drawing on a 28-item survey, this article draws on the editorial experiences of 173 lead authors of articles published in the Academy of Management Journal *and* Academy of Management Review, *over the period 1999 to 2001, to explore some relatively new dynamics that have changed the character of the manuscript review process and given rise to a mounting debate over the proper roles of authors, referees, and editors. Among the survey's more disturbing findings, more than a third of the responding authors reported that recommended revisions in their manuscripts were based on an editor's or referee's personal preferences and nearly 25% indicated that in revising their manuscripts they had actually made changes they felt were incorrect.*

---

*Published in the Journal of Management Inquiry, 2003, 12: 331–338. The vetting of W. Jack Duncan, Hubert S. Field, Mary Ann Glynn, David D. van Fleet, and Thomas A. Wright on an earlier draft manuscript and the helpful suggestions of Hettie A. Richardson are gratefully acknowledged.

In this article, I wish to briefly explore some relatively new dynamics that have changed the character of the manuscript review process and have the potential for corrupting the Management discipline's published record. These dynamics have, in turn, given rise to a mounting debate over the proper roles of authors, referees, and editors. In doing so, I will draw upon survey data collected from lead authors of articles published in the *Academy of Management Journal* (*AMJ*) and *Academy of Management Review* (*AMR*), over the period 1999 to 2001, to remark on various structural features that characterize the review process and contribute to specific sources of dissatisfaction in the relationships between editors and authors, and between authors and referees. In doing so, I do not mean to either put myself forward as a nonpareil judge or critic, but simply to make some informal observations, based on my experience as an author and editor, about various features of the manuscript review process as it has evolved over the past few decades. There are many reasons to be concerned with the editorial policies and practices of our discipline's leading journals. Chief among these is that "the peer review process is at the very heart of scholarly research" and its outcomes affect all members of our community of scholars "both individually and collectively" (Lee, 2002: 9). Moreover, the policies and practices of the discipline's leading journals impact its published record, as well as its public database. The latter, of course, provides a foundation or starting point for future work undertaken by other scholars, as well as a basis for practicing managers interested in understanding and applying current managerial thinking.

As management researchers, we regard the editorial policies and practices of our discipline's leading journals to be a reflection of its scientific norms (Bedeian, 1996). These norms represent standards of behavior and are part of what Robert Merton (1942/1973) described more than 60 years ago as the "ethos of science" that underlies any true academic discipline. Building on an issue Shapiro and Sitkin raised in chapter 5, editors and referees possess considerable power over our discipline's intellectual vitality and future development given established editorial policies and practices. Furthermore, as also argued, the manner in which they perform their roles directly influences the careers of individual scholars vying for academic recognition. Given that the editorial policies and practices enacted by our discipline's editors and referees have important consequences both for our common stock of knowledge and for recognition bestowed upon individual scholars by our academic community, the study to be reported was designed to throw light on various aspects of the manuscript review process that have engendered increasing concern among established, as well as, aspiring authors. These concerns relate to such questions as:

1. Are recommended manuscript revisions ever based on editors' or referees' personal preferences?
2. What right do authors have to protect the intellectual integrity of their work? Do some referees try to find things to object to in a manuscript just to convince an editor that they have done a conscientious job in preparing a review?
3. Do editors and referees treat authors as equals?
4. To what extent do authors feel pressure to conform to the personal preferences of editors and referees?
5. In revising their manuscripts, do authors ever make changes recommended by editors and referees that they believe are incorrect? Are referees willing to consider new ideas relating to theory, study design, and analytical methods?

Method

To explore these concerns, early in 2002, an email survey was sent to the first authors of all articles/research notes published in *AMJ* and *AMR* during 1999, 2000, and 2001. Dialogue commentaries and the prologues/epilogues written by editors of research forums were excluded, as they would not typically be vetted through the normal review process. Individuals who were first authors on more than one article during the study time frame received only one survey. A cover letter informed these authors of the survey's general purpose and that all responses would be anonymous. A follow-up reminder was sent two weeks after the initial survey was posted. Survey items were drawn from three sources: (a) the extensive literature on the manuscript review process, (b) two questionnaires developed by Bradley (1981), and (c) the writer's more than thirty years' experience as both a former journal editor and continuing participant in the peer review system. A total of 288 surveys were distributed. Of this number, 179 surveys were sent to *AMJ* authors and 109 to *AMR* authors. *AMJ* and *AMR* authors were selected to comprise the target population for several reasons. As the discipline's premier journals, it would be expected that the papers published in *AMJ* and *AMR* would be read by a wide audience, be considered among the best in their subject areas, and represent models for others aspiring to publish at the highest levels. The conceptual reasoning and methodologies found in these papers would thus also be expected to have important consequences both for the discipline's common stock of knowledge, as well as its future development.

It is recognized that the targeted population is not necessarily unbiased. On a practical level, however, without direct access to journal files, it is impossible to systematically identify those whose papers have been reviewed and rejected. At the same time, targeting authors whose works have been published avoids bias due to what has been called the "sour-grapes hypothesis," according to which authors whose work has been judged as inadequate engage in rationalization after reading reviews of their manuscripts (Levenson, 1996). Thus, if anything, survey responses from authors whose work was accepted for publication should lend a positive bias to the reported results, by avoiding feelings of rejection and minimizing feelings of anger.

The survey instrument contained 28 items. Of these items, 15 asked that respondents reply with respect to "the most-recent, revised manuscript you had appear in either the Academy of Management *Journal* or *Review*." Eight items requested that respondents reply with regard to "your general experience as a published author." The final five items asked the respondents to indicate their current rank, how many articles they had published in either *AMJ* or *AMR*, to indicate their primary Academy of Management Division membership, and, in space provided for open-ended remarks, to add comments they might wish on their perceptions of the journal review process.

Results

Of the 283 surveys successfully delivered, 173 were returned, for an effective return rate of 61.3%. Exactly 108 of 179 (60.1%) *AMJ* authors and 65 of 109 (59.6%) *AMR* authors returned surveys. The number and percentage returned by Academy of Management division membership were as follows: organizational behavior 47 (27.2%), business policy & strategy 41 (23.7%), human resources 16 (9.2%), organization & management theory 14 (8.1%), international management 10 (5.8%), entrepreneurship 7 (4.0%), organizations & the natural environment 6 (3.5%), managerial & organizational cognition 5 (2.9%), social issues in management 5 (2.9%), organization development & change 3 (1.7%), conflict management 3 (1.7%), technology & innovation management 3 (1.7%), organizational communication & information systems 3 (1.7%), gender & diversity 2 (1.2%), management history 1 (.01%), careers 1 (.01%). Six respondents (3.5%) did not hold or indicate Academy membership. The distribution of respondents' ranks was as follows: full professor 52 (30.0%), associate professor 46 (26.6%), assistant professor 68 (39.3%), and graduate student 2 (1.2%). Five respondents (2.9%) were nonacademics. Perhaps indicative of interest in the survey's topic, 82 respondents (47.4%) provided written comments in the space provided. Selected comments will be quoted later for illustrative purposes; however, because the survey was completed anonymously, will be presented on a nonattributable basis.

Results are presented in Table 7.1, which reproduces the actual survey instrument. Because *AMJ* and *AMR* authors responded similarly to most items, their responses have been combined. Table 1 gives the percentage of respondents selecting each response alternative so that, except for rounding errors, the percentages total 100. The actual number of respondents who selected each alternative is presented in italics and enclosed in parentheses. Due to an error in wording (corrected in the table), Items 25 and 26 are excluded from discussion.

The results indicate that *AMJ and AMR* are indeed seen among the discipline's premier journals, with an overwhelming majority (85.5%) of the responding authors indicating that they had not submitted their manuscripts to any other outlet (see answer to Item 10). An overwhelming majority (89.0%) likewise felt that the net effect of the review process was to improve the quality of their published work (Item 2). As might be expected of a group whose work was ultimately accepted for publication, more than two thirds (71.9%) felt that the editor's or the referees' comments concerning factual matters reported in their manuscripts were correct (Item 5). This same approval pattern is reflected in the belief that "some" (64.2%) or "all" (32.4%) of the referees assigned to review the authors' manuscripts were as competent as the authors themselves (Item 7). The authors also widely agreed that the referees (91.3%) and the editors (91.9%) in question had been carefully read their manuscripts (Items 8 and 9). Further approval is evident in responses to Items 12 through 15, in which the authors expressed satisfaction with the consistency of the editor and referee comments among one another (62.2%), the willingness to consider new ideas (e.g., theories, study designs, analytical methods; 71.0%), referee objectivity (73.4%), and referee competence (80.3%). In addition, a majority (74.2%) of authors agreed that the revisions they were required to make in their manuscripts were beneficial enough to justify the additional labor and delay in publication (Item 11).

These positive responses noted, however, various concerns giving rise to the present study were also recorded. More than one third (38.7%) of the authors reported that recommended revisions in their manuscripts were based on an editor's or a referee's personal prefer-

Table 7.1   Survey of AMJ/AMR Author Editorial Experiences

Instructions: In responding to the following items please fill in ONE of the answer spaces. If you do not find the exact answer that fits your case, use the one that is closest to it. Please answer all items in order.

Answer Items 1–15 with respect to the most-recent, revised manuscript that you had appear in either the Academy of Management *Journal* or *Review*.

1) I will be answering the items in this section with respect to an article published in:
   Academy of Management Journal 62.4 (*108*)
   Academy of Management Review 37.6 (*65*)

2) The net effect of the review process was to improve the quality of the manuscript.
   Strongly Agree 57.2 (*99*)   Agree 31.8 (*55*)   Neutral 6.9 (*12*)
   Disagree 3.5 (*6*)   Strongly Disagree .6 (*1*)

3) Recommended revisions in the manuscript were based on the editor's or referees' *personal preferences*.
   Strongly Agree 8.7 (*15*)   Agree 30.1 (*52*)   Neutral 31.2 (*54*)
   Disagree 25.4 (*44*)   Strongly Disagree 4.6 (8)

4) No pressure whatsoever was exerted by the editor or referees on me to make the revision conform to their *personal preferences*.
   Strongly Agree 5.8 (*10*)   Agree 28.3 (*49*)   Neutral 31.8 (*55*)
   Disagree 24.9 (*43*)   Strongly Disagree 9.2 (*16*)

5) The editor's or referees' comments concerning *factual matters* reported in the manuscript were correct.
   Strongly Agree 17.5 (*30*)   Agree 54.4 (*93*)   Neutral 20.5 (*35*)
   Disagree 6.4 (*11*)   Strongly Disagree 1.2 (*2*)

6) In revising the manuscript, I only made recommended changes that I agreed were correct.
   Strongly Agree 20.8 (*36*)   Agree 44.5 (*77*)   Neutral 11.0 (*19*)
   Disagree 18.5 (*32*)   Strongly Disagree 5.2 (*9*)

7) How many of the referees appeared to be at least as competent in the area in which the manuscript was written as you are?
   Some 64.2 (*111*)   All 32.4 (*56*)   None 3.5 (*6*)

8) The referees seemed to have carefully read the manuscript.
   Strongly Agree 41.6 (*72*)   Agree 49.7 (*86*)   Neutral 5.2 (*9*)
   Disagree 2.3 (*4*)   Strongly Disagree 1.2 (*2*)

9) The editor seemed to have carefully read the manuscript (versus simply summarizing, transmitting, and supporting the referees' comments).
   Strongly Agree 57.8 (*100*)   Agree 34.1 (*59*)   Neutral 4.0 (*7*)
   Disagree 2.3 (*4*)   Strongly Disagree 1.7 (*3*)

Table 7.1   Survey of AMJ/AMR Author Editorial Experiences – *continued*

10) To how many other journals had the manuscript been previously submitted?
    None 85.5 (*148*)   One 11.6 (*20*)   Two 2.3 (*4*)
    Three 0.0 (*0*)   More than Three .6 (*1*)

11) The required revisions to the manuscript improved it enough to justify the additional labor and delay in publication.
    Strongly Agree 33.3 (*57*)   Agree 40.9 (*70*)   Neutral 11.7 (*20*)
    Disagree 9.9 (*17*)   Strongly Disagree 4.1 (*7*)

12) I was satisfied with the consistency of the referees' comments among one another.
    Strongly Agree 16.3 (*28*)   Agree 45.9 (*79*)   Neutral 19.8 (*34*)
    Disagree 12.8 (*22*)   Strongly Disagree 5.2 (*9*)

13) I was satisfied with the referees' willingness to consider new ideas (e.g., theories, study design, analytical methods) presented in the manuscript.
    Strongly Agree 16.3 (*28*)   Agree 54.7 (*94*)   Neutral 19.8(*34*)
    Disagree 8.1 (*14*)   Strongly Disagree 1.2 (*2*)

14) I was satisfied with the referees' objectivity.
    Strongly Agree 11.0 (*19*)   Agree 62.4 (*108*)   Neutral 18.5 (*32*)
    Disagree 5.8 (*10*)   Strongly Disagree 2.3 (*4*)

15) I was satisfied with the referees' competence.
    Strongly Agree 22.5 (*39*)   Agree 57.8 (*100*)   Neutral 12.7 (*22*)
    Disagree 4.6 (*8*)   Strongly Disagree 2.3 (*4*)

Answer Items 16–23 with respect to your general experience as a published author.

16) If there is a disagreement between author and referee about a matter of *opinion*, the author should be required to conform to the referee's position.
    Strongly Agree 1.2 (*2*)   Agree 4.6 (*8*)   Neutral 12.7 (*22*)
    Disagree 57.2 (*99*)   Strongly Disagree 24.3 (*42*)

17) A referee's judgment is probably better than an author's in matters where referee and author disagree.
    Strongly Agree 1.2 (*2*)   Agree 5.8 (*10*)   Neutral 37.0 (*64*)
    Disagree 40.5 (*70*)   Strongly Disagree 15.6 (*27*)

18) Some referees try to find things to object to in a manuscript just to convince an editor that they have done a conscientious[ness] job in preparing their review.
    Strongly Agree 15.6 (*27*)   Agree 48.0 (*83*)   Neutral 21.4 (*37*)
    Disagree 13.9 (*24*)   Strongly Disagree 1.2 (*2*)

19) I have felt that an editor has regarded a referee's knowledge about original research reported in my own manuscript as more important than my own.
    Strongly Agree 9.9 (*17*)   Agree 31.4 (*54*)   Neutral 29.1 (*50*)
    Disagree 26.2 (*45*)   Strongly Disagree 3.5 (*6*)

Table 7.1   Survey of AMJ/AMR Author Editorial Experiences – *continued*

20) I have felt that I was *not* being treated like an equal by an editor or a referee.
Strongly Agree 11.0 *(19)*   Agree 23.1 *(40)*   Neutral 16.8 *(29)*
Disagree 36.4 *(63)*   Strongly Disagree 12.7 *(22)*

21) I have *included* a reference in a manuscript primarily because I hoped that its author would be asked to referee the manuscript.
Strongly Agree 6.4*(11)*   Agree 13.9 *(24)*   Neutral 9.2 *(16)*
Disagree 33.5 *(58)*   Strongly Disagree 37.0 *(64)*

Answer Item 22 only if you have refereed for a scholarly journal.

22) Have you ever been asked to referee a manuscript that you were not competent to review?
Yes. (If "Yes," Go to Item 23.) 93 *(54.7)*
No. (If "No," Go to Item 24.) 77 *(45.3)*

23) Given that you answered "Yes" to Item 22, did you still submit a review of the manuscript?
Yes. 34 *(36.6)*
No. 60 *(63.4)*

24) My current academic rank is:

25) How many articles have you published in *AMJ*?
0   1   2   3   More than 4

26) How many articles have you published in *AMR*?
0   1   2   3   More than 4

27) Please indicate your primary Academy of Management division membership:

28) Please feel free to add any comments you wish on your perceptions of the journal review process.

Note: The actual number of respondents who selected each alternative is enclosed in parentheses and shown in italics.

ences (Item 3). A full one third (34.1%) had likewise experienced pressure to make a revision conform to an editor's or a referee's personal preferences (Item 4). In line with the authors' responses to Items 3 and 4, almost 25% indicated that in revising their manuscript they had actually made changes they felt were wrong (Item 6). More than one third (34.1%) of the authors reported having been treated like an inferior by an editor or a referee (Item 20) and 56.1% felt that an editor had regarded a referee's knowledge about original research reported in their own manuscript as more important than their own (Item 19). Nonetheless, 56.2% believed that their judgment was probably better than that of a referee (Item 17), and 81.5% felt that referees should not have the power to make authors conform to their opinions (Item 16).

Author responses also suggest editors may not necessarily know who would be a competent referee in a particular area. Almost 55% (54.7%) of the authors recorded that they had been asked to referee a manuscript they were not competent to critique (Item 22). Surprisingly, more than one third (36.6%) reported that they still submitted a peer review (Item 23). What relation this last statistic may have to the fact that nearly 25% (Item 6) of the responding authors reported being asked to revise their manuscript by making changes they believed to be incorrect is an interesting speculation. A measure of gamesmanship is revealed in the responses to Item 18, in which 63.6% of the authors reported feeling that some referees try to find things to object to in a manuscript just to convince an editor that they have done a conscientious job in preparing their review, and Item 21, where more than one fifth (20.3%) of the authors admitted including a reference in a manuscript primarily because they hoped that its author would be selected as a referee.

Discussion

The manuscript review process is a subject that does not want for controversy. Indeed, as the above results indicate, although generally pleased, even those authors whose works have "successfully surmount[ed] the peer review process" (Lee, 2002, p. 9) have reservations about the outcome. Moreover, as several authors noted, they would have responded to various survey items differently had their manuscripts been rejected. Whether their judgment would then have reflected the sour-grapes hypothesis mentioned earlier or objective reality (or both) is impossible to say. In searching for reasons why such dissatisfaction might exist, various explanations suggest themselves. The fact that 3 of every 10 responding authors felt that recommended manuscript revisions were based on an editor's or a referee's personal preference, over one third had experienced such pressure to acquiesce and that nearly one fourth had actually made changes they felt were incorrect, is disturbing. Despite protestations to the contrary (Mowday, 1997), the need to "publish or perish" that characterizes major research universities places enormous coercive power in the hands of editors and referees. This power was acknowledged in author comments such as:

- "The pressures to publish are very strong. Reviewers and editors have the power to make or break your career."

- "I believe that *AMX* ... has gone overboard in rewriting manuscripts according to reviewers' and editors' preferences."
- "In the end, [the editor] actually rewrote sections of the paper to include his preferred terminology. I'm somewhat surprised he didn't take authorship credit."
- "I would welcome a process and philosophy that is more respectful of authors on issues of preferences or opinion."

The notion an editor's (or a referee's) demands for revision might be so overly invasive as to boarder on co-authorship is an issue I've addressed elsewhere in asking at what point detailed editing and reviewing end and ghostwriting begins (Bedeian, 1996). As someone who has been a participant-observer of the management discipline for some time, I have seen editor and referee comments become increasingly more detailed and demanding. Others have lamented the same trend and noted that it is common to receive a set of editor and referee comments that rival the length of a submitted manuscript (e.g., Biggart, 2000; Spector, 1998). In turn, author replies to editor and referee comments have, by necessity, grown more particularized and, in some instances, "lengthy companion documents that can be longer than the submitted manuscript ... includ[ing] detailed background, ancillary analyses, references, tables and figures that are not in the submitted manuscript" (Spector, 1998, p. 1). There is no question that peer critiques are an essential element of the review process and that authors can benefit from suggestions that improve their work. One wonders, however, "if there can be too much of a good thing" and whether such a process "actually slows scientific progress by delaying publication, and discouraging many important findings from even attempting publication" (Spector, 1998, p. 1).

Whatever one's view in this regard, it seems indisputable that authors have the right to protect the intellectual integrity of their work. Moreover, in the opinion of some, "a failure to place the authorial voice at the center of a work" (Biggart, 2000, p. 2) is a real loss, with serious implications for the prerogatives and ethics of authorship (for more on this point, see Smith, 1998). This is compounded by the realization that, despite their good intentions, referees' comments are nonetheless subjectively based. What one referee insists is the best way to address an issue, another may be equally adamant is not (or may not even see as an issue). In any case, the resulting manuscript may be as much a function of the idiosyncratic opinions of the referees selected to vet an author's work than the author's own intentions.

Moreover, had the manuscript been read by another set of referees (according to their own subjective perspectives), the final product would likely be quite different.

This state of affairs is confounded by the belief that all too often referee comments are aimed at asking authors to write the manuscript the referees would have written rather than evaluating an author's work on it own merits (Leblebici, 1996). This belief is in no way assuaged by the condescending claim that reviews should serve a "developmental function" and that "developmental reviews are, in the main, teaching reviews" (Schminke, 2002, p. 487). Moreover, it is of no consolation to be told that no matter how one's career may be in the balance, journals also have a concomitant obligation to secure reviews from inexperienced referees as a means of "grooming" future "talent" (Schminke, 2002, p. 489). The notion that such referees, being in the minority, cannot "unduly sway a decision" ignores the fact that authors must respond to all referee comments, and thus the final content, if not outcome, of a manuscript will likely be affected.

Inflation in the manuscript review process may, in part, be a consequence of referees also feeling pressure to convince an editor that they have prepared a conscientious review (see, for example Ashford, 1996; Romanelli, 1996). For ad hoc referees in particular, impressing an editor as being one of the "best of the best" might garner an invitation to be an editorial team member (Lee, 2002, p. 9). Colleagues looking for such recognition are further told that "a thorough review is expected to entail at least two pages of detailed feedback" and that "less seasoned reviewers only dream of completing a review in less than eight hours" (Kinicki & Prussia, 2000, p. 799). Comments from survey respondents confirm the pressure referees feel to be critical and fulfill these expectations. As one offered, "I have, myself felt pressure to find criticisms in works to justify the quality of a review, suggesting there is 'criticism' bias in the review process." The pervasiveness of the belief that a criticism bias prevails is echoed in the view that "editors are 'looking for a reason to reject' manuscripts," and in other author comments such as "reviewers are more interested in slamming a piece than trying to figure it out," reviewing is still mainly about 'stamping out vermin'," and "in my experience editors and reviewers proceed on the 'guilty until proven innocent beyond any conceivable doubt' assumption."

It is of little solace that the tendency of editors and referees to "stress limiting aspects of manuscripts" (SLAM) has been documented in other disciplines (Van Lange, 1999). What is predictable, however, is that as a consequence of authors believing such a bias exists and even recognizing it in their own behavior, the objectivity of the entire review process is cast in doubt. This doubt is exacerbated by the belief among some authors that they have been treated as inferior by editors or referees and that their own knowledge about their own work was considered less important than a referee's. The fact that editors may not know who would be an appropriate referee in a given area is suggested by the 54.7% of the authors who indicated they had been asked to critique a manuscript outside their expertise. Such circumstances may account for the prevalent impression that the fate of a manuscript is determined more by the "luck of the reviewer draw" than its quality (Bedeian, 1996, p. 314). This, of course, again raises the question as to what important work, in such a system, fails to see the printed page. Author confidence that referees have at least peer-level expertise is further eroded when they are informed, that among those asked to serve as ad hoc referees, the "decline-to-review rate appears to be [positively] correlated with reviewing expertise, stature in the field, and professorial rank" (Northcraft, 2001, p. 1079; chapters 2 and 3, this book). This suggests that authors might, in fact, be justified in believing that their judgment may be better than a referee's, and that in disagreements with referees over matters of opinion, they should not necessarily be required to conform to a referee's position, some of whom may simply be seeking vengeance for the harsh treatment that they have suffered at the hands of other referees (Graham & Stablein, 1985).

Conclusion

As noted earlier, the manuscript review process is a subject that does not want for controversy. By and large, the system does work. At the same time, the survey results reported here do suggest that, although peer review is recognized as an essential quality control mechanism, various concerns relating to the proper roles of authors, referees, and editors remain unsettled. As also noted, these concerns have important consequences both for our common stock of knowledge and for recognition bestowed upon individual scholars by our academic community.

Editors are no doubt aware of the frustrations of aspiring authors. Referees (having been authors themselves) doubtless know the disappointment of a less-than-constructive review. This is not to say, however, that we cannot do better without sacrificing the perceived quality and reader appeal of our journals. Whether this circumstance results from our discipline's fairly low level of paradigm development, as suggested by Pfeffer (1993), is a possibility. Whatever the case, we should probably not be satisfied with a process that results in more than a third of the authors whose work appears in our discipline's leading journals reporting that recommended revisions in their manuscripts were based on an editor's or referee's personal preferences and almost 25% indicating that in revising their manuscripts they had actually made changes they felt were incorrect.

Before closing, let me express an additional concern. This concern is related to a growing cynicism among graduate students and new faculty entering the management discipline. This cynicism is evident in both the satirical portrayal of the manuscript review process as a game and a decreasing confidence in having one's work fairly and competently reviewed. Furthermore, realizing that the young are the lifeblood of our discipline, it brings to mind Herbert Simon's observation that "you can always tell a discipline is in trouble when the young people are cynical" (quoted in Biggart, 2000, p. 1).

I make the preceding case braced for the reactions it may evoke. Scientific journals are keystones in the edifice of any serious discipline. They serve as the published record of a discipline's accomplishments and determine the general course of its advancement. Publication is likewise a key ingredient in a successful academic career, influencing who gets promoted, who gets grants, and who advances professionally. The changing dynamics of the manuscript review process are, thus, too important not to be subject to full consideration.

The Review Process as a Professional Problem and Some Thoughts on Solving that Problem Consonant with Bedeian's Article*

John B. Miner

By way of indicating how much (or how little) knowledge of my subjectmatter goes into this commentary, let me start with a review of what I bring to the table. My personal experience includes serving in the roles of author and referee on numerous occasions, plus a stint as editor of the *Academy of Management Journal* back when it contained articles in all four of the areas now covered by the array of Academy publications.

More immediately relevant, I have attempted to prepare myself by doing considerable reading on the subject, starting with Art Bedeian's

---

* This article represents a revision and updating of a previous publication i.e., Journal of Management Inquiry, 2003, 12: 339–43.

references, and then following these back in time to other sources. The net result, I believe, has been to give me a pretty good idea of what people are saying about the adequacy of the professional review process. Others might correct me here to point out that manuscripts are typically involved in a *peer* review process, but my impression is that peer evaluations often are not what take place; more on that later. This literature review led me to seek certain information from the Academy – from the president, the central office, and various editors; we have had a good deal of communication back and forth. Also, I asked Art Bedeian if I might have copies of any reviews and editorial decisions he had received dealing with his manuscript, and he provided me with the feedback that had come to him after a submission to the *Academy of Management Journal*.

An idea of my prior thinking with regard to the review process may be found in Miner (1997). As indicated there, I have long had a deep concern about what this process is doing to the egos of authors and prospective authors – young and old; a concern that on occasion caused me, when serving in the editor role, to delete particularly derogatory comments from reviews before sending them to authors.

This, then, is the context from which I write, including my experience background, knowledge base, and emotional predispositions. Clearly there is a potential for bias here, but anyone who comes to this subject with any amount of information is likely to have absorbed certain predispositions as well. With this in mind I initially looked into Bedeian's (1996a; 1996b) prior publications on the review process to see what his pre-established orientation might be. More recently I have considered his expanded thinking (Bedeian, 2004). One clear concern of his is that editors may on occasion intrude themselves into the writing process in such a way as to invade the intellectual property rights of the author. As a historian, he feels that an editor may in this way distort the record of a person's contribution to the field, and as a scientist he is concerned about misrepresenting the products of that enterprise.

A good example of this phenomenon derives from an article to which Bedeian himself contributed (Ford, Duncan, Bedeian, Ginter, Rousculp, & Adams, 2003). I have discussed this example elsewhere (Miner, 2006) in some detail, but let me outline what was involved here to make the point. The published article describes four notable instances of researcher-practitioner collaboration drawn form Bedeian's (1992, 1993, 1998, 2002) laureate autobiographies. These instances represent what amount to four case histories or narratives of these events, and they are clearly exemplary instances of this type. However, none of them was included in the original paper submitted to the editor of the *Academy of Management Executive*. That paper was an empirical study replete with a sample (the laureates), a measure (based on content analysis), data analyses, and results (Ford, Rousculp, Adams, Duncan, Ginter, & Bedeian, 2001). This original manuscript contains some important material of a research nature, material that was completely deleted in the published version. This transformation occurred at the behest of the editor and reviewers as ghost writers, with the result that any clear authorial voice was lost.

A second point on which Bedeian (1996b) finds himself at variance with established practice has to do with the lack of reliability of the review instrument. He cites Marwell (1992) to the effect that reviewer recommendations on acceptance correlate only about .25, and concludes that authors are often at the mercy of luck alone as they face an editor's reviewer selections; a pervasive and pernicious cynicism is the result. There must be a better way. Additional, more comprehensive data on reviewer agreement indicates a model figure in the .20s and a median of .29 (Weller, 2002).

A second look at the Bedeian data

There are those who argue that Bedeian's concerns are not justified, and that the review process in its present form is working well (see for example Schminke, 2002). Some, including several *AMJ* reviewers of his paper, take the data to mean the opposite of what Bedeian concludes; his evidence in their view is supportive of the status quo. Given these reactions, can we do anything to wring something more from what Bedeian provides to us? Are we really offered only a glass which for some is half-full, and at the same time for others half-empty?

In an attempt to answer these questions, I set up two scales from the Bedeian table on a conceptual basis. There are 13 items that may be construed as clearly reflecting some type of criticism of the review process (#s 2, 3, 4, 5, 6, 7, 8, 9, 11, 18, 19, 20, 22) and 4 more that can be interpreted as indicating some amount of dissatisfaction (#s 12, 13, 14, 15). Note that these items in total extend well beyond the issues about which Bedeian had expressed concern in his prior articles. In conducting my analysis I totaled all responses that indicated some level of criticism or dissatisfaction, and obtained a percentage figure for each item.

The dissatisfaction data do not indicate a great problem. The median figure for the four items is 8.7 and the mean is 10.6. Only item #12 dealing with the inconsistency of referee comments is elevated. The overall pattern here is not unexpected, given that the authors all had their articles accepted and published. One would expect such individuals to experience satisfaction with the outcome of the overall process, and that this satisfaction would permeate more specific components as well.

On the 13 criticism items, however, the results are quite different. The median percentage now is 34.1 and the mean 30.1. There are three items on which over half of the authors indicate some criticism – #7 (incompetent reviewers), #18 (unnecessary objections by reviewers), #22 (editor sending manuscript to the wrong reviewer). Other items with percentage values above the one third mark are #19 (reviewers' knowledge overvalued by editor), #3 (personal preferences of editor or reviewers stressed in recommendations), #4 (pressure exerted to conform to personal preferences), #20 (author treated as inferior by editor/reviewer). And these are criticisms made frequently by people whose articles were in fact published.

Is there a problem?

If what is indicated above is characteristic of the published population, one would have to assume that the problem is even more sizable among those who are rejected; some unknown number of the latter are almost surely lost to the publishing process permanently. Perhaps the actual talent loss from the field at this point is not very large, but it could be considerable; we do not know. Then there is the further possibility of a talent loss because people do not even enter the field due to cynicism surrounding the publication process, or they stay only briefly.

In this cascading process of talent depletion, it seems to me that the key point is that of manuscript rejection. Given that 90% of all manuscripts are rejected by the *Academy of Management Journal* now (Schminke, 2002), we are talking about sizable proportions of people within the field. What is needed is an extension of the Bedeian study into the realm of those who are rejected, but such a study will almost invariably require the cooperation, if not the active participation, of some editor.

Not knowing of any such study, and Bedeian cites none, I have kept an eye out for evidence that data of this kind exist. The only passage that gave me any hope on this score was a statement in Kinicki and Prussia (2000) as follows:

> ... Greg Northcraft recently established a committee of experienced reviewers to advise the editorial staff on issues of importance. This

committee surveyed the customer satisfaction of authors who submitted articles for review at *AMJ* (p. 800).

This statement produced a flurry of e-mails directed to those who might be able to give me more information. In large part this effort failed. I did learn that such a survey existed, that it was not intended for publication, and that items dealt with the following –

initial submission experience
timeliness of feedback
quality of feedback from reviewers
quality of feedback from editor
overall satisfaction with experience
recommendations

There was a report in some form, but repeated efforts to obtain a copy, and thus the actual results, produced only a blank screen. Perhaps others with better access to this information will make these findings more widely available; it would be a real service to the profession.

Yet, in view of the criticism data from published authors that Bedeian has provided; the probability that findings from rejected authors, even if discounted for "sour grapes," would be even more damaging; and in view of the fragmentary evidence from individuals who have written on the subject, it does seem appropriate to conclude that the field faces a real problem. With regard to the latter point I particularly suggest a reading of the chapter by Graham and Stablein (1985) dealing with the newcomers' perspective, several quotes from which follow –

The perils of the publishing process we see include threats to idealistic values and humanistic instincts; rejection and/or ridicule of one's creative labor; thwarted career goals; and perpetuation of a system which batters egos in the name of bettering human understanding (p. 139).

and again –

First-time critical reviews are a shock to newcomers in the field. Some may never try to submit a paper again (p. 146).

Another quote, this time from Ashford (1996), provides insight into the reactions of certain older colleagues –

… several senior members of our field have essentially dropped out of the publication process, viewing the feedback they get from it as coming from "unqualified, incompetent reviewers" (p. 125).

This type of reaction appears to be based on an assumption that some kind of discrimination is occurring, and thus that younger authors are receiving preferential treatment. One factor contributing to this view is that in the past twenty-five years editors and reviewers have increasingly been encouraged to take a developmental role (Feldman, 2004). This fits well with submissions of graduate students and junior faculty; it fits less well when the editor (whose name is known) or reviewer can be assumed to be considerably younger than the author, who is being developed. That older authors get angry at being talked down to by those whom they view as being less capable (and younger) than themselves is not surprising.

Secondly, the blind-review process often is really blind only for junior authors whose work is not yet widely known in the field. More senior authors whose work is part of a program of research extending over many years may need to cite their previous publications and thus reveal their identity (Weller, 2002). Whatever advantages accrue from blind-review are largely restricted to younger authors. There is no such thing as blind review for many pieces written by older authors, and they know it; often reviewers say as much in their reviews. This too seems to imply that the review process is set up to favor those new to the field.

A final point relates to the "conservative" bent in the review process which causes work that departs in significant ways from existing paradigms to have difficulty in getting published (Camic & Wilson, 2001). One could argue either way here as to whether this factor serves to favor the young or the old. Yet any senior member of the field who believes that the ideas presented in a manuscript are novel and out of the mainstream will almost certainly react to evidence of this conservative bent with anger and dismay.

Dealing with more easily corrected problems

My commentary from this point on is predicated on the assumption, documented by Bedeian and the previous discussion, that we do indeed have a problem. Now, I want to take up what can be done about that problem, following upon the lead provided by criticisms from certain *AMJ* reviewers of the Bedeian manuscript. Here I go well beyond what Bedeian attempted. His concern was to serve as a catalyst only, as I understand it, with the objective of sparking debate, further research, and the development of ideas for improvement on the part of others. I wish to go beyond that objective.

One problem in my view is that we reject too many articles. We do publish a mix of quite good articles, but not necessarily the best. A cost inherent in the present reviewing system is that it rejects a substantial number of articles that are just as good if not better than what is published. This occurs because when we get down to something like a 10% acceptance rate, it is impossible to discriminate effectively. The solution as I see it is to shorten the published papers (thus making space available for more articles) and to shorten the editor and reviewer comments (thus making more time available to deal with the work inherent in a higher acceptance rate). Table 1 (p. 1402) in Mowday (1997) indicates that the average article length has escalated in recent years, and what can be accomplished when the editor makes a conscious effort to reduce article length, and thus publish more (Miner, 1997). My belief is that we have experienced a real normative change in this regard; one that we need to reverse.

Related to the issue of a high rejection rate, is the fact that *AMJ* (and *AMR* too) now make it a sine qua non that all accepted papers be theory-based. This means that anything else is automatically rejected, if it is submitted now at all (see Lee, 2002). In particular, I have in mind research which tests existing organizational practice to see if it is accomplishing what is intended. The rejection by *AMJ* of the Bedeian piece under consideration here is a wonderful example, drawn form the practices of our own professional organization, of this exclusionary process at work. The contribution to lowered acceptance rates of such a restriction to theory-based material is compounded by the fact that such a limitation would seem to contribute to the reduced concern with matters of practice and application that now characterizes the field (see Miner, 2003a for documentation). All this is said not with the intent of criticizing the use and development of theory, for which I have had a long-standing personal affinity (Miner, 2002), but to criticize the kind of overemphasis on theory that excludes any other possibility.

Shortening articles to publish more and opening up the publication process to articles beyond those embedded in theory are things that editors can do, and thus they are relatively easily accomplished. The same may be said for restricting the review process to use only true peers of the author(s). I do not believe that manuscripts should be reviewed by people from outside the field represented by their subjectmatter (as has been extolled by Schminke, 2002 for example). There are good reasons for this. In a study of the importance ratings of organizational behavior theories given by strategic management and organizational behavior judges we found that a strong tendency existed to evaluate these theories less favorably among the strategic management people (Miner, 2003a). Thus one would expect that manuscripts reviewed by those whose disciplinary orientation did not fit the material would be recommended for rejection more often. This was the pattern among judges who actually made ratings, but a related finding was that the strategic management judges more frequently declined to evaluate these organizational behavior theories also. I cannot help wondering, from my own experience as an editor, whether the high decline-to-review rate noted by Northcraft (2001) may not have resulted from this same use of field-inappropriate reviewers, i.e. those who are not really peers.

Training reviewers as a remedial process

Schminke (2002) notes that licensing is not required for the critical activity of reviewing. Perhaps something akin to licensing should be required. Reviewers should not learn on the job in the real world of manuscript decision-making; they should already be trained to carry out professional-level reviews as they enter upon their first such experience. We have relied upon doctoral training to serve this purpose, although on occasion apparently reviewers who have not yet completed the doctorate are involved. But at many schools doctoral education does not deal with the specifics of reviewing original manuscripts. Most of us learned by trial and error with little by way of feedback as to how well we were doing.

Building on the experience of sociology (see Marwell, 1992) and on the experiences of Schepmyer and van Emmerik offered in the previous chapter, we should conduct more workshops at professional meetings to train reviewers. This training would involve readings from the literature on the subjectmatter, designed to make trainees sensitive to what constitutes effective reviewing, and what does not. It would also require conducting training reviews on pre-selected manuscripts, comparisons with reviews of these same manuscripts done by experienced reviewers, and seminar discussions of the results. Such a training process should produce a clearer set of standards for what represents an effective review, and at the same time it should foster an increase in the reliability of the review instrument across individuals by establishing consistent guidelines. In my opinion no one should be permitted to conduct reviews for a major journal unless that person had either conducted or participated in a workshop of this kind; no grandfathering should occur. Individual journals would either bid into this process or they would not, and each would clearly indicate whether they had such a training requirement.

Instituting an appeal process above the editor

As has often been noted, reviewers do not make final acceptance decisions, editors do (see for example Northcraft, 2001). Editors are the real gatekeepers. However, unlike the judicial system, the manuscript publication system has no formal appeal process above the level of an individual editor. Where associate or action editors are employed, there may be some appeal to the editor, but that is the extent of what is typically possible.

The only exception of which I am aware has occurred on occasion within the Academy of Management. There have been appeals of editorial decisions at *AMJ* where the president has set up a review panel to reconsider an editor's rejection decision. The existence of this procedure does not appear to be widely known, and I have had no success in tracking it beyond those few instances of which I am personally knowledgeable. Inquiries to the current president of the *Academy,* and extending to the central office as well as all current journal editors, have produced no indication of any familiarity with such a process. My impression is that the operation of such appeal processes within the Academy is intermittent at best, and generally ineffectual when appeals are considered.

What I propose is that a standard appeal procedure above the editor level be instituted, staffed, and given widespread publicity (Epstein, 1995). Such appeals could support the editor, result in a re-review, or reverse the editorial decision. They would normally operate in cases of manuscript rejection, but they could apply in other instances, as when the editor's revision requirements are unacceptable to an author. The appeal process would serve primarily to hold editors accountable for their actions (Fine, 1996). The very existence of such a procedure should serve to make most editors think twice before engaging in certain practices, such as bridging the void into obvious ghostwriting.

The appeal would be made to a panel whose members have no ties to a current editor, personal or professional, and particularly no involvement in the appointment of that editor. The panel would draw upon advisory expertise as it saw fit in a particular case before it. It would have access to all records including names of authors and reviewers. Appeal panel members would be publicly known and would be of a professional stature sufficient to give legitimacy to their opinions. Their decisions would be published.

Some current editors might be expected to oppose this type of limitation on their authority, and accordingly the introduction of the appeal process should probably occur during the interval between editorial terms. One clear objection that a current editor might raise is that the appeal panel would be flooded with author complaints to the point where it could not function effectively. This effect could be handled by establishing a statute of limitations, a priority schedule, standardization of cases, and perhaps even some rationing of appeals. However, as Fine (1996) has noted, authors may hesitate to criticize an editor when there is the prospect that doing so might jeopardize the chances of subsequent submissions to the same journal. It is not at all clear what type of case load would be elicited were such an appeal process to be installed; we should take action, and then determine empirically what the result is.

I have tried here to build upon the excellent argument that Bedeian presented for some type of restructuring of our manuscript review systems; then, going beyond what Bedeian attempted, to make some firm proposals for change. I can only hope all this will not fall upon deaf ears.

Turning Lemons into Lemonade: Where is the Value in Peer Reviews?*

William H. Starbuck

Abstract

Authors need to view reviewers' comments not as judgments about the value of their work, but as data about the potential readers of their articles. Reviewers give good data about readers' reactions, and such data are hard to obtain.

The editorial review process does have deficiencies, the most serious of which is the premise that reviewers should decide what articles warrant publication. "Peer review" should mean that reviewers and authors are indeed peers. But editors typically act as if reviewers have more competence and more valid opinions than authors, and as if they themselves have the wisdom and knowledge to impose constraints on manuscripts.

---

* Published in the Journal of Management Inquiry, 2003, 12:344–51.

Empirical evidence indicates that editorial decisions incorporate bias and randomness. In chapter 3, Ryan offers a systematic overview of several biases that could be valid grounds for declining an invitation to review. However, authors need to persuade potential readers to read their articles and to convince actual readers that the ideas and theories in articles are plausible and useful. To do these things, authors must adapt their manuscripts to the perceptual frameworks of potential readers. Nevertheless, authors should remember that editors and reviewers are not superior and that the ultimate decisions about what is right must come from inside themselves.

My Golden Rule

Many years ago, when I was a junior instructor and had been receiving editorial feedback for only a couple of years, I formulated a rule for myself. This rule has subsequently proven to be very valuable to me, and so some years ago, I began to call it my Golden Rule. The rule states:

No reviewer is ever wrong!

Why is this rule valuable? Well, the main reason is that it makes an assertion that seems patently ludicrous and bizarre. Obviously, any human being, even an editor or reviewer, may err. Sometimes editors or reviewers make comments that appear stupid, or they recommend changes that are misguided or unethical. Occasionally reviewers seem arrogant, disrespectful, even nasty. So, to declare that reviewers' comments are never wrong might appear irrational, but this apparent irrationality draws attention to a more fundamental truth: Every editor and every reviewer is a sample from the population of potential readers. Indeed, a reviewer is likely to be an unrepresentative sample in that reviewers probably read more carefully than do most readers, and nearly every reviewer plows through an entire manuscript instead of giving up in disgust or boredom after only a few pages.

The central purpose of my Golden Rule is to compel me to regard reviewers' comments not as judgments about the value of my research or the quality of my writing, but as data about the potential audience for my articles. If a reviewer interprets one of my statements in a different way than I intended, other readers, possibly many other readers, are likely to interpret this statement differently than I intended, so I should revise the statement to make such misinterpretations less likely. If a reviewer thinks that I made a methodological error, other readers, possibly many of them, are also likely to think that I made this error, so I should revise my manuscript to explain why my methodology is appropriate. If a reviewer recommends that I cite literature that I deem irrelevant, other readers are also likely to think that this literature is relevant, so I should explain why it is irrelevant. In general, I should attend very carefully to the thoughts of anyone who has read my words rather carefully. These are much more realistic data than the polite but superficial comments of close colleagues, who may have read my manuscript hastily and who do not want to hurt my feelings. Good data about readers' reactions are hard to obtain and good data can never be "wrong".

My Golden Rule does not assert that I should always follow reviewers' advice. Absolutely not! Their advice derives from their interpretations of what they thought I was trying to say, which may not be what I actually intended to say. What reviewers advise often conflicts with advice I get from colleagues, so I have to decide what advice is more useful. Most of the time, reviewers' advice also conforms to widely accepted beliefs about proper methodology, which, in my experience, are often incorrect. Indeed, there would be no point in doing research if all widespread beliefs were reliably correct.

Current editorial practices do have serious deficiencies, and the main deficiency, I believe, is the premise that reviewers should decide what articles should be published. The act of rendering judgment creates a hierarchical relation between a reviewer and an author that benefits neither of them and that may – likely does – keep innovative research from appearing in prestigious journals. Even when a reviewer intends to say "perhaps this might be a useful suggestion," the author is likely to hear "do this or we will reject your manuscript."

"Peer review" should mean that reviewers and authors are indeed peers. But editors typically act as if reviewers are more competent than authors and as if reviewers' opinions have more validity than authors' opinions. Editors also typically act as if they themselves have the wisdom and knowledge to impose constraints on manuscripts. Such behaviors create power differences that not only contradict the concept of peer review but also invite reviewers and editors to indulge their idiosyncrasies. As Lord Acton's hoary dictum implies, editorial power tends to corrupt, and absolute editorial power… . Very few editors or reviewers remain able to refrain from thinking, "I could say this better," "I see a more interesting problem," "I could design a better study."

Before, during, and after my period as the editor of *Administrative Science Quarterly*, the journal sent every accepted manuscript to a botanist for copyediting. *ASQ* employed this botanist as a way to further its effort to communicate to an interdisciplinary audience, the premise being that a management article that a botanist could understand would also be understandable to a wide variety of readers. Over time, however, the botanist increasingly made imperious and detailed demands of authors and increasingly expressed disdain for authors' own writing. We sometimes received complaints from authors who were protesting the botanist's style preferences or the tone of the botanist's remarks. A crisis occurred when the botanist wrote on the manuscript of a very famous and distinguished author, "This looks like the ramblings of a senile old man speaking before a Rotary Club!" Thereafter, with every copyedited manuscript sent back to authors, I attached a letter explaining (a) that the copyeditor was a botanist, (b) that *ASQ* used a botanist to copyedit precisely because the botanist might not understand nuances and jargon, and (c) that the author was free to ignore the botanist's suggestions and comments because they were merely suggestions. Of course, I also told the botanist what I was saying to authors. The botanist's comments developed a different tone, and we never again received a complaint from an author, yet it appeared that authors were following the botanist's suggestions more thoroughly than before.

Two personal experiences

Two stories exemplify some issues with peer review as journals now use it. The first story illustrates the dependence of reviewers' evaluations on their personal frames of reference. The second shows the randomness inherent in editorial decisions.

In 1999, I participated in a five-person committee that chose the winners of the Academy of Management's William Newman Award for the best paper presented at the annual meeting that was based on a recent doctoral dissertation. Each division could nominate only one paper, so each of the nominated papers represented very high quality according to the values and norms of the division that nominated it. Ten divisions submitted nominations. The papers reflected the diversity of the Academy's divisions; and likewise, the committee members represented diverse methodological and topical interests. Each committee member rated three papers as "high", four papers as "medium", and three papers as "low". Nine papers received "high" ratings from at least one committee member, and nine papers received "low" ratings from at least one committee member. The difference was small between the highest average rating and the lowest. As a result, the committee members themselves inferred that the ratings had not really identified an ordering of shared beliefs about quality but rather echoed the mutually inconsistent beliefs of the committee members. Seeing no way to resolve our differences, and feeling some guilt because we were not recognizing all forms of excellence, we made the award to the three papers with the highest average ratings, three being the maximum number of awards we were allowed to make.

When I became the editor of *Administrative Science Quarterly*, my predecessor gave me a thigh-high stack of manuscripts that were awaiting review. He said he had sent no manuscripts out for review for several months because he thought I would like to have a low backlog of accepted articles. Embarrassed that so many authors had been waiting so long for feedback, I weeded out the obviously inappropriate topics and then sent manuscripts to hundreds of reviewers. At that time, *ASQ* was seeking to encompass all aspects of management, so the manuscripts and reviewers were quite diverse. After two or three months, I had received well over 500 pairs of reviews. The property of these reviews that struck me most vividly was their inconsistency: A surprisingly (to me) small fraction of the reviewers agreed with each other. Counting an "accept" as 1, a "revise" as 0, and a "reject" as –1, I calculated a correlation. It was 0.12. Given the large sample size, this correlation was statistically significant, but it was practically insignificant. It was so low that knowing what one reviewer had said about a manuscript would tell me almost nothing about what a second reviewer had said or would say.

I also observed that about 25% of the reviews recommended "accept", about 25% recommended "revise", and about 50% recommended "reject". If any two reviews are utterly independent, the probability of a manuscript receiving two "accepts" should be about 25%*25% = 6% and the probability of a manuscript receiving two "rejects" should be about 50%*50% = 25%. The remaining 69% should receive mixed reviews. These frequencies are close to the ones I experienced as *ASQ*'s editor. I responded by accepting the 6% that received two "accepts", rejecting the 25% that received two "rejects", and soliciting revisions from the 69% that received mixed reviews.

Beyond my personal experiences

Was my experience atypical? Acceptances are probably less frequent and rejections more frequent than I observed. Table 7.2 shows the frequencies with which reviewers for four journals recommended "accept", "revise", or "reject".

Table 7.2   Frequencies of Recommendations by Reviewers

	Academy of Management Journal and Review[2]	*Journal of Personality and Social Psychology* (Scott, 1974)	*American Psychologist* (Cicchetti, 1980)
Accept	13%	9%	19%
Revise	34%	25%	18%
Reject	53%	66%	63%

Studies of peer review in psychology and sociology suggest that agreement between reviewers is low throughout the social sciences. The Consumer Psychology division of the American Psychological Association ran a contest that both resembles and differs from the William Newman award. The division set out to choose the best paper submitted to a meeting, using ten former presidents of the division as raters. Bowen, Perloff and Jacoby (1972) observed the ratings and found that the coefficient of concordance among raters was only 0.11. As was the case for the Newman Award, all these papers were ones that someone deemed excellent; but unlike the Newman Award, these papers all fell into a common topic domain where norms should be rather uniform.

Cicchetti (1980) reported the highest inter-rater correlations that have been published. He examined reviewers of manuscripts submitted to the American Psychologist and calculated several inter-rater correlations that fell between 0.52 and 0.54. However, when he repeated this study one year later, the inter-rater correlation dropped to 0.38.

Later, Cicchetti (1991) reported inter-rater Kappas[3] for ten psychological and sociological journals, which ranged from 0.21 to 0.44. Inter-rater Kappas were somewhat lower for the various criteria that the journals asked reviewers to consider; these ranged from 0.07 to 0.37. Although a few authors and editors have speculated that inter-rater agreement tends to be higher where journals have narrower foci, the evidence for this notion is weak.

Low agreement between reviewers is also an issue in the medical sciences. For instance, Cicchetti (1991) reported inter-rater Kappas for six biomedical journals that ranged from 0.26 to 0.37. Rothwell and Martyn (2000) reported much lower inter-rater Kappas for two neuroscience journals. In journal A, the accept-reject Kappas averaged 0.08; and in journal B, these Kappas averaged 0.28. These journals also asked reviewers to rate the "priority" that a manuscript should have. In journal A, the "priority" Kappas averaged –0.12; in journal B, these Kappas averaged 0.27.

Gottfredson (1978), Gottfredson and Gottfredson (1982), and Wolff (1970) found that reviewers for psychological journals agree rather strongly with each other about the properties that manuscripts ought to exhibit. Unfortunately, reviewers do not agree strongly when asked about the properties of specific manuscripts; the correlations range from 0.16 to 0.50. Gottfredson (1977, 1978) found that reviewers do distinguish between the quality of a manuscript and its probable impact on its field, but reviewers' ratings of impact correlate only 0.14 with later citations. In fact, the practical correlation is nil because reviewers' ratings of impact correlate 0.03 with later citations for most articles. The 0.14 correlation occurs because a few articles receive high impact ratings from reviewers and also many later citations.

Mahoney (1977, 1979) submitted five manuscripts to 75 people who had recently reviewed for the *Journal of Applied Behavior Analysis*. The manuscripts were nearly identical except that some of them reported negative results, some positive results, and some mixed results. Mahoney chose reviewers who were likely to prefer positive results, and indeed the reviewers did generally give higher ratings of scientific contribution to manuscripts that reported positive results and the reviewers were much more likely to recommend acceptance or minor revision of manuscripts that reported positive results. The inter-rater correlations were 0.30 for recommendations about publication and ratings of scientific contribution, but close to zero for ratings of methodology, relevance, and the quality of discussion. Yet, the ratings of methodology correlated 0.94 with recommendations about publication. It appears that reviewers criticize the methodology of studies that contradict the theories they prefer and they applaud the methodology of studies that support the theories they prefer. Ryan (chapter 3) refers to this as a methodological bias.

Other studies have also reported reviewers' biases. Mahoney, Kazdin, and Kenigsberg (1978) found that reviewers are more likely to render favorable opinions about manuscripts that cite in-press studies by the manuscripts' authors. Nylenna, Riis, and Karlsson (1994) found that reviewers give higher ratings to a manuscript in English than to the same manuscript in the author's native language. Horrobin (1990) is one of several authors who have complained that reviewers with investments in prior research impede the publication of innovative research, with one result being that more innovative research tends to appear in lower-status journals. Ellison (2002) found that review processes of economics journals take longer when manuscripts fall into editors' areas of specialization, possibly because the editors do more nitpicking.

Ellison (2002) also observed that reviews were taking about 12 to 18 months longer in 2000 than in 1970. He attributed this slowdown to (a) manuscripts growing longer, (b) manuscripts having more coauthors, and (c) increasing focus on publishing in a few very prestigious journals. Ellison estimated, however, that these factors accounted for less than half of the slowdown that has occurred, and he turned up no evidence that published articles had significantly higher quality in 2000 than in 1970.

Perhaps the most discussed and controversial study of peer review was the one by Peters and Ceci (1982), who resubmitted 12 articles to the journals that had published them just 18 to 32 months earlier. All 12 journals were highly regarded ones, and the articles had originally been written by authors from prestigious psychology departments. However, the resubmissions bore fictitious authors' names and return addresses at obscure institutions. The submissions went to 38 editors and reviewers. Three of these editors or reviewers detected that the articles had already been published, which cut the sample to nine articles that had 18 reviewers. Sixteen of the 18 reviewers recommended rejection, and the editors rejected eight of the nine articles. The most prevalent reasons for rejection were "serious methodological flaws," including inappropriate statistical analyses and faulty study design.

Why do these statistics matter?

Of course, everyone who has submitted several manuscripts to journals has experienced inconsistent reviews, and every academic has heard many stories about the inconsistent reviews received by colleagues. Nevertheless, such experiences inevitably leave us wondering if we are the unfortunate ones, if others of more talent and greater skill receive helpful, positive reviews.

Statistical studies put our individual experiences in perspective and provide credible evidence that we are not the only ones who must deal with conflicting demands, many of which seem to be ill-founded. With rare exceptions, the data indicate that there is little agreement among reviewers. Agreement between reviewers is especially low concerning specific properties of a manuscript, and somewhat higher for ratings of scientific contribution and their recommendations about publication. However, the correlations are very low between reviewers' ratings of scientific contribution and later citations of published articles, so there may also be low correlations between reviewers' recommendations about publication and manuscripts' contributions to knowledge as appraised by readers generally.

So how should one react? At a social level, the spectrum of reactions has been remarkably wide, as demonstrated by the numerous commentaries accompanying the articles by Cicchetti (1991) and by Peters and Ceci (1982). Peer review arouses very diverse emotions, beliefs, and ambitions. It angers, it reassures, it intimidates, it tramples egos, and it puffs them up. For some, peer review demonstrates the vacuousness and unreliability of social science; for others, the substance and reliability of social science. Responses range from abstract to quibbling, from idealistic to pragmatic, from outraged to philosophical (Baumeister, 1990; Bedeian, 1996a, 1996b; Holbrook, 1986).

Harnad (1986) observed that attitudes toward peer review depend on whether people believe that most published research is "significant and essential" or "neither significant nor essential". But does not this phrasing implicitly understate the role of social construction? It is people, acting collectively, that determine what is "significant and essential". Processes of communication, social influence, and consensus building transform the insignificant into the significant, the inessential into the essential, the irrelevant into the interesting, perceptions into facts, conjectures into theories, beliefs into truths. For instance, Davis (1971) analyzed the properties that help sociological contributions to attract attention and to exert influence. He inferred that such contributions have presentational ingredients that create tension in readers and make the topics seem "interesting". Faddishness is also involved: Meehl (1991) noted that psychologists have lost interest in older theories.

Disagreements about what is "significant and essential" play quite important parts in the development of widely shared perceptions and beliefs. Kuhn (1970) argued that some scientific fields develop for long periods around stable paradigms that determine the criteria for choosing problems and the methods of research. A new paradigm does not emerge until doubt about the existing paradigm grows strong and spreads widely. Such is not the world of management thought, however. In the social and economic sciences, including management, paradigms are multitude and vague and ever changing. Researchers do not behave as if agreements exist about some beliefs and perceptions being correct. Almost every researcher discards prior "findings" and proposes new "laws", and minor revisions of existing theories get distinctive names and attract enthusiastic adherents. Consequently, the research process tends to follow dialectic trajectories: a new assertion elicits a contrary assertion; indeed, merely stating a hypothesis may be sufficient stimulus to elicit a contrary hypothesis. The ensuing debates often yield syntheses that combine the opposing hypotheses in more complex frameworks; such integration expands perceptions. But until such syntheses occur, the proponents of alternative viewpoints continue to quarrel about terminology and methodology and to spurn each other's manuscripts. Partly because researchers have not agreed about what they know, knowledge has not accumulated and today's theories work no better than do those of fifty years ago (Webster & Starbuck, 1988).

The statistics about acceptance rates and reviewers' inconsistent opinions also support a basic truth: Every manuscript can be said to deserve rejection. Every manuscript contains poorly phrased statements. Every manuscript fails to mention some relevant literature. Every manuscript makes arguments that could be more cleanly reasoned. Every theory overlooks some potentially important contingencies. Every design for a study has defects. All data have limitations and defects. Every analytic technique makes unrealistic assumptions. Every useful study demonstrates its own inadequacy by revealing aspects of the studied situation(s) that the researchers did not anticipate. One finding of every empirical study is that the research could have been done better.

How should we deal with it?

So, we can interpret the inconsistency of reviewers' opinions as evidence that social science is progressing normally and also as reason to place our own judgments alongside or ahead of the judgments of reviewers and editors. Nevertheless, we still have to cope with muddled and hostile environments for our research.

Peter and Olson (1983: 111) contended that social scientists should view research as "the marketing of ideas in the form of substantive and methodological theories". Authors need to win audiences for their work – to persuade potential readers to read their articles and to convince actual readers that the ideas and theories in articles are plausible and useful. Social scientists who believe they have something valuable to contribute have to be willing to persuade others of this value; and to do that, they must adapt their manuscripts to the perceptual frameworks of potential readers.

For example, an author's taking credit for ideas makes writing less persuasive and reduces the ideas' influence on readers. Highly persuasive writing gives readers the impression that what they are reading makes such perfectly good sense that it expresses their own thoughts. When authors refer explicitly to themselves by saying "I", "we", "us", "my", or "our", they remind readers that they are reading the authors' ideas, not the readers' own ideas; and consequently, make it more difficult for readers to perceive the ideas as their own. Authors who want their ideas to have wide influence have to give their ideas away. After reading our manuscript "Camping on seesaws" (Hedberg, Nystrom, & Starbuck, 1976), a reviewer said, "This is so obvious that I can't figure out why no one has said it before." Although I thought the reviewer intended this remark as criticism, I smiled with satisfaction.

Also, if authors want innovative ideas to receive wide acceptance, they need to frame their innovations to make them acceptable to as many readers as possible. People generally resist radically new ideas that devalue their current beliefs, whereas they welcome incrementally new ideas that enrich their current beliefs (Normann, 1971). Thus, authors can increase acceptance of their innovations by portraying them as being incremental enhancements of widespread beliefs, but doing this makes the ideas less radical and less "interesting". The essential skill is to present interesting enhancements, not obvious ones.

Peter and Olsen (1983) discussed several "product attributes" that may make theories more marketable, they advocate test marketing theories, and they advise authors to evaluate alternative distribution channels and alternative pricing policies. The reports we receive from reviewers can help with all of these issues. Reviews implicitly identify some "product attributes" that impede acceptance of our theories, they signal the likely appropriateness of specific distribution channels, and they point out elements of manuscripts that make them expensive from the viewpoints of some readers. Of course, one should also seek such information by presenting research seminars and soliciting feedback from colleagues, and it makes sense to do these things before submitting manuscripts to journals.

During my term as editor of *Administrative Science Quarterly*, only about half of the authors whom I invited to revise actually submitted revisions that differed noticeably from the earlier manuscripts. The other half either submitted very superficial revisions or took their manuscripts elsewhere. Thus, authors' motivation and belief in their work play large parts in determining whether their manuscripts make it into print. Some authors respond to negative feedback by withdrawing or refusing to comply, whereas other authors respond by demonstrating persistence and some degree of compliance. Baruch and Altman (chapter 13) offer a thorough discussion of the five choices an author can make in response to an invitation to revise and resubmit a manuscript; they also share their research on how often four of these choices occurred among a sample of scholars in management and the behavioral sciences. Although noisy and inconsistent environments pose challenges, ambiguity creates opportunities for authors to engineer success through persistence, adaptation, symbolic behavior, and intelligent marketing.

Although those who seek success as social science researchers should observe and adapt to the consumers of their work, researchers dare not depend on editors and reviewers to tell them what is right. Researchers should regard editors and reviewers as peers, not as betters. If one tries to follow their inconsistent advice slavishly, one is going to say and do some very silly things. The ultimate decisions about what is right must come from inside oneself, expressing one's own expertise, way of thinking, and ethics.

Notes

1 This article has benefited from suggestions by Mike Barnett, Joan Dunbar, Roger Dunbar, Gerard Hodgkinson, Frances Milliken, Roy Payne, Susan Salgado, and Linda Smircich.
2 Statistics for the *Academy of Management Journal* and *Academy of Management Review* are taken from 1996 reports by Angelo DeNisi and Susan Jackson.
3 Kappa is a coefficient that represents the consistency with which nominal variables were classified on repeated occasions. Like a correlation coefficient, Kappa ranges from –1 to +1 and it equals zero when there is no consistency. Fleiss (1981) argued that Kappas over 0.75 indicate agreement stronger than chance; Gardner (1995) recommended that one should not analyze data further unless Kappa exceeds 0.70; and Landis and Koch (1977) offered the following recommendations:

Kappa Value	Interpretation
Below 0.00	Poor
0.00–0.20	Slight
0.21–0.40	Fair
0.41–0.60	Moderate
0.61–0.80	Substantial
0.81–1.00	Almost perfect

References

The Manuscript Review Process: The Proper Roles of Authors, Referees, and Editors

Ashford, S. J. (1996). The publishing process: The struggle for meaning. In P. J. Frost & M. S. Taylor (eds) *Rhythms of academic life: Personal accounts of careers in academia*, 119–28. Thousand Oaks, CA: Sage.

Bedeian, A. G. (1996). Improving the journal review process: The question of ghostwriting. *American Psychologist, 51*, 1189.

Biggart, N. W. (2000, Spring). From the chair. *Organizations, Occupations, and Work,* 1–2. [Newsletter of the Organizations, Occupations, and Work Section, American Sociological Association].

Bradley, J. V. (1981). Pernicious publication practices. *Bulletin of the Psychonomic Society, 18*, 31–4.

Graham, J. W. & Stablein, R. E. (1985). A funny thing happened on the way to publication: Newcomers' perspectives on publishing in the organizational sciences. In L. L. Cummings & P. J. Frost (eds) *Publishing in the organizational sciences,* 138–54. Homewood, IL: Irwin.

Kinicki, A. J. & Prussia, G. E. (2000). From members of the editorial board. *Academy of Management Journal, 43*, 799–800.

Lee, T. W. (2002). From the editors. *Academy of Management Journal, 45*, 9–11.

Leblebici, H. (1996). The act of reviewing and being a reviewer. In P. J. Frost & M. S. Taylor (eds) *Rhythms of academic life: Personal accounts of careers in academia,* 269–74. Thousand Oaks, CA: Sage.

Levenson, R. L., Jr. (1996). Enhance the journals, not the review process. *American Psychologist, 51*, 1191–3.

Merton, R. K. (1942). A note on science and democracy. *Journal of Legal and Political Sociology, 1*, 115–126.

Merton, R. K. (1973). Priorities in scientific discovery. In N. Storer (ed.) *The sociology of science,* 267–78. Chicago: University of Chicago Press. (Original work published 1942.)

Mowday, R. T. (1997). Celebrating 40 years of the *Academy of Management Journal. Academy of Management Journal, 40*, 1400–13.

Northcraft, G. B. (2001). From the editors. *Academy of Management Journal, 44*, 1079–80.

Pfeffer, J. (1993). Barriers to the advance of organizational science: Paradigm development as a dependent variable. *Academy of Management Review, 18*, 599–620.

Romanelli, E. (1996). Becoming a reviewer: Lessons somewhat painfully learned. In P. J. Frost & M. S. Taylor (eds) *Rhythms of academic life: Personal accounts of careers in academia,* 263–8. Thousand Oaks, CA: Sage.

Schminke, M. (2002). Tensions. *Academy of Management Journal, 45*, 487–90.

Smith, L. Z. (1998). Anonymous review and the boundaries of "intrinsic merit." *Journal of Information Ethics, 7*, 54–67.

Spector, P. E. (1998, Fall). When reviewers become authors: A comment on the journal review process. *Research Methods Forum,* 1–4.

Van Lange, P. A. M. (1999). Why authors believe that reviewers stress limiting aspects of manuscripts: The SLAM effect in peer review. *Journal of Applied Social Psychology, 29*, 2550–66.

The Review Process as a Professional Problem and Some Thoughts on Solving that Problem Consonant with Bedeian's Article

Ashford, S. J. (1996). The publishing process: The struggle for meaning. In P. J. Frost & M. S. Taylor (eds) *Rhythms of academic life: Personal accounts of careers in academia,* 119–27. Thousand Oaks, CA: Sage.

Bedeian, A. G. (1996a). Improving the journal review process: The question of ghostwriting. *American Psychologist, 51,* 1189.

Bedeian, A. G. (1996b). Thoughts on the making and remaking of the management discipline. *Journal of Management Inquiry, 5,* 311–18.

Bedeian, A. G. (1992, 1993, 1998, 2002). *Management laureates: A collection of autobiographical essays.* Vols. I, II, V, & VI. Greenwich, CT: JAI Press.

Bedeian, A. G. (2004). Peer review and the social construction of knowledge in the management discipline. *Academy of Management Learning & Education, 3,* 198–216.

Camic, C. & Wilson, F. D. (2001). A dialogue about ASR: The editorial team talks. *American Sociological Review, 66,* v–ix.

Epstein, S. (1995). What can be done to improve the journal review process. *American Psychologist, 50,* 883–5.

Feldman, D. C. (2004). Editorial – Being a developmental reviewer: Easier said than done. *Journal of Management, 30,* 161–4.

Fine, M. A. (1996). Reflections on enhancing accountability in the peer review process. *American Psychologist, 51,* 1191–2.

Ford, E. W., Duncan, W. J., Bedeian, A. G., Ginter, P. M., Rousculp, M. D. & Adams, A. M. (2003). Mitigating risks, visible hands, inevitable disasters, and soft variables: Management research that matters to managers. *Academy of Management Executive, 17(1),* 46–60.

Ford, E. W., Rousculp, M. D., Adams, A. M., Duncan, W. J., Ginter, P. M. & Bedeian, A. G. (2001). Scaling the ivory tower: Consequential experiences in the lives of contemporary management laureates. Working paper, University of Alabama at Birmingham.

Graham, J. W. & Stablein, R. E. (1985). A funny thing happened on the way to publication: Newcomers' perspectives on publishing in the organizational sciences. In L. L. Cummings & P. J. Frost (eds), *Publishing in the organizational sciences,* 138–54. Homewood, IL: Irwin.

Kinicki, A. J. & Prussia, G. E. (2000). From members of the editorial board. *Academy of Management Journal, 43,* 799–800.

Lee, T. W. (2002). From the editors. *Academy of Management Journal, 45,* 9–11.

Marwell, G. (1992). Let's train reviewers. *American Sociological Review, 57,* iii–iv.

Miner, J. B. (1997). Participating in profound change. *Academy of Management Journal, 40,* 1421–9.

Miner, J. B. (2002). *Organizational behavior: Foundations, theories, and analyses.* New York: Oxford University Press.

Miner, J. B. (2003a). The rated importance, scientific validity and practical usefulness of organizational behavior theories: A quantitative review. *Academy of Management Learning and Education, 2(3),* 250–68.

Miner, J. B. (2003b). Commentary on Arthur Bedeian's "The manuscript review process: The proper roles of authors, references, and editors." *Journal of Management Inquiry, 12,* 339–43.

Miner, J. B. (2006). *Organizational behavior: Historical origins, theoretical foundations, and the future.* Armonk, NY: M. E. Sharpe.

Mowday, R. T. (1997). Celebrating 40 years of the *Academy of Management Journal. Academy of Management Journal, 40,* 1400–13.

Northcraft, G. B. (2001). From the editors. *Academy of Management Journal, 44,* 1079–80.

Schminke, M. (2002). From the editors: Tensions. *Academy of Management Journal, 45,* 487–90.

Weller, A. C. (2002). *Editorial peer review: Its strengths and weaknesses.* Medford, NJ: Information Today.

Turning Lemons into Lemonade: Where is the Value in Peer Reviews?

Baumeister, R. E. (1990). Dear journal editor, it's me again: Sample cover letter for journal manuscript resubmissions. *Dialogue, 5 (Fall),* 16.

Bedeian, A. G. (1996a). Thoughts on the making and remaking of the management discipline. *Journal of Management Inquiry, 5,* 311–18.

Bedeian, A. G. (1996b). Improving the journal review process: The question of ghostwriting. *American Psychologist, 51,* 1189.

Bowen, D. D., Perloff, R., & Jacoby, J. (1972). Improving manuscript evaluation procedures. *American Psychologist, 27,* 221–5.

Cicchetti, D. (1980). Reliability of reviews for the American Psychologist. *American Psychologist, 35,* 300–3.

Cicchetti, D. V. (1991). The reliability of peer review for manuscript and grant submissions: A cross-disciplinary investigation. *Behavioral and Brain Sciences, 14,* 119–86.

Davis, M. S. (1971). That's interesting! Towards a phenomenology of sociology and a sociology of phenomenology. *Philosophy of Social Science, 1,* 309–44.

Ellison, G. (2002). The slowdown of the economics publishing process. *Journal of Political Economy, 110,* 947–93.

Fleiss, J. L. (1981). *Statistical methods for rates and proportions* (2nd ed.). New York: Wiley.

Gardner, W. P. (1995). On the reliability of sequential data: Measurement, meaning, and correction, 341–59 in J. M. Gottman (ed.) *The analysis of change.* Mahwah, N. J.: Erlbaum.

Gottfredson, S. D. (1977). Scientific quality and peer-group consensus (Doctoral dissertation, Johns Hopkins University). *Dissertation Abstracts International, 38,* 1950B. (University Microfilms No. 77–19).

Gottfredson, S. D. (1978). Evaluating psychological research reports: Dimensions, reliability, and correlates of quality judgments. *American Psychologist, 33(10),* 920–34.

Gottfredson, D. M. & Gottfredson, S. D. (1982). Criminal justice and (reviewer) behavior: How to get papers published. *Criminal Justice and Behavior, 9(3),* 259–72.

Harnad, S. (1986). Policing the paper chase. *Nature, 322,* 24–5.

Hedberg, B. L. T., Nystrom, P. C., & Starbuck, W. H. (1976). Camping on seesaws: Prescriptions for a self-designing organization. *Administrative Science Quarterly, 21,* 41–65.

Holbrook, M. B. (1986). A note on sadomasochism in the review process: I hate when that happens. *Journal of Marketing, 50 (July),* 104–6.

Horrobin, D. F. (1990). The philosophical basis of peer review and the suppression of innovation. *JAMA, 263(10),* 9 March 1990, 1438–41.

Kuhn, T. S. (1970). *The structure of scientific revolutions* (2nd ed.). Chicago: University of Chicago Press.

Landis, J. & Koch, G. G. (1977). The measurement of observer agreement for categorical data. *Biometrics, 33,* 159–74.

Mahoney, M. J. (1977). Publication prejudices: An experimental study of confirmatory bias in the peer review system. *Cognitive Therapy and Research, 1,* 161–75.

Mahoney, M. J. (1979). Psychology of the scientist: An evaluative review. *Social Studies of Science, 9(3),* 349–75.

Mahoney, M. J., Kazdin, A. E., & Kenigsberg, M. (1978). Getting published. *Cognitive Therapy and Research, 2,* 69–70.

Meehl, P. E. (1991). *Selected philosophical and methodological papers.* Minneapolis: University of Minnesota Press.

Normann, R. (1971). Organizational innovativeness: Product variation and reorientation. *Administrative Science Quarterly, 16,* 203–15.

Nylenna, M., Riis, P., & Karlsson, Y. (1994). Multiple blinded reviews of the same two manuscripts: Effects of referee characteristics and publication language. *JAMA, 272,* 149–51.

Peter, J. P., & Olson, J. C. (1983). Is science marketing? *Journal of Marketing, 47(Fall),* 111–25.

Peters, D. P. & Ceci, S. J. (1982). Peer-review practices of psychological journals: The fate of published articles, submitted again. *Behavioral and Brain Sciences, 5,* 187–255.

Rothwell, P. M. & Martyn, C. N. (2000). Reproducibility of peer review in clinical neuroscience. Is agreement between reviewers any greater than would be expected by chance alone? *Brain, 123,* 1964–9.

Scott, W. A. (1974). Interreferee agreement on some characteristics of manuscripts submitted to the *Journal of Personality and Social Psychology. American Psychologist, 29,* 698–702.

Webster, J. & Starbuck, W. H. (1988). Theory building in industrial and organizational psychology. In C. L. Cooper & I. Robertson (eds) *International Review of Industrial and Organizational Psychology 1988,* 93–138. Chichester: Wiley.

Wolff, W. M. (1970). "A study of criteria for journal manuscripts." *American Psychologist, 25,* 636–9.

Section 3

Reviewing Different Types of Works

8
Reviewing for Academic Journals: Qualitative-Based Manuscripts

Cary L. Cooper and John Burgoyne

We are presenting this chapter in two parts. In the first we deal with general issues about the place of reviewing, and particularly that of "qualitative" research in the overall process of research based knowledge production, publication, consumption and use. In the second, to meet the specific objective of this book, we take the process of reviewing from beginning to end and consider the choices the reviewer has to make at each stage of the process, and our thoughts and advice on how to make these choices. We are writing primarily for "the reviewer" – someone called on by an editor to review a piece of work. We believe that there is a spectrum of issues that a reviewer needs to attend to from the macro and philosophical to the micro and technical, and that there are issues of style and attitude in terms of how reviewers treat the author(s) of the work they are reviewing.

The big picture

In contemporary society research based knowledge competes for attention with many other sources of ideas and information. Potential users of knowledge and research output are overwhelmed with choice and material that they could attend to – particularly with the resources available on the Internet. Users of knowledge wish to and need to discriminate between that which is useful and reliable, and that which is questionable opinion, made up, serving the cause of getting publicity or selling something. Consider someone looking for medical advice for a health condition – how do they distinguish sound knowledge from quackery or well-meaning but ill-informed advice?

The publication of peer-reviewed research material is the cornerstone of the process of assurance of the quality of knowledge that can be taken seriously.

There is no mechanical or procedural way of assessing the quality and reliability of knowledge and its production. This is particularly so in an area like management and business studies where there is no single and universal research methodology that is accepted as right for all purposes. Indeed appropriate research methodology, including the debate between "qualitative" and "quantitative" research is highly contested.

Peer review is the process of mutual inspection and judgement amongst the community of researchers in a field, which is the best idea anyone has come up with for quality control in the production of knowledge. The notion of publication in a peer-reviewed journal has become the guarantor of knowledge quality.

However there are complications. Who counts as the peer-review community is one of the main ones. Is it only the older, more experienced, researchers? If so is there a danger of younger, newer researchers with radical new ideas being rejected because their ideas do not fit with the establishment? In a field like management and business studies with many sub-disciplines and tribes championing different methodologies, who is the appropriate peer to judge a particular piece of work?

In a field like management and business studies the potential users of knowledge extends beyond the community of researchers that produce it. Managers as practitioners look for useful knowledge to guide their actions. Managers as practitioners are also in a sense lay researchers – they try to work out what makes sense of their actions and what "works" for them. What is the status of this knowledge? In the field of management and business studies there is a debate about mode 2 research – research involving a broader user community, contrasted with mode 1 research – producing "pure" knowledge within the defined researcher community (Gibbons et al, 1994; Huff and Huff, 2001). There is a related proposition (Van Aken, 2004) that management and business studies should be considered to be, at least in part, a design science as well as an analytical science. Physics is an analytical science, devoted to understanding the material world, engineering is a design science – designing and making things that work on the basis of physics knowledge. Similarly biology is an analytical science, medicine a design science. Since management is arguably about making organizational arrangements that work, management and business studies needs to be, in part at least, a design science – drawing on social and other sciences for a basis of confidence about what will and can work. The implication of this for the peer review process is that, in principle, there is a case to be made for the involvement of practitioners, knowledge users, and lay knowledge producers, in the peer review process. Custom and practice around leading peer-review journals does not currently extend very far in using this broader peer community. Some criticisms of "academic" knowledge can be attributed to this – that it is expressed in esoteric language that is not easily comprehensible to practitioners and tends not to address questions and issues on which they believe they need guidance.

The term "qualitative research", usually in contrast to "quantitative research" is well-established and in common use in the field. However it is far from clear what it means, and indeed it appears to have many meanings.

At the simplest (and perhaps simplistic) level you can tell the difference on the basis that qualitative research, when written up, is all words, whereas quantitative research accounts contain numbers, mathematical equations, tables and graphs, report data that is expressed in quantitative terms and is analyzed by statistical methods. The qualitative or quantitative leanings of a journal can be simply and accurately judged by flipping through the pages to see how many numbers and equations they contain and whether statistical analyses are reported.

In management and business studies the different sub-disciplines have different leanings. Economics, finance, accounting and management sciences are more likely to be quantitative, organizational behavior and strategy are more likely to be qualitative, but there are exceptions either way. Economic historians are qualitative; some branches of psychology are very quantitative. The correlation coefficient was allegedly invented for psychologists to analyze the data from intelligence tests.

Arguably no field of inquiry outside pure mathematics is purely quantitative. Whatever may exist in some quantity also has some quality. Six apples have the quantitative dimension of six and the qualitative dimension of appleness (which distinguishes them from oranges). It plays the other way too – whatever exists with some quality also exists in some quantity. This makes it likely that much research will be both. Arguing that textual statements and mathematical statements are all parts of language, they are just different grammars can further erode the distinction. Textual statements tend to have subject, object and verb. $2 + 2 = 4$ has a similar structure. The statements "most people.." and "80% of people.." are saying something quite similar. Quantitative fans will say that 80% is more precise, which is fair enough. Quantitative grammar has the capability of being more descriptively precise. "+" is more precisely defined than "and".

Another take on the qualitative – quantitative debate is that it is another name for the long running debate, in terms of research methodology, between scientific positivism (quantitative) and the rest: phenomenograpy, ethnomethodolgy, discourse analysis and many others. The difference is about ontology – what we take to exist, and in consequence epistemology, how we can get to know about it. The positivist position is that the world is a stable machine, the properties of which can be discovered by the collection of factual data and the analysis of this within an experimental or other research design. The other position, often referred to as constructionism (the preferred term from sociology) or constructivism (the psychology take on this), is that the world is a flat sea of meaning with ebbing and flowing currents of ideas expressed in language. The new(er) kid on the block is critical realism (Sayer, 1999) that argues that both of these are wrong, and makes the case for the ontological position that the world is made up of interacting entities with emergent properties which are real, but which can only be viewed through lenses of linguistic meaning. In this sense the qualitative – quantitative debate hovers over the top of a seemingly bottomless pit of philosophical debate on ontology and epistemology. The debate seems bottomless because there seems little prospect of a definitive resolution to these questions, though philosophers will continue to earn a living by trying. The trouble is that to do research, in the sense of an empirical activity, requires the taking of a position on ontological and epistemological issues to get to the starting gate. This is why much research writing begins with extensive philosophical foreplay, and in some cases never gets beyond it. When they do get beyond it this is by making assumptions or taking a position that can be contested on philosophical grounds. These debates are one of the features of academic writing that frustrates managers looking for useful knowledge to guide their actions, and may lead them to turn to sources of ideas other than the peer-reviewed academic journals.

What this tells us for the purpose of this chapter – how to review qualitative work – is that it can be thought of as all the research approaches that are not scientific – positivist. This constitutes a multitude of types with their different followings and communities of research practice, with no clear way of adjudicating between them.

For practical purposes, and the purposes of this chapter, we will define qualitative research as research that tends to come out of some non-positivist approach, tends to deal with meanings and descriptive phenomena, tends not to attempt to model the world, and interpret and analyze data about it, via mathematical modelling and the use of statistical techniques to draw meaning from numerically represented data. Qualitative research can to some extent be defined as a family of research "methods" used, and some of the main examples of these are ethnography (Hammersley & Atkinson, 1983), ethnomethodology (Benson & Hughes, 1983), phenomenology (Edie, 1987), phenomenography (Brookfield, 1994), discourse analysis (Fairclough, 1990), case method (Yin, 1989), stakeholder analysis (Burgoyne, 1994), grounded theory (Glaser & Straus, 1968), and at a more technical level, interviews (Kvale, 1996), focus groups (Krueger, 1988), open-ended questionnaires (Oppenheim, 1968), participant and non-participant observation (McCall & Simmons, 1969), analysis of textual and archival data (Webb, Campbell, Schwartz, & Sechrest, 1966), and many forms of action research (Bradbury & Reason, 2002).

So in the light of all this what advice can we offer about the conduct of the process of reviewing qualitative research?

The review process and reviewer choices

We have chosen to structure our practical advice to reviewers in terms of the sequence of events starting with an enquiry or request from a journal editor to review a paper, through to the final decision and its implementation by the editor in terms of publishing, or not, the paper in question, very often with revisions to the paper by the author(s) in the light of the reviewers comments and the editors interpretation of these. Puffer, Quick and McCarthy in chapter 10 provide a similarly detailed model of the review cycle that may also be of interest to those who are working on qualitative manuscripts. Good practice by editors includes telling reviewers their final decision and the reasons for it, and sharing the advice from other reviewers. We will deal with it in phases.

The first phase is the "decision-making" phase, that is, should I do it. The decision process is usually broken down into two parts: the costs and benefits of doing it; and am I qualified to judge and comment on this particular article.

Part of the decision-making process is to calculate your own cost-benefit analysis. The costs may be the significant amount of effort and time you need to devote to it when you already are overloaded or the lost opportunity costs of doing your own research or fulfilling your writing commitments. Another cost may be that it is unpaid and in some cases unappreciated or not professionally acknowledged in a way that you personally need. There are potential benefits of keeping up to date with the literature, in networking with the editor or associated editors, in gaining access to the editorial board, in getting a free copy of the journal, in being perceived by the research community as a "good citizen". We would argue that in the long run reviewing is a good investment in your own education and continuing professional development and an essential aspect of research life.

Each individual will make their minds up on the balance of these costs and benefits, taking into account the perceived quality of the journal concerned and where this fits into their career plan.

Having made a decision that the benefits outweigh the costs, the next decision is "am I qualified to review this particular article, is it in my area of expertise?" If it is not remotely in your field, the answer may be an easy one to reach. More often than not it may not be directly in your area of expertise but you have the skill base to review it in terms of research design, or methods used, or implications for other research or practice. The problem occurs in qualitative research, that many quantitative researchers feel they have the expertise to evaluate this type of article, allowing their bias against less empirically orientated research to drive them to do it without either declaring their bias or demonstrating an open mind, leading to unhelpful and unconstructive reviews. When considering whether to do a qualitative review, it is important to understand your own biases and research preferences, and reflect on whether they are likely to get in the way of a constructive and developmental review. In doing this you might ask yourself some of the following questions: what are my methodological preoccupations and will they get in the way of my review? If it is interdisciplinary research, can I cope with leaving my single discipline comfort zone? Am I so entrenched in my micro area of research and its accompanying methodological approaches that I would feel unable to cope with diverse methods and approaches? In addition to asking yourself these questions, you may also consider the questions that Ryan raised in chapter 3 to assess your biases and determine if they are a cause for not doing a review. In accepting a reviewing assignment we often need to make the choice of using it as an opportunity to strike a blow for our own preferred method – criticise or praise the work according to its fit with our preferences, or whether we are prepared to judge whether a piece of work is "good of its kind", even if we are not particularly keen on the kind.

If you feel comfortable with these two parts of the decision-making processes, then you will have to consider some simple technical issues: can I devote the time available to do a very good and comprehensive job?; can I do it quickly enough, given that the editor and author/s are anxiously awaiting my reply?; and where can I build this into my timetable for commitments?

Broader editorial considerations

Having made the decision to review the article from your personal point of view, there are broader editorial issues to consider. First, given the editorial statement/objectives of the journal, and what you have observed by exploring past issues, does this particular article fit with the mission of the journal? If it does not, then you ought to let the editor know at this stage, but suggest alternative journals or practitioner orientated outlets for them to try. There is no point in spending time to review an article that is wholly inappropriate for the journal it was submitted to. Second, you may receive a paper from a colleague in a developing country where English is their second or third language, and the grammar is very poor. You should, however, read through the article to see if the ideas and/or methods within it are novel, innovative, etc., before deciding that it is inappropriate from a "language or communications" perspective. It may be that it is so novel or innovative that one can overcome its language deficits, and that a recommendation might include, in addition to particular substantive points, that an associate editor work developmentally with the author to edit the language problems – so don't dismiss out of hand scholarly work that comes from parts of the world less represented in Anglo/American English language journals.

Criteria for evaluation

We all have our different ways of reading papers. It may be a good idea, ideally, to read it several times. You may want to start by reading the overall synopsis and summary and conclusions to get an idea of the kind of paper it is. Another practice is to try to work out what the overall "story line" is for the paper. This (with the possible exception of extreme forms of post-modernist writing) should be relatively clear. See if you can summarize it. Some papers fail because they have too many or too complicated storylines, or ones that do not join up in the middle.

If you have explored the paper, you are now ready to consider the criteria for evaluation. Some of these are laid out for you by the editor or in the manuscript review documentation. These usually include the following: originality, adequacy of research design, adequacy of data analysis, clarity of writing, appropriateness of interpretation of results and adequacy of the discussion, including understanding the conceptual and practical implications of the findings. When it comes to research in the qualitative arena, there are some subtle distinctions in the criteria that should be included, given that usually we are not referring to large data sets analyzed by structural equation modelling or other sophisticated statistical techniques, but data in a different format and used for a different purpose. Nevertheless, some of the criteria should be similar but with a slightly different orientation. We would suggest some of the following criteria and in this order of priority: originality, contribution to the literature or field, rigour, adequate empirical base (in other words some data to support the work), adequate location in the field of knowledge, technical competence of execution, clarity of structure and storyline and readability (taking into account the caveat about non English speaking authors). You can often take the reviewers' guidelines to give you a structure for your report, and quite often they contain a form to structure your judgements.

In quantitative research there is the question of whether appropriate statistical analyses have been chosen and competently carried out, which can call for a high degree of technical knowledge. For some kinds of qualitative research there is the equivalent. When, for example, some form of content analysis of interview transcripts or field notes is involved, the technical process needs to be described and evidence of its thorough execution provided. There are some computer-based content analyses in use currently (ENVIVO, NUDIST), and a reviewer will need to be able to judge their effective use.

In defining qualitative research we pointed out that there is a broad spectrum of "methodologies": ethnography, ethnomethodology, phenomenology, phenomenography, discourse analysis, case method, stakeholder analysis, grounded theory, and at a more technical level, interviews, focus groups, open-ended questionnaires, participant and non-participant observation, and many forms of action research, that fall within this category. Each of these has its own (often contested) "rules" for the collection and analysis of data, and the reviewer needs to know those rules and be able to judge whether a specific piece of qualitative research is "good of its kind" according the sub-school of qualitative research being followed. Some authors will claim to work with a mix of these methods, and in this situation the reviewer needs to consider whether the work is carried out from a clear and consistent position in terms of epistemological an ontological assumptions, in relation to the substantive theory being developed or tested.

There is a challenge in presenting research based on qualitative data. Quantitative data can be presented in a brief and compressed way, but raw qualitative data, as in transcripts, is extensive and can only be quoted very sparingly in the typical five to eight thousand-word paper. Good writing involves showing the analysis process, overall summary categories of meaning extracted from qualitative data and a very selective use of quotes to illuminate and validate points. A guiding principle that applies to both quantitative and qualitative research is that it should be written up, in methodology terms, in enough detail for someone else to be able to repeat the investigation or something like it. This is the principle of replicability. Questions about validity, depending on research paradigm, need to be addressed in qualitative research – what is important is that authors address the issue in one way or another. One appropriate practice in many situations is for researchers to check back with the researched whether their interpretations make sense to them. Qualitative researchers need also to be clear on generalizability. They may wish to claim that they are only describing the uniqueness of a situation but they need to say so and why this might be of broader interest, as in identifying patterns that might occur elsewhere, or illuminating generative interpretative frameworks that could be used elsewhere.

You may have a different weighting of the above criteria than us or even different from the editor, but as long as you make clear your criteria and evaluate the article accordingly, the transparency will add to the editor's in the final decision-making process. For example, you may find that an article you have reviewed is highly original, making a quantum leap in the field but without much qualitative or quantitative data to support it … as long as your recommendation is based on clear-cut and transparent criteria the editor will be able to make a better final judgement call.

There are other issues to consider as well: does this paper represent research of a type that there is too little or too much of?; is this a "less good paper" but on an important new topic?; it doesn't quite fit the mainstream of articles usually published in this journal but could create a whole new field of valuable research even though it would stand out in the first instance; etc.. The overall background criteria, rather like examining Ph.D.s, are whether there is an original contribution to knowledge here.

Preparing your review

You have now decided on your criteria and reviewed the paper, and now need to come to a decision. Although the final decision might be quite easy in terms of the normal "decision categories" (e.g., accept without revision, accept with minor revisions, revise and resubmit, major rewrite required on a revise and resubmit basis, or reject), the mode of delivery of your comments is very important. It is important, particularly in qualitative research, to provide "constructive feedback" whether in a revise and resubmit mode or in a reject mode. It is important not to denigrate, demean or devalue the research or paper in any way. Being a "critical friend" who is helping the author(s) to develop further their ideas, methodology and the like is the approach that should be taken. You should go as far as you feel will help the people to develop their work, the clarity of their argument, the clarity of their writing, etc. Put yourself in their position on receipt of your comments, how would you feel if you received the review you are considering sending? Empathy, as described in chapters 4, 5 and 6, is a good guideline of your approach. Some reviewers provide very little constructive feedback, with a one-liner such as "it isn't good enough, go back to the drawing board" or "don't waste my time, submit this to a magazine instead". You should not accept the invitation to review unless you plan on doing a thorough and comprehensive review for the purposes of developing the author and his/her ideas, methods, theories, constructs and the like. This is particularly in the case in qualitative research where constructive feedback might prove extremely useful in fuelling a new theory or methodology or different way of exploring human behavior.

As well as making judgements about the publishability of papers, referees often get involved in detailed editorial comments on spellings, grammar, typographical errors, correctness of referencing and references, compliance with journals layout and presentation guidelines. While these may not be essential to academic quality they are important to comprehensibility and part of the refereeing process. One trick is simply to mark any errors of this kind (on paper or through "track change" in electronic form) while reading a paper, and return the paper thus marked with the review.

Ethical issues

Ethical issues relate to qualitative reviewing at three levels.

Firstly, there are ethics of the reviewing process itself. The principle is that it is the work not the author/researcher that is being evaluated. For this reason papers are usually sent to reviewers' anonamatized, and reviewers' identities are usually withheld from authors. This can be challenged since it does rather imply that we do not trust ourselves and each other to focus on the work in itself, however it is the norm. It is of course, in a closely-knit research field, often possible to guess who the authors (and reviewers) are or for this to "leak" informally. The ethical principle for personal reviewer conduct is to stay focused on the question "is this good work"?

At the second level is the question of whether the research reported has been conducted ethically. Ethical principles for research are contested, but one can at least see if the issue has been considered, and whether there are any obviously questionable practices, ones, for example, that are damaging to the researched or their interests. Informed consent to be researched by those being researched is often an ethical principle to be observed, however some common sense is needed – informed consent can reasonably be expected in individual interviews, but may be inappropriate or impossible for observations of mass public behavior.

Thirdly and finally there is the possibility that as a reviewer you find yourself reading about activity and behavior in a researched situation that raises ethical issues – e.g. actual accounts or fraudulent or criminal activities, or personally damaging behavior in work settings. This is a dilemma for researchers and reviewers – are they there like war reporters and photographers to report, record and publicize, or should they do something about certain situations? It is perhaps surprising how infrequently issues like this arise in research, perhaps because researchers are more interested in broad theoretical issues that can be illuminated by research rather than the rights and wrongs of specific episodes. Our main thought on this is that reading research that appears to report ethically or morally dubious practices in researched settings would probably merit a discussion with the editor on what to do.

Conclusion

In conclusion we would simply like to assert that reviewing of qualitative (and perhaps other) work is in the long term a rewarding and essential part of activity in the research community, and is itself a qualitative judgement making process, and one that calls for the qualitative communication and expression of your judgements in a way that is critical and constructive to the world of knowledge, and those who generate and apply it.

We have suggested that qualitative research is not a single entity, but constitutes a family of methods and approaches with quite different philosophical underpinnings, technical issues and challenges, alignments with different sub-disciplines (e.g. psychology, sociology, economics), and boundary definitions in relation to quantitative research. The reviewers job is therefore to work out what kind of qualitative research any given piece is claimed to be, whether this is made clear and transparent, and whether the research is "good of its kind", i.e., follows the rules and procedures, and is executed rigorously it its own terms.

References

Benson, D. & Hughes, J. A. (1983). *The Perspective of Ethnomethodology*. London: Longman.

Bradbury, H. & Reason, P. (eds) (2002). *The Handbook of Action Research*. London: Sage.

Brookfield, S. D. (1994). Takes from the darkside: A phenomography of adult critical reflection. *International Journal of Lifelong Education, 13*(3).

Burgoyne, J. G. (1994). Stakeholder Analysis. In C. Cassell and G. Symon (eds) *Qualitative methods in organizational and occupational psychology*. London: Sage.

Edie, J. M. (1987). *William James and Phenomenology*. Bloomington: Indiana University Press.

Fairclough, N. (1990). *Language and Power*. London: Longman.

Gibbons, M. L., Limoges, H., Nowotney, S., Schwartman, P., Scott, P. & Trow, M. (1994). *The new production of knowledge: The dynamics of science and research in contemporary societies*. London: Sage.

Glaser, B. G. & Straus, A. L. (1968). The *discovery of grounded theory*. New York: Weidenfield and Nicholson.

Hammersley, M. & Atkinson, P. (1983). *Ethnography: Principles in practice*. London: Tavistock.

Huff, A. S. & Huff, J. O. (2001). Re-focusing the business school agenda. *British Journal of Management, 12*, S49–S54.

Krueger, R. A. (1988). *Focus groups: A practical guide for applied research*. London: Sage.

Kvale, S. (1996). *Interviews: An introduction to qualitative research interviewing*. London: Sage.

McCall, G. J. & Simmons, J. L. (1969). *Issues in participant observation*. Reading, MA: Addison-Wesley.

Oppenheim, A. N. (1968). *Questionnaire design and attitude measurement*. London: Heinemann.

Sayer, A. (1999). *Realism and social science*. London: Sage.

Van Aken, J. E. (2004). "Management research based on the paradigm of the design sciences: The quest for field-tested and grounded technological rules". *Journal of Management Studies, 41*, 219–45.

Webb, E. J., Campbell, D. T., Schwartz, R. D. & Sechrest, L. (1966). *Unobtrusive measures: Non-reactive research in the social sciences.* Chicago: Rand MacNally.

Yin, R. (1989). *Case study research.* London: Sage.

9

Reviewing by the Numbers: Evaluating Quantitative Research

S. Gayle Baugh, James G. (Jerry) Hunt and Terri A. Scandura*

The three authors of this chapter have three different perspectives on the reviewing process. The first author is an experienced reviewer who still struggles to "get it all right" in trying to provide, with a supportive tone, appropriate feedback to manuscript authors. The second author is a very experienced reviewer and journal editor – experienced enough to get cranky at times, but professional enough to hide such feelings from manuscript authors! The third author is a very experienced reviewer and relatively new journal editor who has made the transition from "critic" to "coach" (these terms will be used later in this chapter). All three of us have been recipients of both supportive and develop-mental reviews and of harsh, critical, and sometimes outright nasty reviews. We hope that this chapter will help you to write reviews of quantitative manuscripts that are helpful to both the author(s) and the journal editor.

The purpose of the chapter is to provide an overview of the process of reviewing a manuscript which involves the quantitative analysis of data. We first offer a definition of what we consider a "quantitative" manuscript, then we look at concerns about the overall value of the manuscript – what has been termed the "after dinner" question. We next discuss the framing of the hypothesis, which is also an important concern. We turn our attention after that to the actual quantitative analysis included in the manuscript and the extent to which the ana-lysis fulfills the promise that the introduction offers. As we discuss the reviewing of quantitative manuscripts, we will touch upon ethics (covered more thoroughly in chapter 5) and the overall tone of the review (covered more thoroughly in chapters 4 and 6).

---

* Note: Author ordering is alphabetical.

A qualitative definition of quantitative research

It seems wise to begin this discussion by defining what we mean by "quantitative research." A very loose definition could be "anything that includes numbers," in which case the telephone directory would qualify as "quantitative research." We will include in our definition any research which involves the presentation of quantitative data to test research questions or hypotheses explicitly proposed by the author of the manuscript. This definition includes techniques such as meta-analysis (a method of cumulating results from multiple studies), event analysis (a method of determining whether or not a specific event has had an effect on some outcome) and structural equation modeling (a method of determining if data conform to a particular theoretical model that has been proposed). It excludes studies which present only descriptive statistics with no attempt made to test hypotheses or studies which analyze qualitative data (even if numerical counts or per-centages of response categories are presented). Despite this description of quantitative research, we acknowledge that, at times, the lines become blurred. For example data may be collected with qualitative methods (e.g., in-depth interviews) and then coded or content ana-lyzed at a later point and become quantitative. Also, some research employs mixed methods in which qualitative and quantitative methods are employed in the same study.

The "After Dinner" question – is it interesting?

A wise colleague was asked to look over a manuscript based on a part of a newly-minted dissertation. After completing the task, the wise person responded that the manuscript did not pass the "after dinner" test. The "after dinner" test is, of course, an informal test of the interest that the manuscript arouses. Many, perhaps most, readers of scholarly journals will catch up on their reading after putting in a full day at work and then eating dinner. Thus, the manuscript must be engaging enough to capture one's attention after dinner, or at least not to put the reader to sleep. Typically, this means that the title and the first paragraph or two must be interesting enough for the reader to keep reading.

A good quantitative manuscript offers a "hook" in terms of a promise of what the reader can learn by continuing through the rest of the paper. If that promise is not engaging enough, then the published article will be set aside by the reader with a low probability of ever returning to it. The reviewer, unlike the journal reader, is committed to reading the full manuscript. Thus, a helpful and supportive reviewer will let the author know when the manuscript does not pass the "after dinner" test. If the manuscript as a whole has value, however, then the reviewer may provide suggestions for the author so that the manuscript can more quickly capture the reader's attention. It would truly be a waste if a valuable paper failed to get the attention it deserved because fatigue and work overload caused too many potential readers to set it aside as "uninteresting" based on the first couple of paragraphs.

Some authors, of course, carry this idea to the extreme, with the result that their manuscript or manuscript title is "cute," rather than "interesting." We have heard stories, for example, of a manuscript examining the validity of the "Faces" job satisfaction measure that was titled "Face Validity." A second example comes from one of the authors, with a manuscript titled "The Great Hi-Hi Leader Behavior Myth: A Lesson from Occam's Razor" (Larson, Hunt, & Osborn, 1976). One reviewer of this manuscript commented that, if nothing else, the work should win a prize for the best title. It did win publication, although one of the authors now admits that it might have been right on the edge of "cuteness." Another example is the now classic "R.I.P. LPC: A response to Fiedler" (Schriesheim & Kerr, 1977). This title is not only catchy but effectively captures the essence of this critical analysis of the Least Preferred Coworker Scale and the Fiedler Contingency theory of leadership. From a reviewer's perspective, you want to look carefully at the title to see how "catchy" it is. You want to help the author develop a title that is descriptive but also gets attention. In the next chapter, Puffer, Quick and McCarthy devote an entire section to the topic of assessing a manuscript's title and its executive overview.

The "Value-Added" question

There are, of course, those manuscripts that make very little substantive contribution to the field, whether or not they "read" well. On occasion, you will review a manuscript that sounds interesting only because the author is an excellent writer, but there is really very little that the manuscript offers in terms of substantive findings. In a more discouraging scenario, you may review a study that offers little substantive contribution and is, in addition, not well-written. Manuscripts with limited substantive values may offer a replication of well-established results, exhibit serious methodological errors, or offer "marginally significant" results (discussed later) but few or no significant results. If the manuscript has weaknesses which the author will not be able to repair (e.g., the initial data collection is flawed), it is incumbent upon you, as a reviewer, to indicate why the manuscript cannot be considered a contribution. You may find that the conceptual model has value, however, even if the operational testing is fatally flawed, in which case your comments can be directed toward strengthening research and analytic procedures for future quantitative studies.

While it is very easy to become annoyed with the author of a manuscript that offers very little to you as the reader and reviewer, remember the "Pareto principle." The Italian economist Alfred Pareto developed a formula in the 1700s that is quite useful to reviewers in the current era. Simply stated, the principle is that 80% of results come from 20% of effort. So as a reviewer, try to look for the 20% of what the author has done that might be a contribution. Sometimes it is a challenge to find it, but usually it is there. A manuscript that is poorly written with very limited or no substantive contribution often will not reach a reviewer, but will instead be rejected by the editor on editorial review. As there has already been some pre-screening, make sure that whenever possible you point out to the author what is valuable in the manuscript, not just the weaknesses.

That's a good question! – evaluating research hypotheses

Any good quantitative manuscript requires the statement of a hypothesis or hypotheses. Gone are the days of "dust bowl empiricism," when one could just study relationships to see what one could deduce from them. Many new entrants into the competition to publish are so eager to demonstrate strong empirical results that they forget that such results must be grounded in a good theoretical reason to predict them (a hypothesis) and must also be interpreted in terms of the contribution that they can make to theory-building. It is no longer acceptable to conduct research on an issue simply because "it is interesting" or because it is currently a "hot" issue. A colleague reading an early draft of a manuscript commented: "You know exactly what you found, but you appear to have no idea why you found it." Reviewers cannot always count on the author's colleague to point out this defect in an empirical manuscript. It is probably wise to be a little gentler than the comment above, but the author must be aware that theorizing precedes hypothesizing, and interpretation involves re-theorizing.

One indication of poor theorizing is offering the null hypothesis as the research hypothesis. This problem occurs quite often, and it slips by reviewers unidentified more often than one would think. While it might seem obvious that a hypothesis could be rephrased so that it is no longer null, that process may be more difficult than it appears. This problem occurred to one of the authors of this chapter, who wanted to hypothesize no differences in perceptions between the partners in a mentoring dyad.

This hypothesis is, of course, a null hypothesis, and "supporting" such a hypothesis would be subject to alternative explanations, especially a lack of sufficient power to detect real differences. The solution (still unpublished at the time of this writing) was to find a different type of dyad, in this case supervisor-subordinate pairs, and to compare the level of perceptual agreement in the mentoring dyad to the level of perceptual agreement in the supervisor-subordinate dyad.

A similar problem occurred in a published study by Hunt, Boal, and Dodge (1999). In this study, the authors posited that vision-oriented and crisis-responsive charismatic leadership would be equally effective under crisis conditions – a null hypothesis. The solution in this case was to find two other forms of leadership, exchange-oriented and low expressive leadership, both of which were predicted to be less effective than the two charismatic forms of leadership.

Clearly, in the two examples provided above, the authors exercised some creativity to develop testable hypotheses. A reviewer cannot be expected to solve all such problems for the author. However, it is important for reviewers to read each hypothesis presented in the manuscript carefully to determine if it is logically derived from the theoretical model presented, if it can be disconfirmed, and if it is stated in a non-null form.

A subtler, more insidious problem is one termed HARKing (Hypothesizing After Results are Known) (Kerr, 1998). HARKing involves "cheating" in the sense that an author develops a hypothesis after looking at the results and then presents the hypothesis in the manuscript as if it had been developed a priori. This approach is inappropriate because it allows the author to "lead" the reader and reviewer into the hypothesis as if it is quite logical, knowing, of course, that the hypothesis will be supported. It will take a very careful reviewer to realize that often there are equally logical alternative predictions. Thus, the author has built in a bias toward acceptance of the manuscript by ensuring that the predictions made are supported by the data. It is difficult for a reviewer to assess whether or not HARKing might have occurred in a manuscript, but it is always wise to consider whether alternative hypotheses could be derived from the theory presented.

You do not want to be the not uncommon reviewer who encourages HARking without being aware of what you are doing – i.e., suggesting to the author post hoc why the results obtained could have been predicted from a different theoretical perspective. While it would be ideal for all authors to develop "strong inference" tests (Platt, 1964) – developing two competing hypotheses based on two different theoretical perspectives and then determining which of the theories can be disconfirmed and which supported based on empirical results – competing hypotheses cannot be established post hoc. It is incumbent upon the reviewer to indicate alternative theoretical perspectives that could equally well fit the results obtained, but as a reviewer you must make your suggestion in terms of the *interpretation* of results or suggested future research directions rather than in terms of predictions.

Methodology and analysis

There are many issues with respect to the methodology used to develop research instruments and collect data, as well as the analytic tools used to analyze data, that are worthy of comment. We have chosen only a few, which we consider to be common sources of error in quantitative manuscripts. There is no intent here to provide a "checklist" of issues to consider in reviewing a quantitative paper, although such guidelines are available (e.g., Campion, 1993; Rynes, 2005).

Research population. There are some journals that simply will not accept organizational research that is conducted utilizing student samples. It seems obvious conducting research in an academic setting using student samples means that many of the processes that are active in organizations, and which affect individual and group behavior, are absent. Studies which focus on student response to "vignettes" or "paper people" are a prime example of research which lacks realism. In these types of studies, the absence of distracting features of a real organization, coupled with the fact that the research participant need not actually produce results or experience consequences of decisions, allow the participant to focus only on the essential features of the research (i.e., the manipulated variables). Arguments that students have work experience or are "going to be" managers notwithstanding, effects sometimes emerge in studies using student samples that are not found in real systems (Gordon, Slade, & Schmitt, 1986).

There are instances in which results in a student sample may be appropriate, however. A student sample can be very useful as a preliminary indicator of effects that might be found in a sample of employed individuals or to show that the phenomenon in question <u>could</u> occur in more "real world" settings (cf. Mook, 1983). Research with student samples is frequently undertaken to investigate the psychological processes underlying or influencing organizational phenomena and offer the author an opportunity to conduct research which might not be possible in an organizational setting (Greenberg, 1987a). In addition, student samples are clearly appropriate for pedagogical research, which focuses on learning in an academic environment. While it would be unwise to reject all research utilizing student samples for that reason, the reviewer should expect that the author using student samples for research on organizational phenomena has provided some strong rationale for the appropriateness of such a sample. If the rationale is not presented, it is the reviewer's responsibility to prompt the author to provide it, if the quality of the manuscript is such that it is not rejected on first review.

Sample size. Most authors live by the rule that "more is better" with respect to sample size. It is important, however, to determine if the sample size is appropriate to the effects which the author wishes to identify (Austin, Boyle, & Lualhati, 1998). With a sample that is too small, real effects may go undetected because the study lacks sufficient statistical power to uncover them. A sample that is very large, however, may result in findings that are statistically significant but too small to be of any practical importance. Unfortunately, power analyses are reported in quantitative studies only infrequently (Finch, Cumming, & Thomason, 2001). You may wish to request a power analysis in order to draw the author's attention to the issue of sample size.

Another concern with respect to sample size is the necessity of determining the actual number of observations on which hypothesis tests are based. Sometimes authors will report large numbers of respondents to surveys or other types of research, but the actual number of observations that meet the criteria for the research in question is much smaller. In a manuscript on mentoring in an organizational setting reviewed recently by one of the authors of this chapter, the sample size was reported as over 500. However, observations could only be included in the study if the participant reported having been a protégé, which reduced the sample size to less than half of the original number of respondents. Multiple inclusion criteria can reduce a sample dramatically, so it is important to determine how restrictive the inclusion criteria are for the study under review.

An issue related to sample size is response rate. The author should report the response rate for the study in order for the reviewer to have some sense of how representative of the population the sample might be. In addition, the methods used to increase the response rate should be identified, and the number of additional responses received at each follow-up should be noted. Obviously, response rates will vary depending on the population sampled (Baruch, 1999; Gupta, Shaw, & Delery, 2000) and "rules of thumb" are hard to come by (for an exception see Roth & BeVier, 1998), but extremely low response rates should arouse suspicion that either the sample is not representative of the population or that the hypotheses studied are irrelevant or uninteresting to the population sampled (Cycyota & Harrison, 2002).

Measurement concerns. Measurement may well be the "Achilles' heel" of organizational research. There is a great deal of effort and little reward for developing good measures of constructs. It is very easy for authors to write a list of items or observe some behavior and give it the label that they desire, but measuring constructs cannot be done in so casual a manner. As one early methodologist put it, "The point is <u>not</u> that adequate measurement is 'nice.' It is <u>necessary</u>, crucial, etc. Without it, we have nothing" (Korman, 1974, p. 194).

It is the reviewer's responsibility to think carefully about whether or not the measure actually matches the theoretical construct that it is supposed to represent and does so without contamination or deficiency (Brogden & Taylor, 1950; Nunnally & Bernstein, 1994). Even well-established measures may suffer from contamination or deficiency. The Position Analysis Questionnaire has been criticized as contaminated by the reading level it requires (thus confounding job dimensions with reading ability) (Ash & Edgell, 1975) and the commonly used measure of role conflict and role ambiguity developed by Rizzo, House, and Lirtzman (1970) has been subject to charges that it confounds item wording with the substantive dimensions (Tracy & Johnson, 1983). In a study conducted by two of the authors of this chapter, a measure which was designed to assess turnover intentions was found to be deficient because it lacked items assessing intended behavior and instead assessed only perceived alternatives to the current position.

This assessment of the adequacy of the measures used is not simple, and the results of the assessment must be communicated to the author of the manuscript as something more than "This is not a good measure of the construct in question." It is not sufficient for the reviewer to point out that the author simply wrote items, subjected them to exploratory factor analysis, and settled upon a name for those items – even if it is true. The reviewer must be ready to indicate the sources of contamination or deficiency, and it is extremely helpful to suggest alternative methods of measuring the construct.

Research setting. The "realism" of the research setting has been debated among organizational researchers, often in conjunction with a discussion about the "realism" of the research population, mentioned earlier (e.g., Greenberg, 1987b). Typically, the realism argument concerns external validity (degree to which the study's results can be generalized across the entire population of people, settings, and other similar conditions, Davis & Casenza, 1993). In turn, external validity is conceptualized in terms of ecological validity (faithful reflection of "real people in the real world") or mundane realism (similarity of the setting and events at the surface level) (Berkowitz & Donnerstein, 1982). Zelditch (1969) in an article entitled, "Can you Really Study an Army in the Laboratory?" provides effective counter-arguments for criticisms regarding the absence of ecological validity or mundane realism. The author suggests that we do not really need to study the Army as such, but instead what is necessary is experimental realism (the reproduction of relationships and psychological processes as such (cf. Berkowitz & Donnerstein, 1982; Greenberg & Tomlinson, 2004; Mook, 1983). Laboratory studies offer relatively stringent control over extraneous variables to eliminate alternative hypotheses and focus on the underlying processes of interest to the researcher.

From the reviewer's perspective, the author's discussion of the findings is most important here. An emphasis on experimental realism is easier to justify than ecological or mundane realism. A careful review of the discussion of results is necessary to ensure that they are neither over- nor under-generalized.

Cross-sectional studies. Despite increasing emphasis on dynamic and processual or at least longitudinal work (e.g., Bluedorn, 2002; Graen, Wakabayashi, Graen, & Graen, 1990; Hunt, 1991) much of the research produced in the field is cross-sectional in nature. While there are certainly strong arguments to be made to require temporality in all publishable research, this requirement has not yet been imposed by any journal with which we are familiar. Reviewers must, as a result, be wary of authors that overgeneralize cross-sectional findings. While it seems trite to state that causality cannot be inferred or implied from cross-sectional data, many authors become so enthused with significant results that they forget this very basic requirement. Worse yet, sometimes reviewers get caught up in the same enthusiasm and the author's interpretation stands. Such overstepping the interpretive bounds of cross-sectional data is a relatively minor violation, but it can result in some embarrassment for the author, the reviewer, the editor, and the journal.

Given the frequency of calls for longitudinal research, reviewers must be ready to read manuscripts that incorporate temporal analysis. These methodologies require sophisticated reviewing, and if a reviewer does not feel that his or her methodological background is up to the task, there is honor in acknowledging this fact (see chapter 3 of this volume). It is far easier to quickly return a manuscript to the editor without review than it is to supplement one's methodological background in order to adequately review the paper.

Same-source data. Data collected from the same source may give rise to a problem referred to as "common method variance" or "common method bias" (Campbell & Fiske, 1959; Campbell, 1996). Common method bias occurs when the proportion of shared variance due to the method used to measure the variables (i.e., same source) accounts for variance beyond that of the real relationship between/among variables. The issue is most prominent when all or most of the measures in a study are self-reports. What was once expressed as a concern about a manuscript is now gaining virtual "fatal flaw" status. Where it was at one time sufficient to acknowledge the issue and beg forgiveness in the discussion of limitations of the research, this approach no longer suffices.

The reliance on self-report measures has been a source of controversy in organizational behavior, but self-reports are not the only types of measures that may be influenced by common method variance (see Conway, 2002 and Campbell, 1996). Thus, reviewers should be aware of common method variance when it has the potential to affect the results obtained in the study under review (Donaldson & Grant-Vallone, 2002; Williams & Brown, 1994). Clearly, there are some phenomena, such as individual feelings, beliefs, and perceptions, which can only be measured using self-report approaches (Spector, 1994). Further, some authors have demonstrated that problems of common method variance may not be equally threatening to all types of conclusions (e.g., Conway, 2002; Crampton & Wagner, 1994; Spector, 1987). While Spector (1994) cautions that research should not be rejected simply because common method variance might be a concern, it is incumbent upon the author to demonstrate that the issue has been carefully considered and, in the particular study presented, mitigated to the extent possible (see Podsakoff, MacKenzie, Lee, & Podsakoff, 2003; Schmitt, 1994).

Marginally significant results. It is common in studies that present results of several statistical tests for authors to present significant results, which indicate clear support for the research hypothesis, to note non-significant results, which do not support the research hypotheses, and then to discuss "marginally significant" results (sometimes authors will discuss results that are "approaching significance"). This terminology should raise a red flag to a reviewer that the author is attempting to enhance a paper with scant statistical and practical significance. As we have been taught from our first statistics class, the significance level is the probability of erroneously rejecting the null hypothesis based only upon sampling error. If sampling error were the only threat to our research conclusions, then most of us would live with a 5% error rate over a lifetime of research conclusions. Of course, sampling error is never the only threat to the conclusions of a study, and increasing the significance level serves only to further muddy the waters as to the true error rate for the research. We would argue that the reviewer should ignore any discussion of the "marginally significant" results and then determine if the manuscript still has value as a research study.

The "law of the hammer." The "law of the hammer" suggests that almost every object we find requires pounding as soon as we take ownership of a hammer. Likewise, it is common to find that new analytic techniques are adopted by authors because they are new and presumably "better" than the old techniques simply because they are more complex. Structural equation modeling (SEM) is a case in point. While this technique represents a great advance in the field of data analysis, it is not the solution to every analytical problem. Recalling the lesson of Occam's razor, if a simpler technique is sufficient to analyze the data, then the simpler technique should be employed in the interest of both accessibility for more readers and ease of presentation of results.

Simple techniques are not always sufficient, however. If a more sophisticated statistical technique is appropriate and will facilitate stronger conclusions for the study, then the reviewer should be willing to suggest both the technique and some published sources to assist the author in learning about it. It is something akin to cruel and unusual punishment for a reviewer to suggest that an author should employ, for example, negative binomial regression as an analytic tool, then leave the author to search desperately through the research methods literature in an attempt to find a good introductory source.

What was the question? The reviewer's primary concern in reading the sections of the manuscript on methods and analysis is to determine if the author has answered the questions that were set out in the introduction to the paper. In order to do this, alternative explanations for the observed results should be minimized. This requirement does not mean that the author cannot or should not speculate as to reasons why observed results were not as initially predicted (an indication that HARKing is unlikely to be a serious concern in the study). But alternative explanations might include such concerns as measurement error and same source bias, as discussed previously. If you, as a reviewer, are not convinced that the author of the manuscript has appropriately minimized alternative explanations for the results, it is important not just to indicate what the alternative explanations are, but how they might be countered.

In addition, the reviewer can assist an author by indicating how easy or difficult it is to determine if the author has addressed the questions posed in the introduction. If you, as a reviewer, find that you must return to the introduction in order to "match up" analyses with hypotheses, then it is almost certain that a less careful reader will become frustrated. It is a great boon to both the author and the potential audience for the paper if you can offer a structure that will simplify the "matching" of results to hypotheses. In one paper by the one of the authors (now in press), a table was created to summarize the propositions since there were a number of them (twelve).

Another problem that occurs more frequently than might be expected is the inclusion of additional analyses that were not discussed in the introduction. Sometimes these additional analyses represent appropriate elaboration of significant results of the study. But on occasion, an author will include additional analyses because they are "interesting." A common example is the inclusion of analyses of gender differences when none was initially hypothesized simply because significant differences emerge.

An author should not surprise the reviewer or reader of the manuscript with analyses that were not suggested in the introduction and method sections of the manuscript. If the author has not provided in advance a good rationale for looking at the analyses, then the results, even if they are statistically significant, will be difficult to interpret. It is wise to be alert to such insertions and make recommendations to the author with regard to their inclusion. Unfortunately, a suggestion that the author revise the introduction to the manuscript so as to include hypotheses regarding the analyses in question at this point in the manuscript development is something akin to HARKing, which, as we have said, is very serious, indeed.

It's not what you say, it's how you say it

Given that this chapter focuses on quantitative research, we thought it would be interesting to examine research on the effectiveness of the reviewing process. Such empirical research is scant, but Cummings and associates examined a sample of manuscript reviews completed while Cummings was the editor for the *Academy of Management Journal* (Cummings, Frost, & Vakil, 1985). Based on the reviewer style, reviewers were categorized as being primarily "coaches" or "critics." Coaches emphasized the developmental aspect of their role, reinforcing work well done and promoting improvement or follow-up work, in addition to providing reasons for recommendations to the editor. Critics emphasized the evaluative role, with comments that were almost exclusively critical sans constructive suggestions, and seemed relatively insensitive to the form and tone of their communication. Cooper and Burgoyne's idea of the reviewer as a critical friend, described in the previous chapter, would fall somewhere in the middle of these two. Despite the expectation that author behavior would differ based on reviewer style, the predicted differences were not found (Cummings et al., 1985). The conclusions of this study merit further study, but we will note that they are *not* consistent with our personal observations in the editorial role and as recipients of such reviews. We emphasize in this chapter the coaching aspects of the reviewer role.

Ethical Concerns

There are two ethical issues that are specific to evaluating quantitative manuscripts – data retention and sharing and multiple publications from a single data set. We limit our consideration of ethical issues to these two concerns, recognizing that a more extensive discussion of the ethics of reviewing is offered in chapter 5 of this volume.

Data retention and sharing. Both the American Psychological Association (the APA) and the Academy of Management codes of ethics require retention of data used to support analyses in published papers. The APA specifies retention for a period of five years after publication and explicitly states that the author is obligated to share those data for verification purposes (APA, 2001), whereas the Academy of Management code of ethics is silent with respect to these issues (Academy of Management, 2003). Further, the APA's position is that shared data may only be used for verification purposes, and any other usage is a violation of ethical principles. If, on reading the Method section of a manuscript, you find that the description is the same or similar to that of a published article, you should be alert to the possibility that the author has violated the constraint imposed or that the author is deriving multiple publications from the data set (discussed next). The appropriate response is to enlist the aid of the journal editor in determining whether an ethical violation has occurred.

Multiple publications from a single data set. As any researcher knows, data collection is very labor intensive, so every author hopes to squeeze as much value as possible from the data collected. Publication of data that have previously been published is proscribed by both the Academy of Management, the APA, and journal editors, unless the publications are directed at identifiably different audiences through different types of outlets. We have recently become aware of a case where authors submitted a paper that included analyses of both previously published data and original data. The notification came to the editor from a perceptive reviewer and resulted in a rejection of the manuscript with a suggestion that the manuscript could be revised to include only data not previously published. A good reviewer can save the journal editor some embarrassment by pointing out multiple publications based on the same data set, and allowing the editor to determine if the level of overlap is unacceptable.

Conclusion

Reviewing quantitative manuscripts is a demanding task and requires a strong grounding in research methods and quantitative analysis. Good methodology allows the author to rule out alternative explanations for results, and you must be able to determine when such alternative explanations are possible or even likely as a result of flawed methodology.

A good reviewer of quantitative manuscripts must also consider issues beyond research methods and analysis. You must be able to determine if the manuscript makes a valuable contribution to substantive knowledge and also engages the reader early on so that the reader is willing to discover the manuscript's value. You must be able to assist authors in stating hypotheses, as well as testing them appropriately. We have emphasized in this chapter the developmental aspects of reviewing, and we hope that you are willing to use your skills to help your colleagues become better at the research and publication processes.

References

Academy of Management (2003). Code of ethical conduct. http://myaom. pace.edu/octane8admin/websites/ProfessionalDevelopment.

American Psychological Association (2001). *Publication manual of the American Psychological Association (5th ed.)*. Washington, D.C.: American Psychological Association.

Ash, R. A. & Edgell, S. L. (1975). A note on the readability of the Position Analysis Questionnaire (PAQ). *Journal of Applied Psychology, 60*, 765–6.

Austin, J. T., Boyle, K. A., & Lualhati, J. C. (1998). Statistical conclusion validity for organizational science researchers: A review. *Organizational Research Methods, 1*, 164–208.

Baruch, Y. (1999). Response rate in academic studies: A comparative analysis. *Human Relations, 52*, 421–38.

Berkowitz, L. & Donnerstein, E. (1982). External validity is more than skin deep. *American Psychologist, 37*, 245–57.

Bluedorn, A. (2002). *The human organization of time: Temporal realities and experience*. Stanford, CA: Stanford Business Books.

Brogden, H. E. & Taylor, E. K. (1950). The theory and classification of criterion bias. *Educational & Psychological Measurement, 10*, 159–86.

Campbell, D. T. (1996). Unresolved issues in measurement validity: An autobiographical overview. *Psychological Assessment, 8*, 363–8.

Campbell, D. T. & Fiske, D. W. (1959). Convergent and discriminant validation by the multitrait-multimethod matrix. *Psychological Bulletin, 56*, 81–105.

Campion, M. A. (1993). Article review checklist: A criterion checklist for reviewing research articles in applied psychology. *Personnel Psychology, 46*, 705–18.

Conway, J. M. (2002). Method variance and method bias in industrial and organizational psychology. In S. G. Rogelberg (ed.), *Handbook of research methods in industrial organizational psychology*, 344–65. Malden, MA: Blackwell Publishers.

Crampton, S. M. & Wagner, J. A. (1994). Percept-percept inflation in microorganizational research: An investigation of prevalence and effect. *Journal of Applied Psychology, 79*, 67–76.

Cummings, L. L., Frost, P. J. & Vakil, T. G. (1985). The manuscript review process: A view from the inside on coaches, critics, and special cases. In L. L. Cummings & P. J. Frost (eds) *Publishing in the organizational sciences*, 469–508. Homewood, IL: Irwin.

Cycyota, C. S. & Harrison, D. A. (2002). Enhancing survey response rates at the executive level: Are employee- or consumer-level techniques effective? *Journal of Management, 28*, 151–76.

Davis, D. & Casenza, R. M. (1993). *Business research for decision making*. Belmont, CA: Wadsworth.

Donaldson, S. I. & Grant-Vallone, E. J. (2002). Understanding self-report bias in organizational behavior research. *Journal of Business & Psychology, 17*, 245–60.

Finch, S., Cumming, G., & Thomason, N. (2001). Reporting of statistical inference in the Journal of Applied Psychology: Little evidence of reform. *Educational & Psychological Measurement, 61*, 181–210.

Gordon, M. E., Slade, L. A., & Schmitt, N. (1986). The "science of the sophomore" revisited: From conjecture to empiricism. *Academy of Management Review, 11*, 191–207.

Graen, G. B., Wakabayashi, M., Graen, M. R., & Graen, M. G. (1990). International generalizability of American hypotheses about Japanese management progress: A strong inference investigation. *The Leadership Quarterly, 1,* 1–24.

Greenberg, J. (1987a). The college sophomore as guinea pig: Setting the record straight. *Academy of Management Review, 12,* 157–9.

Greenberg, J. (1987b). Real people + real situations = real research: Really? *Contemporary Social Psychology, 12,* 47–51.

Greenberg, J. & Tomlinson, E. C. (2004). Situated experiments in organizations: Transplanting the lab to the field. *Journal of Management, 30,* 703–24.

Gupta, N., Shaw, J. D., & Delery, J. E. (2000). Correlates of response outcomes among organizational key informants. *Organizational Research Methods, 3,* 323–47.

Hunt, J. G. (1991). *Leadership: A new synthesis.* Newbury Park, CA: Sage.

Hunt, J. G., Boal, K. B., & Dodge, G. E. (1999). The effects of visionary and crisis-responsive charisma on followers: An experimental examination of two kinds of charismatic leadership. *The Leadership Quarterly, 10,* 423–48.

Kerr, N. L. (1998). HARKing: Hypothesizing after the results are known. *Personality and Social Psychology Review, 2,* 196–217.

Korman, A. K. (1974). Contingency approaches to leadership: An overview. In J. G. Hunt & L. L. Larson (eds), *Contingency approaches to leadership,* 188–95. Carbondale, IL: Southern Illinois University Press.

Larson, L. L., Hunt, J. G., & Osborn, R. N. (1976). The great hi-hi leader behavior myth: A lesson from Occam's razor. *Academy of Management Journal, 19,* 628–41.

Mook, D. G. (1983). In defense of external invalidity. *American Psychologist, 38,* 379–87.

Nunnally, J. C. & Bernstein, I. H. (1994). *Psychometric methods (3rd ed.).* New York: McGraw-Hill.

Platt, J. R. (1964, October 16). Strong inference. *Science, 146,* 347–53.

Podsakoff, P. M., MacKenzie, S. B., Lee, J. Y., & Podsakoff, N. (2003). Common method biases in behavioral research: A critical review of the literature and recommended remedies. *Journal of Applied Psychology, 88,* 879–903.

Rizzo, J. R., House, R. J., & Lirtzman, S. I. (1970). Role conflict and ambiguity in complex organizations. *Administrative Science Quarterly, 15,* 150–63.

Roth, P. L. & BeVier, C. A. (1998). Response rates in HRM/OB survey research: Norms and correlates, 1990–1994. *Journal of Management, 24,* 97–117.

Rynes, S. L. (2005, April 22). *Academy of Management Journal: Guidelines for reviewers.* Retrieved from http://aom.pace.edu/amjnew/reviewer_guidelines.html.

Schmitt, N. (1994). Method bias: The importance of theory and measurement. *Journal of Organizational Behavior, 15,* 393–8.

Schriesheim, C. A. & Kerr, S. (1977). R.I.P. LPC: A response to Fiedler. In J. G. Hunt & L. L. Larson (eds) *Leadership: The cutting edge,* 51–6. Carbondale: Southern Illinois University Press.

Spector, P. E. (1987). Method variance as an artifact in self-reported affect and perceptions at work: Myth or significant problem? *Journal of Applied Psychology, 72,* 438–43.

Spector, P. E. (1994). Using self-report questionnaires in OB research: A comment on the use of a controversial method. *Journal of Organizational Behavior, 15,* 385–92.

Tracy, L. & Johnson, T. W. (1983). Measurement of role stress: Dimensionality of scale items. *Social Behavior and Personality, 11,* 1–7.

Williams, L. J. & Brown, B. K. (1994). Method variance in organizational behavior and human resources research: Effects on correlations, path coefficients, and hypothesis testing. *Organizational Behavior & Human Decision Processes, 57,* 185–209.

Zelditch, M., Jr. (1969). Can you really study an army in the laboratory? In A. Etzioni (ed.) *A sociological reader on complex organizations,* 529–39. New York: Holt, Rinehart & Winston.

10
Reviewing for Scholarly Practitioner Journals

Sheila M. Puffer, James Campbell Quick and Daniel J. McCarthy

Introduction

This chapter is intended for those who review papers for scholarly practitioner journals, which have different audiences, objectives, formats, and writing styles from those of academic as well as strictly practitioner journals. The first section focuses on the ways in which these journals differ from others. As a complement to what Oliver (chapter 6) lists as the characteristics of high-quality reviewers, characteristics of effective reviewers of this type of journal are covered in the second section. The subsequent section covers the crucial topic of communications in the review process, especially reviewers' communications with associate editors and editors. Included is a discussion of the relationship between reviewers and the editorial team covering such topics as developing working relationships and assisting the editorial team in publication decisions. Feldman's chapter (14) is devoted entirely to providing both reviewers and authors with strategies for communicating effectively with editors. The next section covers the review process itself and develops suggested steps that reviewers might follow when reviewing for scholarly practitioner journals. This section is followed by one that further elaborates on the importance of communications, focusing on communicating results and decisions to authors. The final substantive section examines getting closure and is a summary section that considers the review cycle from submission to editorial decision, including rejections, invitations to revise and resubmit, and acceptances. While Priem and Rasheed discussed the wide-ranging rewards of reviewing, this chapter concludes with a discussion of the rewards that reviewers can realize from their contributions to reviewing for scholarly practitioner journals.

Scholarly practitioner journals are different

Scholarly practitioner journals are different from scholarly academic journals as well as purely practitioner journals since the three have different audiences, objectives, formats, and writing styles.

Scholarly practitioner journals are targeted at practicing managers, as well as academics who teach, consult, and otherwise work with managers and aspiring managers, particularly business school students. These journals have the objective of advancing the practice of management by serving as a bridge between theory and practice. For instance, articles might be based on established theories of leadership and draw implications for managers from those theories. Additionally, articles might be based on findings and conclusions from empirical studies of topics like the influence of organizational culture on leadership effectiveness, again providing implications for improving leadership effectiveness. By providing such bridges between theory and practice, articles are often prescriptive rather than purely descriptive or analytical.

Regarding format and writing style, scholarly practitioner journals typically attempt to operationalize theory by providing lessons, guidelines, or recommendations to managers. In doing so, they seek to answer the "so what"? and "how to"? questions to help managers implement research-based practices in their organizations. Articles are written in a manager-friendly style with many examples and caselets to illustrate concepts and help make the material accessible and relevant to practitioners.

An illustration of a scholarly practitioner journal is *The Academy of Management Executive*, a journal with which the three authors of this chapter have had extensive experience. The first author served a three-year term as editor from 1999 to 2001, having been an associate editor from 1995 to 1999 and an editorial board member from 1992 to 1997. The second author was an associate editor from 1998 to 2001 and served on the editorial board from 1990 to 2004. The third author was a member of the editorial board from 1999 to 2005. Additionally, all three authors have published frequently in *The Executive*. Other leading scholarly practitioner journals in the management field include *California Management Review*, *Sloan Management Review*, *Organizational Dynamics*, *European Management Journal*, *Long Range Planning*, and *Thunderbird Journal of International Business*. The material in this chapter dealing with scholarly practitioner journals applies to these journals as well as others of this type.

As noted earlier, some practitioner journals, because of their audiences, objectives, format, and writing style are not considered scholarly practitioner journals. Probably the best known example of such a practitioner journal, one that focuses primarily on the practical aspects of management, is *Harvard Business Review*. It and other such journals have as their primary objective helping managers understand more about the current challenges of their jobs. Most articles do not usually rely on theory or extensive empirical evidence, but provide tools and ideas that can be implemented right away to help managers improve their performance and that of their companies. In addition to articles by academics, these tools and ideas often come from consultants and executives with substantial practical experience in best company practices or new practices and techniques that have been successfully utilized in various settings. While these experiences are based in practice, often in numerous organizations, they do not usually reflect or rely on rigorous research methodologies or accepted theories. They are not usually developed or presented in the structured fashion of a scholarly practitioner journal.

Scholarly academic journals again differ from scholarly practitioner journals and other practitioner journals in their target audience, objectives, format, and writing style. Examples of leading scholarly academic journals are the *Academy of Management Review*, the *Academy of Management Journal*, *Administrative Science Quarterly*, *Organization Science*, *Strategic Management Journal*, and the *Journal of Management*. Their audience consists of research-oriented scholars, thus these journals focus on theory development and/or empirical research. Implications for managerial practice, if offered, are presented in ways that cannot be immediately implemented, but the research results might affect practice over time. Scholarly academic journals follow prescribed formats used in social science research for conceptual or theoretical contributions and empirical results. The writing style is tight and controlled, with careful use of hypotheses and specialized terms. Generalizations that go beyond the data or beyond the bounds of a theory being developed are avoided.

Characteristics of effective reviewers

The most important characteristics of reviewers for scholarly practitioner journals are the willingness and ability to carry out that role effectively. Many reviewers perform this service for the different types of journals described earlier, and they need to keep the type of journal in mind, in this case, scholarly practitioner journals. Good reviewers for scholarly practitioner journals have backgrounds in both theory and practice, or at least clearly understand the relationship between the two. They also have a good understanding of the journal's guidelines for authors as well as those for reviewers. Reviewers should also be objective and refrain from showing bias and personal preferences. For instance, if reviewers personally don't subscribe to a particular theory or line of research and feel they cannot be objective, it might be best to respectfully decline to review. See chapter 3 for more information on these and other types of biases.

Reviewers should also try to put themselves in the shoes of the authors by being positive and developmental while still providing a rigorous critique. There is never a reason to hurt. Some authors are new to the field, do not have English as their first language, have been trained in other styles or paradigms, or educated at institutions outside North America. Some academically trained authors might have difficulty making linkages to practice that provide insights for executives, while practitioner authors might be unfamiliar with academic theories and research in which to ground their papers. Reviewers should be prepared to help both types of authors bridge the gap in their knowledge and experience if their manuscript has potential for publication.

Reviewers should also be prepared for changes in editorial policy that could affect the nature of the review. For instance, a scholarly practitioner journal might become more scholarly or more practitioner-oriented. The *Journal of World Business*, for example, appears to have become more scholarly in content and format since the early 2000s. Such redirections may occur with changes in editorship, sponsoring organization, or publisher.

Reviewing for a special issue rather than a regular issue can also affect reviews. Reviewers might want to ask the editor or associate editor whether the review cycle and timing of publication are expected to be longer, shorter, or similar to the regular cycle. Special issues of scholarly practitioner journals might have shorter cycle times than regular issues if the topic is very timely or time sensitive. For instance, in 2005, outsourcing was a hot topic, was highly controversial and timely, and was of high interest to practitioners seeking guidance from research-based theories and data.

Reviewers should also tailor their reviews to the fit between the quality of submissions and the quality of the journal. A large number of scholarly practitioner business journals exist, particularly in various areas of general management and human resources. One clear quality measure of a journal is the acceptance rate, which is often available in such publications as *Cabell's Directory*, in the journals themselves, or in articles and reports comparing acceptance rates across journals. Other measures include journal rankings such as those published annually by the *Financial Times* and *BusinessWeek*, which include selected scholarly practitioner journals, as well as scholarly academic journals. Given the wide range in quality of scholarly practitioner journals, recommendations regarding manuscript publishability, as well as the rigor and detail of reviews, should be guided by the quality of the journal.

The reviewer – associate editor – editor relationship

To perform well as a reviewer for scholarly practitioner journals, at least two things are important to keep in mind. First is a good understanding of the relationship you as a reviewer have with the associate editor and editor. Much reviewer contact occurs with the associate editor rather than the editor, so it is important to determine who your primary contact is as well as his or her expectations of you. The reviewer's role may vary, depending on the journal, including expert advisor to the associate editor and editor, mentor for authors, and judge and jury over manuscripts. Dipboye (chapter 1) explores in great detail the various roles reviewers can play in the generation of knowledge. An essential aspect of this role clarification process is to understand the workload you are taking on. How many manuscripts are you expected to review in what period of time? Can you devote the required time to do a good job?

Second is a clear conceptual understanding of the theory and research linkages to practice. The editor and associate editor(s) should help you with this conceptualization. As a reviewer, you must have an eye and ear for the audience of peers as well as the practicing manager and executive, as noted earlier. If scholarly practitioner journals fail to connect with managers and executives, they ultimately fail in their mission. However, you as a reviewer are a guardian of the theoretical and research underpinnings of the best information aimed at practice. So, you should review information about the specific scholarly practitioner journal. Some things to develop information about are the number of manuscripts the journal receives annually, the targeted and actual acceptance rates, the names and affiliations of other reviewers and associate editors for the journal (especially important in the case of new journals), and you may want to query your home institution as to whether this is an opportunity which the institution considers of value. In addition, give consideration to the number of editorial boards on which you serve. You honor your home institution as well as yourself through board service, yet if you are a member of too many boards, the quality of your reviews is likely to decline, doing a disservice to all parties.

Being an ad hoc reviewer is another way of participating in the review process, usually without the workload of a board member. Your industry-specific and/or company-specific experience can be especially valuable in helping authors and/or editors or associate editors develop manuscripts that make sound connections to the practitioner community from the academic side of the bridge. While lending your applied expertise as an ad hoc reviewer is a great asset for editors and associate editors, make sure they do not overwork you. All of the authors of this chapter have experienced this situation. To resolve it, we have asked the editors to either reduce the number of manuscripts sent or make an editorial review board appointment.

Associate editors and editors want to know the scope of each reviewer's expertise, so in the case of scholarly practitioner journals, share both your academic expertise and your professional experience in the private sector, public sector, and/or military organizations. You may not be aware of and probably do not need to try and catalogue all of your potential biases for the associate editor and editor. However, each of us does have biases, informed opinions, and judgments about a range of subjects for which we may review. When you get a specific manuscript, you should probably ask yourself if you are sufficiently knowledgeable and adequately objective to provide a professional, high quality review. Be especially alert to conflicts of interests and/or prejudices related to specific companies, industries, and/or occupational categories when it comes to scholarly practitioner journals. Balance and fair treatment is a hallmark of good practice as well as good scholarship; infomercials and corporate bashing are two inappropriate extremes. If you have particular biases or caveats that could bear upon the manuscript, it is very acceptable to state these openly to either author, editor, or both as appropriate. Alternatively, if your biases are such that you cannot render a constructive review, it may be best to return the manuscript promptly. Each of us has done so, for various reasons, on occasion.

As you accept manuscripts to review, be sure to respond to the associate editor's and/or editor's particular criteria with your quantitative rankings on the sheets they provide. If you cannot respond to a specific criterion or two, state so and indicate your rationale if that's appropriate. As the editor develops experience with you based on a track record of your reviews, s/he is likely to know you as a "tough" reviewer, a "soft" reviewer, an "inconsistent" reviewer, and the like.

In addition, state any dilemmas, caveats, recommendations, judgments, concerns, or questions to the editor in an explicit and complete way. Managers respect experience, so use yours effectively. Editors must rely on the best information they can get to make good decisions. If the editor receives more and higher quality information, it is more likely that the editor will be able to make a high-quality decision. While receiving conflicting information from reviewers may pose a dilemma for the editor, you should not withhold your professional judgment for that reason. The editor always can ask for help if needed. For example, one of us served as one of three reviewers on a very controversial manuscript and was the minority voice in advocating publication. The editor presented all three reviews to a consulting editor for another opinion. The consulting editor affirmed the minority review because of its thoroughness and soundly reasoned confidential comments to the editor. The manuscript was published.

You must display integrity in your confidential and "off-line" comments to the editor. Specifically, do not communicate glowing comments to the authors while you give the editor scathing remarks. This demonstrates not only your duplicity but it also presents the editor with a dilemma as to what and how to communicate his or her decision to the author. While all editors should reserve the right to override reviewer input for any number of reasons, they need a basis and rationale that makes sense to an author. If there is an inconsistency between the reviewer's comments and the editor's decision, let it be because of additional factors considered by the editor, not because you as a reviewer told the editor one thing and the author something quite different.

Suggested steps in reviewing a paper

The review process for scholarly practitioner journals involves numerous people and many steps. The steps in this section should be especially helpful to relatively newer reviewers, but seasoned reviewers might also gain insights to further hone their reviewing skills.

To review or not review?

The first step for reviewers is to decide whether they feel qualified and are willing to undertake a review. This point is raised in each chapter of this section because the requisite skills for one to feel qualified vary slightly for each type of manuscript. It is usually not necessary for a reviewer to be an expert in the subject matter. However, reviewers need to be well versed in and confident enough of their knowledge of the topic to provide a thorough review. If not familiar enough with the subject matter, theory, or methodology, reviewers should be willing to respectfully decline, and in a timely fashion. However, reviews can still be valuable if reviewers have knowledge of some aspects of the paper. For instance, one might know the subject matter well but be unfamiliar with the methodology, or vice versa. In such cases, reviewers should clearly state in the review the areas in which they are providing expertise as well as the areas or points of view about which they do not feel they can provide fully informed feedback. Most importantly, reviewers for scholarly practitioner journals should be confident in their ability to communicate with practitioners and see the possibilities of linkages between theory and practice.

Make an initial assessment

Having accepted a reviewing assignment, an early step is to read over the paper and arrive at a tentative conclusion about its suitability and value for the journal, as well as the overall quality of the potential contribution. If the paper seems to be relatively weak and/or unsuitable for the journal, the review will likely focus on those aspects rather than providing more exhaustive detail about the full content of the article. For instance, if the paper appears to be a "rotten egg," written initially for a scholarly academic journal and resubmitted to a scholarly practitioner journal without revision, it would fall in the unsuitable category.

If the paper appears to be a good fit, with the potential to make a meaningful contribution to the field, the essence of the review will likely cover in some detail the paper's strengths, along with substantive comments, criticisms, help, and recommendations for improvement. Even at this early stage, before conducting a thorough review, reviewers form an overall opinion of the work. A positive opinion would likely emerge when the manuscript is clearly based on theory, and developed and applied to the interests and needs of executives.

Still, the more strongly the reviewer feels that he or she will eventually recommend it for acceptance, the more detailed and specific the review is likely to be. But even probable rejections deserve a thorough reading in which reviewers provide some help for the authors to develop the paper. One form of help, for instance, is recommending other outlets that might be more appropriate for the paper, almost certainly after revision. Under all circumstances, reviewers should stay positive in their comments, recalling that reviews are for developmental purposes and should never be hurtful. This is especially the case when reviewing for scholarly practitioner journals, since many manuscripts will have been authored by individuals or teams unfamiliar with how to link theory and practice.

Assess the title and executive overview

Consider whether the title and executive overview are clear and true to the paper, and whether they will capture the attention and interest of practitioners. Assess how well they convey the objectives, content, and conclusions. For a scholarly practitioner journal, the title should not be overly academic or stilted. For instance, in place of "Contrasting types of enterprises in the privatized Russian economy," you might suggest something like "Diamonds and Rust on Russia's Road to Privatization," the title of an article published in 1995 in the *Columbia Journal of World Business* (renamed the *Journal of World Business*) by two of the authors of this chapter. Additionally, reviewers should consider whether the paper lived up to the title, and if not, recommend a new title that better reflects the content and orientation of the paper. The same caveats generally apply to the executive overview. Reviewers should determine, for example, whether it is too long or too short given the content of the paper. The executive overview should clearly and succinctly introduce the reader to the most important aspects of the paper, including its objectives and, if appropriate, whether the paper presents results or recommendations. In the spirit of a scholarly practitioner journal, the content of the executive overview should emphasize the value of the article to practitioners, but also include something about the theory upon which the article is based.

Keep an open mind

At this point, reviewers must be mindful of the need for reviewer objectivity. A paper should be reviewed on its own merits and not in light of reviewers' personal biases or preferences. Since a thorough review has not yet been done, reviewers must consider thoughtfully the reasons they arrived at a tentative opinion. They should make notes to themselves detailing those reasons and convince themselves that they do not represent personal biases. One test is to ask oneself whether these reasons would convince others in the field and/or the associate editor managing the manuscript. For instance, one might have a bias against articles framed around too many or too few case studies, but reviewers should keep in mind that executives like cases that illustrate real-life situations they can relate to. Another bias might be for or against the way in which statistical results are reported. Or, one might not personally care for the author's approach to a discipline, such as a microeconomic approach to strategic management. In all cases, responsible reviewers will separate themselves from such biases and consider whether the paper in total can make a contribution to the field, perhaps in a controversial way. Guidelines for an open mind include the mission of the journal, suggestions for authors and reviewers, and particularly a focus on the needs of executive readers who are the target audience.

Check for the theory-practice link

Closely related to the subject of personal bias is forgetting that one is reviewing for a scholarly practitioner journal, and not a scholarly academic journal, since many reviewers serve both types of journals. So from the initial reading of the paper, reviewers should gauge how well the authors build the relationship between theory and practice, and how clearly they convey that relationship to the reader. This is the appropriate reviewer insight, rather than looking negatively at a paper that does not conform to the style of a scholarly academic journal. It is important early in a review to ascertain whether the paper contains clear implications for managerial practice, but also builds on theory. These implications should be clear for practitioners and might be summarized as recommendations for action or lessons learned. This liaison is in fact the heart of scholarly practitioner journals. So dig deeply into the paper to see how well this linkage is developed. Typically, papers draw upon existing theory rather than develop new theories. The paper should clearly explain the theoretical basis it is grounded in and provide key references, including classic works as well as current ones. Even if the paper does not clarify its theoretical foundations, but is otherwise a promising contribution, reviewers can pose questions and offer suggestions for authors to strengthen the theoretical underpinnings of the piece.

Would it capture practitioners' attention?

Practitioner journals, including scholarly ones, are intended to communicate with managers and influence their attitudes and behaviors. Essential to these outcomes is that papers must not only be useful, but also capture readers' interest. In contrast, scholarly academic journals carefully describe the research objectives, theory, methodology, results, and limitations in a prescribed format. For scholarly practitioner journals, the executive summary can be used not only to summarize the paper's content, but also to capture readers' attention. Early on in the paper and elsewhere, vignettes or caselets are useful for illustrating major points in a way that practitioners find relevant. Examples of best practices and worst practices, or learning from failures, can also be compelling. Exhibits can also generate interest since they summarize information in a graphic format, and can be organized around recommendations or lessons. They can also contain comparisons of such things as company experiences, managerial practices, country differences, or executive characteristics. Graphics using arrows and various geometric shapes showing relationships among important components also provide useful visualization of the material. All these ways of presenting information add interest for managers and executives, and when building upon or applying theory, such illustrations can help busy practitioners more easily grasp the messages of the article. Where possible, graphics should focus on actionable knowledge or processes for practitioners who, in addition to potentially applying them, can use them when explaining ideas to members of their organizations and other practitioners.

In contrast to these attributes of interesting papers, others will contain exhibits that are unwieldy, overly complex, or virtually undecipherable. Although exhibits containing some scholarly material or results, such as basic descriptive statistics, can be appropriate, scholarly practitioner journals are not the outlet for reporting results using sophisticated methodologies and analytical techniques. Such approaches do not mean that a paper is unsuitable. Again, if the paper shows promise otherwise, reviewers should recommend that such material be deleted or offer solutions to recast it in a more practitioner-friendly format.

Are the writing style and format appropriate for the journal?

The audience for most scholarly practitioner journals, as noted above, consists of practitioners as well as academics and students. The papers that reviewers will work with, then, should be written in a style that is reader friendly for practitioners, while including terminology and ideas from the academic literature as appropriate. Many authors, however, have been trained to write primarily in a scholarly academic publication style, which is not appropriate for the type of journal discussed here. For instance, hypotheses should not be overused in scholarly practitioner journal articles, and when used, should be oriented to executives' understanding of implications for action in their own world. Reviewers of scholarly practitioner journals, then, can be very helpful by providing suggestions to make the writing style and format more appropriate for the journal's readers.

It is certainly fitting for authors to refer to academic theories, such as resource-based theory in strategy or expectancy theory of motivation. However, when doing so, excessive use of highly technical or esoteric terms or academic jargon, such as "operationalization" or "received theory," should be avoided. Also look for and encourage wording that is action oriented, and written in the active voice rather than the passive voice. For example, "Managers reported an overload of information," is preferred over "An overload of information was reported by managers."

Writing style extends into the references and footnotes or endnotes. They too should be in the journal's format, and journals vary widely on that dimension. For instance, one scholarly practitioner journal, *Organizational Dynamics*, requires a selected bibliography, which is presented in paragraph form annotating key reference works and their general thrust or conclusions as they relate to the paper. In contrast, *The Academy of Management Executive* requires endnotes containing references to support assertions made in the paper. In addition to noting deviations from the journal's required format, reviewers should not hesitate to recommend additional references that would strengthen the paper.

Is the paper well-structured?

Beyond the wording and sentence structure, determine whether the paper is well-crafted. Does the paper flow smoothly and logically from the objectives to the development and support of the major messages to conclusions and recommendations? If the paper develops a framework or model, be sure that each component is covered in a logically sequential manner, rather than being subsumed in sections that have little relevance to the model. Conversely, if the paper does not include a model, but your reading of the paper tells you there is one inherent in the work, you should explain the possibilities to the author. And wherever possible, frameworks should be oriented to the executive world, and contain activities, or at least thought processes or policy steps that can apply to them.

Another aspect of structure deals with the organization of sections. Are there enough, too few, or too many sections and subsections throughout the paper? Are important areas given the proper attention by having their own sections and strong introductory sentences or paragraphs to highlight their importance to practitioners? Are headings true to the content of the section, and do they carry the reader from one section to another in a smooth fashion? It is also helpful if the headings catch readers' interest, rather than being simply "introduction," "conclusion," and the like. As noted earlier, executives appreciate illustrations, concepts, and examples that these can provide suggestions for interesting section titles.

With that said, good papers still need an ending, which might be a summary or conclusion, but often with a different title like "View from the Top," or "Insights for Executives." Also, papers for practitioner journals, including scholarly ones, have more impact if they provide recommendations or lessons to be learned. Practitioners value works containing guidelines for action, and many articles are amenable to this approach. If you believe a paper has potential for such an ending, be sure to recommend it in your review.

Completing the review

The last step as a reviewer is to complete the evaluation form provided by the editors. This typically consists of assigning numerical ratings to a number of criteria, such as the appropriateness of the article for the journal, the clarity of the writing, and the degree to which the paper is grounded in relevant theory. Also included is an overall recommendation ranging from "accept without revision" to "reject." This information is crucial for the associate editor and editor to factor into their editorial decision. Even more important is your response to the authors, which includes the detailed rationale for your overall recommendation. A major aspect of this should be how well the paper has lived up to the message contained in the preceding steps. In essence, these steps focus on the appropriateness of the theory base of the article, but even more importantly, on how well the theory is linked to the various aspects noted as being important to practitioners. All the information in your review will allow the editor and associate editor to make a reasoned decision about publication and provide the author with valuable feedback.

Getting closure

After completing the substantive aspects of the review process, the reviewer needs to take two, and sometimes three, steps to get closure.

The first two steps are the reviewer's communication with the author and with the editor. One of the authors of this chapter had a colleague who received a review in the early 1980s with the opening line: "This manuscript has absolutely no redeeming scholarly value." Not only had the reviewer engaged in unprofessional and unconstructive feedback to the author, but the reviewer came across as mean-spirited and demeaning. Reviewers can, and should, do better. In addition, managers and executives typically do not understand the way academicians talk to each other and it is not uncommon for a manager, executive, or other practitioner to be a co-author on a scholarly practitioner journal article. So, you are not just talking within the profession in such reviews, you are potentially communicating to those outside as well.

In his *Academy of Management Executive* article with Chaparral Steel Company's CEO Dr. Gordon Forward and others, Dennis Beach talked about the importance of managing people by "adultery;" that is, treating people like adults and expecting them to act like adults (1991, p. 43). That principle of "adult" respect for all people applies to authors, reviewers, and editors alike. As a reviewer, remember to respect the process and the people you are engaged with, display dignity, and, under the right circumstances, show humor, as Dennis Beach did.

In addition, keep in mind that the focus needs to be on the manuscript, not on the person, so refrain from personalizing your feedback to either the author or the editor. In another example, one of us experienced as a young author, during the third revision and review of his manuscript, one of the three reviewers becoming exasperated at not getting his or her way. That reviewer inserted in his/her communication to the authors a snide comment: "Well, at least this manuscript is better than a number the editor is publishing." This is disrespectful to the editor and serves no value to the author. What is the author to do?

Therefore, as you get closure on the review, remember to be authoritative without arrogance and be humble without subservience. From Aristotle's virtues perspective, seek excellence in both the content and the communication process of your review. Play your part well and mind your lines, literally.

Communicating reviewer comments to authors

A useful way to begin your communication with the author is to show that you understand what the author is attempting to accomplish. By providing a broad summary of what you saw in the paper, you are practicing a common reflective communication technique. This technique is to feed back to a speaker or an author a summary or paraphrase of what you understand to be the main thoughts, ideas, concepts, and arguments communicated in the original manuscript. This establishes your basic understanding of the author's ideas and lines of reasoning. If the author has failed to clearly or completely communicate what was intended, this short, opening paragraph in the review can quickly identify the "missed" communication between author and reader (in this case the reviewer). Keep in mind that not all authors are academic peers, as in the case above of Gordon Forward, who was a CEO at the time, and Dennis Beach, who was a vice-president of human resources. Whether your review is positive or negative, and whether you recommend acceptance or rejection, may not be as critical in scholarly practitioner journals as your contribution to building an effective dialogue with practitioners. You have the opportunity to construct a bridge from the academy to those who apply theory and research in their decisions.

From that point of departure in the written review, you may proceed in several ways to structure the review in a logical way. Two such alternatives are to follow the structure of the manuscript in your written review, or distinguish your major and minor review points. If you choose the second alternative, you should then follow up the opening summary with major comments on broad areas – key areas referring to the steps noted earlier in this chapter. Make sure you are specific and tie your comments to manuscript page numbers where possible and where appropriate.

In either case, we encourage reviewers to be thoughtfully critical. Critical feedback is tied to careful observation and understanding. As the father of scientific management and one of the first members of the management profession to effectively bridge the theory-practice gap, Frederick Taylor displayed excellence in critical observation. Use your own critical thinking skills to identify both strengths and limitations or weaknesses in the manuscript. In doing so, we encourage you to be consistent with your own intellectual integrity. Do not communicate false positives nor withhold honest criticism, and always work to achieve constructive comment. In order to avoid giving authors false hope, it is important to prepare what Sullivan et al called a realistic review in the last section of chapter 4. When identifying major weaknesses or areas for improvement, be specific, refer to ideas, and provide quotations and page numbers from the paper to guide the authors. Remember, your aim is to help authors improve or strengthen their papers.

We encourage you to draw on your own expertise and knowledge where appropriate, sharing with the author specific references, source materials, and perspectives which may enrich their own work. For scholarly practitioner journals, suggest concrete examples, specific illustrations, and companies, industries, or contexts. Some may come from purely practitioner journals, trade publications, or even news items. However, in your written review and communication, display your expertise, authority, and/or experience in an objective manner. Do not be overbearing with an attitude of "I am right and you are wrong." Nor do you need to be apologetic or overly tentative in your written review. Provide all your input for the author and editor to see. Once you have done that, trust the author to use your information, sources, and examples wisely, while trusting the editor to make a good, informed decision.

Reviewers offer help by providing references in their written reviews that support areas throughout the manuscript, particularly for the author's major themes, frameworks, and/or models. References that give theoretical depth to the manuscript may not be intended to go directly into the text so much as provide endnote or footnote materials for the thinking manager or leader as well as the academician or student who reads the scholarly practitioner journal. In this process, the reviewer should be sensitive to counterarguments or alternative perspectives which the author may not have considered or to which the author has not previously been exposed. "Have you considered?" is a powerful question for a reviewer to pose.

Throughout the written review, remember that you are not a decision-maker. Rather, as a reviewer you are an independent voice who is sharing expertise with authors and editors alike. The reviewer is an advisor to the editor, coach and counselor to the author, and an independent professional with their own perspective. Good editors may well find themselves educated by star reviewers, and these editors often acknowledge their appreciation of such reviewers in a variety of ways, such as offering them associate editor positions. So, while the written review is for the primary benefit of the author, the editor too is part of your audience.

We offer a final caveat for reviewers as they prepare their written communication to the author. Given the global context within which our profession now operates, we encourage reviewers to be sensitive to the wide variance in authors beyond scholarly versus practitioner. Authors range from non-native English speakers, newly-minted doctorates, seasoned professionals and/or scholars, and even renowned authors. It is important to distinguish substance from style or process. Non-native English-speakers may have an important message, and yet find difficulty in expressing it, so reviewers need to be helpful with language and style. One of us spent a year working with a German author to guide him in publishing an important message for English speakers with an interest in the practice of occupational health psychology. Similarly, for the academic author writing in a scholarly practitioner journal, the potential problem may be a style that is too academic or written in the passive voice. Help them convert to the active voice and to translate academic jargon or technical terms into clear prose.

The renowned author poses a different challenge, more so for the editor than the reviewer. Former journal editor Paul Gordon described an exchange with the world-famous management expert, Peter Drucker, which showed diplomacy, tact, humor, and an adherence to high standards. After receiving two very critical and unfavorable reviews of one of Peter's manuscripts, Paul wrote:

> Peter,
> Unfortunately we cannot publish your manuscript.
> You can do better.
> Paul

To his credit, Peter's response went something like:

> Paul,
> Thank you for saving me the embarrassment.
> Peter

Just because a person is a renowned author for scholarly practitioner journals does not mean everything s/he writes is appropriate to publish.

Communicating with editors

Your communication with editors, including associate editors, guest editors, or consulting editors, should be timely and appropriately confidential. All journal editors have difficult and challenging jobs, a key aspect of which is the requirement for managing a complex process in a timely manner because of the production deadlines to which they must be responsive. Therefore, one of the most helpful things you can do for the editor is to provide your review by the deadline requested.

Editors appreciate thoroughness in reviews and in communication with them because it helps them not only in their decisions but also in their letters to the author. The more thorough and complete you are in expressing your ideas, thoughts, opinions, and reasoned judgments, the more information or variance you are introducing into the review process. Increased variance from the editor's point of view adds information richness and detail, leading to a higher quality editorial decision in the long run. However, do not box an editor into a corner nor put him or her on the defensive with an author in an effort to manage the outcome of the review process. That is not your job.

The gist of our guidance to reviewers is to put all your substantive comments into the review, while being appropriately discriminating in your communication with editor and author. However, we strongly encourage reviewers to self-monitor their own emotions and biases in both these lines of communication. Considering the editors, some exercise a quality control function before a review gets to the author. So if the editor thinks you are out of line or questions whether you really want to communicate a word, phrase, or idea, that editor might discuss this with you before your words gets to the author. You don't have this second chance in your communication with the editor. Therefore, carefully proof your comments before you submit them to make sure you are not saying things you really do not want to say upon more careful reflection.

It takes time to develop a reputation as a first-rate reviewer who has serious influence in the peer-review process. To earn credibility in scholarly practitioner journals, you must also demonstrate a clear eye for application and practice. Theory and research alone are not sufficient. Over time, every reviewer develops a reputation of some sort. We believe you would want that reputation to be good, positive, and of high value. Errant reviewer communication with an editor may cause you to lose quickly what has taken years to develop.

A final consideration in your relationship with the editor is to see how the editor views his or her role. Some editors are deeply involved in the review process, contributing their own reviews in addition to those of associate editors and reviewers. Other editors function more as managers, insuring a healthy and positive set of exchanges between authors and reviewers without adding their own opinions. Therefore, you might to give thought to, and even ask questions about, the degree of editor involvement in the review process. This could affect the degree to which your review is presented to authors in its totality or in the context of the editor's views.

The review cycle

Your role as reviewer may end when you communicate with the author and editor, and it is customary for an editor to provide reviewers with feedback about the communication to the author. Alternatively, it may not end then if the editor requests that the author prepare a revision of the manuscript for resubmission. Thus, the review cycle may include one, two, three, or even more iterations before a final decision is made. The most likely weakness will be that there is insufficient theory for a scholarly practitioner journal, or that there is no clear linkage to practice. Either weakness is reparable if the second element is strong and well done.

The final decision most often takes one of two forms, either accept or reject. On rare occasion, an editor may suggest that the original manuscript be redirected to an alternate journal or other publication outlet. However, at the end of the first review, the typical communication from good-quality journals is rejection of the manuscript. A very small percentage of manuscripts are accepted for publication at the end of the first review. The third and most common category is revise-and-resubmit. Some journals even include a "high-risk" version of the revise-and-resubmit category, signaling to the author that the probability of success appears low. The reviewer should at this point attempt to understand the essence of the revise-and-resubmit decision and provide detailed guidance to the author. For instance, your role may be to help explain to the author how better to utilize the theory in more depth, including providing references, or to explain and provide examples of how the theory has influenced or could influence practice in organizations.

If the editor decided upon a revise-and-resubmit for one of the manuscripts which you have reviewed, your work is not done. The editor may, on occasion, request a revise-and-resubmit that is not seen by the reviewers but rather provides the editor with the additional information s/he needs to make a final decision on the manuscript. A review cycle with more than two revise-and-resubmit iterations is uncommon but can occur. As a reviewer, your role may vary after the first review. The editor may guide the reviewers in their roles after the first review, requesting specific input to aid him or her toward a final decision.

In the absence of specific guidance from the editor, we recommend reviewers use a three-step process once they receive a revised manuscript. Step one is to review the editor's letter inviting the revision from the author. Step two is to review the author's response to the first set of reviewer, and editor, comments on the original manuscript. Implicit in this second step is ensuring that you understand the reviewers' critique of the original manuscript. Step three is to read the revised manuscript and prepare a new set of comments for the author and the editor. A reviewer's focus at this point should be upon the linkage between theory and practice, and whether this has been accomplished effectively, since this is the central mission of scholarly practitioner journals.

A successful review process, and ultimately the journal's success, depends upon giving great care to the communications involved among reviewers and editors, and of course to authors. In addition to the mutual respect needed among all parties, effective communication enhances the reputations of all involved in the process. Reviewing is one of the major professional services one can render to colleagues who are committed to advancing scholarship through publication of their creative work. And reviewing for scholarly practitioner journals carries unique responsibilities and opportunities to develop manuscripts, contribute to the experience of authors, and make a difference in the operational decisions and practice of executives.

Rewards for reviewers

Although material rewards are seldom offered for reviewing, there are nonetheless numerous sources of satisfaction, gratification, and personal growth for those taking on the role of reviewer of scholarly practitioner journals. The first is the opportunity to learn about and stay current with one's fields of interest by being exposed to the most current work being done by researchers. Reviewers can learn new concepts and theories and applications to practice within those fields, as well as observe how new methodologies have been applied. Scanning a bibliography can provide sources of work in the field that may have eluded one's purview. For instance, a reviewer with interests in international business may be exposed to new ideas from sociology, psychology, economics, and even historical perspectives that are found in many articles in international business. Learning how business and management function in various environments is especially rewarding, since executive practice is inherent in the manuscripts submitted to scholarly practitioner journals. Such real-life experiences can also enrich one's teaching repertoire.

Another personal learning opportunity arises from reading the decision package described earlier that is usually sent as feedback by the editors to reviewers in addition to the authors. The package typically consists of the editorial team's decision letter and the reviews of all reviewers. Seeing these various points of view of a paper can provide a broader perspective, offering additional insights into the paper and at times to the topic in general. For instance, the editors or other reviewers might have seen the paper in a more positive or negative light than you, and seeing their reasons and arguments provides the opportunity for your additional personal development. The review may make contributions to the theory underlying the paper, or explain how it could influence practice.

A second major source of gratification is the opportunity to contribute to the development of colleagues. Much as reviewers have the opportunity to learn from the ideas and points of view of other experts in the review process, reviewers' ideas and viewpoints can add to their knowledge and expertise. Additionally, many articles will be authored by newer or junior faculty members, or those from other countries. The opportunity to contribute to their progress as scholars by providing expert and developmental reviews will hopefully hasten their growth as professionals in their fields. Although reviewers typically remain anonymous in the blind-review process, knowing that you have undertaken your role in a serious and professional manner can provide the best reward that true professionals can hope for. Reviewers' contributions to these authors, particularly with regard to assessing, and even helping to develop, the linkage between theory and practice, will aid their development as authors and academics. Thus, their careers and what they offer to students and executives can be greatly enhanced by reviewers' work.

Another clear reward from reviewing for scholarly practitioner journals is continuing to develop one's expertise as a bridge between theory and practice, since this is the fundamental objective of such journals. Most reviewers have more experience in the academic world than the world of practice, even though most reviewers for scholarly practitioner journals have had at least a reasonable level of practical experience. This is usually gained through consulting, sabbaticals, case writing in companies, or working in companies or other organizations before or during their academic careers. So in the process of reviewing for these journals, reviewers have the opportunity to continue to build their own expertise in the linkages between theory and practice. Additionally, they might also help build new bridges between the two spheres by providing insightful and helpful reviews of papers with significant potential for that possibility. A byproduct of this activity might be the opportunity to have a direct influence on business practice, which might otherwise be seen as being limited to one's own research or teaching.

Although the role of reviewer may not bring financial rewards, some journals have recognition awards such as those for best reviewers or best newer reviewers. Receiving such recognition enhances one's professional reputation among colleagues associated with the journal, authors, and colleagues in one's own institution. Additionally, there is prestige for individuals and their institutions in being a member of editorial boards, with one's name and affiliation typically published on the masthead of every journal issue. Also, many journals acknowledge the work of ad hoc or non-board member reviewers in lists published periodically in the journals, such as reviewing for special issues or conferences sponsored by the journals. And some scholarly practitioner journals have advisory boards of practitioners, and occasionally invite practitioners to serve on the editorial board. The opportunity exists to work with such practitioners and possibly establish relationships that can lead to consulting or other such work with their firms. At this point, there is the possibility of communicating with executive advisors to broaden one's own perspective and experience, which can be helpful in developing linkages between theory and practice.

In fact, networking with the many professionals with whom reviewers become associated is an important aspect of the role. It can allow reviewers to become more effective in that role as well as lead to other opportunities and collaborations with those parties. Continuous collaboration with the editorial team can lead to invitations to make presentations at various universities with which they have meaningful ties. The same can be said over time of relationships with fellow reviewers, usually members of the editorial board. At professional meetings, reviewers find much in common with that group, which can lead to friendships as well as professional opportunities to collaborate in publication, case writing, consulting, or even periodic teaching opportunities or sabbaticals at their institutions. Additional networking can take place at events such as writers' workshops sponsored by a journal where reviewers act as mentors for newer authors or those exploring scholarly practitioner journals as a new outlet. In all cases, the opportunity exists to enhance one's knowledge, experience, and appreciation of how theory can influence practice and provide an opportunity to improve one's own teaching, consulting, and even writing for scholarly practitioner journals.

Although reviewing for scholarly practitioner journals entails a substantial amount of work and contribution of service to the profession, it also brings with it many sources of satisfaction, gratification, and opportunities for growth and development. Reviewing for these journals, then, is different in many ways from scholarly academic or purely practitioner-oriented journals. The rewards can also be different and varied. This gratifying experience can make an important difference in the professional lives of those who review for scholarly practitioner journals as well as the colleagues they serve.

References

Forward, G. E., Beach, D. E., Gray, D. A. and Quick, J. C. (1991). Mentofacturing: A vision for American industrial excellence. *Academy of Management Executive, 5*, 32–44.

11
Reviewing Scholarly Books
Walter Nord*

As a two-term book review editor for the *Academy of Management Review*, one of my objectives has been to increase the perceived value of books in the scholarly pursuits of my colleagues. "Good" book reviews, in addition to aiding scholars in their search for knowledge, can foster the appreciation of books. Unfortunately, however, many book reviews are done in a rather mechanical and non-analytical fashion (specifically such reviews tend to offer summaries with little analysis, little passion, and little critical thought). Therefore, these book reviews do not make the contribution that they could. My hope is that this essay will stimulate and guide future reviewers to write better reviews.

This is my hope, but, for several reasons, giving advice on how to write reviews of scholarly books is a hazardous undertaking. First, as far as I know, there is no template for writing them. Second, in my view, a "good" review is itself an intellectual contribution and clearly, there is no program for doing that. Thus, to a considerable degree, writing "good" reviews is probably best viewed as an art. Treating the process as an art suggests viewing it as a creative task. Consequently, the advice is directed to aiding potential reviewers to tap their creativity fully. Further the artistic metaphor suggests that aesthetic criteria are used in judging what constitutes "good".

The best way I know to illustrate what introducing aesthetic criteria implies, is by borrowing a thought from the Nobel laureate physicist Steven Weinberg (1993) that he used to explain how physicists use a

* Thoughtful comments by Ann Connell, three anonymous reviewers and James Walsh helped to improve this essay. Their efforts are gratefully acknowledged.

sense of beauty to evaluate theories; it is more than a sense of aesthetic pleasure. Rather it is closer "to what a horse trainer means when he looks at a racehorse and says that it is a beautiful horse. The horse trainer is of course expressing his personal opinion, but it is an opinion about an objective fact: that, on the basis of judgments that the trainer could not easily put into words, this is the kind of horse that wins races." (p. 133)

In this context, the suggestions I advance in this paper are a function of my sense of beauty.

To set the context, I need to comment on some functions that I believe reviews of scholarly books perform. As I see it, reviews serve the scholarly community by providing a snapshot of what a book may mean for the scholars for whom it was intended. Ideally, a review helps members of that community know how they might benefit from careful study of the book and alerts them to potential deficiencies. For seemingly obvious reasons, most reviews tend to be published very near a book's own publication date. I refer to these reviews as <u>current</u> reviews. Current reviews provide the community with an early read on the work – keeping its members abreast of new developments.

However, it is worth noting that there might be advantages to <u>deferred</u> reviews. I have tried to institutionalize these in my role as *AMR* book review editor by inviting book review essays (see Nord, 2003). By deferred reviews I mean reviews that are written some years following the book's date of publication showing the book's value to the intellectual community at this later point in time. Deferred reviews perform quite different functions from the more typical current reviews. Specifically, a deferred review might alert the community to an important body of work that has been over looked. In addition, a deferred review might alert the community to problematic interpretations a book has received. For example, Walsh's (2005) deferred review of Freeman's (1984) *Strategic Management: A Stakeholder Approach* demonstrated that the field had misinterpreted a central concept in the now classic book. Such a review serves a corrective function.

Both types of reviews can also serve students who are not directly in the specific research community for whom the book was intended. Being someone whose research relates to a wide number of topics, many beyond my specialized competence, often book reviews have led me to important material which I would otherwise not been aware of. A prime example was a *New York Times* book review of Ross' (1991) study of the history of American social science that led me to a virtual goldmine.

I have long considered my lack of knowledge of history to be an important intellectual shortcoming. When I first learned about the Ross book through the book review, I was convinced that if I ever was going to take the time to try to better understand the history of American social science, this would be a good place to start, so I purchased a copy. Some years later, for a book I am writing, I was trying to determine how fruitful the model for doing research borrowed from the natural sciences had been for adding substantive knowledge in the social sciences. When I went to my bookshelves to explore this question, Ross' book, that I had long wanted to read, was the first thing I turned to. Her book, without using the term, made a compelling case that what organizational theorists would term an institutional theory accounts for the hegemony of natural science methods in the social sciences. The methods gave them legitimacy by making them appear to be like the more prestigious natural sciences. In addition to this interesting substantive insight, the book pointed to a host of crucial materials for understanding the process that took place.

To sum up so far, good book reviews are scholarly creations that help other scholars learn of potentially important ideas, aid them in digesting the ideas, and point to morsels that are potential sources of indigestion. In addition, when reviews appear after the book has been around awhile, they can retrospectively serve corrective functions (correcting both misinterpretations and uncovering overlooked gems).

The fact that they are potentially very valuable, points to the need to consider what makes a "good" review. As I indicated earlier, creating "good" reviews resembles art. Rather than attempting to delineate the aspects of good reviews, which is done quite thoroughly in section 2 of this book, I will note the aspects that I find pleasing and then sketch how a person may best prepare himself/herself to create such art.

Quality scholarly critiques

I like critiques that are intellectually deep – i.e., they examine the underpinnings of the manifest message. Gouldner's (1970) discussion of sub-sociology provides a guide for such subterranean investigation. He began by noting that all inquiry rests upon assumptions. Because of their foundational nature, assumptions can unobtrusively direct attention to and privilege some perspectives and types of evidence over others. Among other things, the assumptions heavily influence what one takes as problematic and, equally important, one's lacunae. The latter, because they are by definition omissions from the text, are particularly difficult to discover. The difficulty is compounded by the fact that the reviewer is likely to be part of the same scholarly community as the book's author. Therefore, the reviewer faces the problem of the proverbial fish that cannot find the water.

To help discover the underpinnings, Gouldner pointed to the need to study contexts and personal realities that shape scholarly inquiry. This approach helps to reveal an author's "... personal commitments that he [sic] wishes to defend." (p. 44) Further, "... the personally real and problematic often enough becomes the starting point for systematic inquiry. ..." (p. 45) Gouldner went on to show how the work of the heralded sociologist Talcott Parsons was shaped by Parsons' personal social context. Specifically, Gouldner found Parsons' "grand theory" a bit presumptuous and suggested that this attribute could be partially explained by Parsons' Olympus complex that afflicted him as a result of his holding a position at a highly esteemed university such as Harvard. Furthermore, Gouldner suggested that like all scholars, Parsons' picture of the world had both permitted and not permitted aspects. The permitted became central to his theory and the unpermitted became lacunae.

While of course such speculative suggestions do not by themselves provide convincing evidence of their truth, they do call attention to the role that personal and social context might play in the work of scholars and the books that they write. From my perspective, good reviews reflect insights stemming from awareness of such a possibility.

Undoubtedly, similar forces to the personal and social ones that influenced the scholar who wrote the book one is reviewing, probably affect the reviewer as well. Thus, the creator of "good" reviews not only considers the context of the author, but is reflexive about his/her own.

Since I place a high value on understanding context, I prefer broad-based reviews. Further, I prefer reviews that build on this broad base to provide me with understanding of the intended contribution of the work, an assessment of its value, and an analysis of the contribution the reviewer deems the book actually made as well as its lacunae. Then, of course, the reviewer provides convincing rationale for the reviewer's judgments.

Ideally, the reviewer compares the book's apparent contribution with the intended one. Finally, I like it when the reviewer indicates the implications of his/her own reflexivity for the judgments.

Obviously, these are ambitious aspirations and not every reviewer may be ready to meet them. Thus, it is worth considering the personal attributes and actions that might prepare one for doing so.

What it takes

Without a doubt, a *sine-qua-non* for such a review is a deep understanding of knowledge related to the book's subject and its position in the broader intellectual enterprise. The person must know the field. A further aid is a passion to promote excellence of scholarship on the subject. In combination, these attributes should drive the reviewer to a deep reading of the book. Walsh's (2005) essay exemplifies this approach.

An exemplar

Walsh's essay provides some helpful specifics about what I have been discussing: attention to context, a passion to get things right, and attention to implications.

Here, I will only deal with one portion of Walsh's essay – on his analysis of R. Edward Freeman's (1984) *Strategic Management: A Stakeholder Approach*. Note that Walsh's review was a deferred one – he was writing two decades after the book's publication, on a book that had become a classic.

Walsh demonstrated the book's classic status by referring to citation counts. But, then he noted:

> The problem with "classic" writings is that they may be cited more than they are read ... even worse, they may be known for something the author never intended. The Freeman (1984) book is a classic book that is also a classic case of becoming something that it is really not. [p. 427]

Specifically, the book has become a rallying cry against stockholder theory but Walsh demonstrated effectively that such use entailed a serious misreading of the book. Clearly, such a review can serve an important corrective function.

To recognize the influence of the book's context, Walsh observed it was written in the turbulent economic times of the early 1980s; consequently, the book focused on managing in turbulent times – times that stimulated the need for the stakeholder approach. Possibly, Walsh suggested, Freeman's purpose was to awaken managers to the new reality of the times; times that demanded a radical externalism and an expanded sense of leadership. Reading this message in the light of Pfeffer and Salancik's (1978) resource dependence model, Walsh made it very clear that Freeman's book should not be read, as many of its users seem to have, as a call to serve stakeholders in an altruistic sense.

To reiterate, Walsh's essay was not a typical book review. Further, he had the advantage of seeing how others had interpreted the book. Still, it is an instructive example for several reasons. First, it shows how informative deferred reviews can be. Second, it showed the value of a deep reading that gets in touch with the author's intent and the historical context of the time. We learn even more through Walsh's relating the book to parallel literature.

Unlike many reviews that mechanically guide the reader through the text, Walsh's essay demonstrates how some of the elements of a "good" review that I noted earlier, such as deep reading, attention to context, effort to understand the author's intent, and assumptions – can lead to reviews that are beautiful and are themselves examples of creative scholarship.

In short, book reviews that emerge from deep readings by experts who are reflexive and sensitive to context can be very valuable for the scholarly community. Among other things, they can help our field overcome what I, and a number of colleagues, believe is a proclivity to underutilize books.

Overview

Believing as I do that: 1) scholarly books have a great deal to offer the intellectual community, and that reviews of such books can facilitate this function; 2) quality reviews can themselves be important intellectual contributions and 3) quality reviews have an aesthetic character, I have tried to summarize some attributes of such contributions and implicitly provide some general guidance for producing such reviews.

At this point, let me try to make some of the implicit somewhat explicit. For many reasons, including the fact that some of these are not under the control of a potential reviewer, this list should not be read as a "how-to-do-it-program". Rather, it should be read as a brief inventory of elements that might help a person prepare himself/herself to produce such good art.

1. Deep immersion in the scholarly area that is the subject matter of the book.
2. A passion to understand and advance knowledge that the book deals with.

3. An inquiring stance that seeks to explain why the book contains what it does and why it omits crucial elements that it in fact omits.

4. A deep intellectual orientation that permits matters of context to be employed in analysis of the book and reflexivity on the book review itself.

References

Freeman, R. E. (1984). *Strategic management: A stakeholder approach*. Boston, MA: Pitman/Ballinger.

Gouldner, A. W. (1970). *The coming crisis of Western sociology*. New York: Basic Books, Inc.

Nord, W. R. (January 2003). Augmenting the role books play in organization management studies. *Academy of Management Review, 28*(1), p. 154.

Pfeffer, J. & Salancik, G. R. (1978). *The external control of organizations: A resource dependence perspective*. New York: Harper & Row.

Ross, D. (1991). *The origins of American social science*. Cambridge: Cambridge University Press.

Walsh, J. P. (2005). Book review essay: Taking stock of stakeholder management. *Academy of Management Review, 30*, 426–52.

Weinberg, S. (1993). *Dreams of final theory*. New York: Vintage Books.

Section 4

Answering Reviews to Get Published

12
Revising to Be Published: Building Trust to Win the Acceptance of Journal Editors and Reviewers

Shaker A. Zahra and Donald O. Neubaum*

Anyone who has ever submitted their work for publication can surely sympathize with the perilous journey of the peer-review process. As reviewers we appreciate authors' aspirations and apprehension. Authors painstakingly craft their theoretical arguments and sweat over every last detail of their empirical analysis in hopes of creating a publishable piece. Authors endeavor to dot every *i*, cross every *t*, and look upon the final draft with the same affection as they would their own newborn child. After much hard work, authors send their intellectual offspring out for peer review. They wait expectantly for weeks and months at a time for a single letter, and its accompanying reviews, the content of which will determine the manuscript's fate. Authors do this knowing that the best possible outcome is "revise and resubmit," a verdict that is sometimes fraught with even greater fear, anxiety and trepidation. The pain associated with academic review process is so great that one editor has described the process a sado-masochistic ritual (Feldman, 2005).

As reviewers, we see an invitation for a revision as an occasion for celebration. Revising and resubmitting a paper for additional review offers authors an opportunity to refine their work, rethink through their arguments, reflect on their logic and reconsider their conclusions. These changes are likely to improve a paper's clarity and make

* We appreciate the helpful suggestions of Yehuda Baruch, Daniel Feldman, Michael Levy, Dhruv Grewal and Patricia H. Zahra for her useful comments.

its contribution more evident. Revisions also ensure rigor and currency in scholarly research. Still, some authors hold somewhat different views arguing that the review process induces angst, if not terror.

We understand that the review process itself has evolved into an institution with its own norms and traditions that perpetuate strong and deeply felt reactions, even among well-established and published scholars. The fact that peer review remains relatively unchanged since 1750 demonstrates its usefulness (Day, 1998). We, the reviewers, are also authors. As a result, many of us have experienced one or more disappointing episodes with this process. Given the considerable personal investments associated with our intellectual work, it is easy to understand why authors get exceedingly nervous, anxious or even fearful. Jobs, careers, professional reputations and self-esteem depend on the outcome of this uncertain and, at times, seemingly random process.

Over the years, we have reviewed for many leading journals. This has given us insights into how to address some of the uncertainties associated with the academic peer-review process. We have come to view this process as one of "social exchange" among authors, reviewers, and journal editors, with each of these groups holding different needs and expectations. One of the key lessons we have learned is that trust and reciprocity are the cornerstones of this exchange process. As with any reciprocal social exchange, uncertainty awaits around every corner. Authors are unsure of the competence or attentiveness of the anonymous reviewers, or how they will judge their work. Editors are also unsure of how careful reviewers will be in their appraisals, or how likely authors will improve the quality of a flawed manuscript. Reviewers do not know if editors will carefully consider their points of view, or if authors will pay attention to their comments and suggestions.

As Dipboye pointed out in chapter 1, uncertainty in the review process stems from the complementary but seemingly competing goals and roles of editors, reviewers and authors. Editors would like a productive and efficient process that reliably identifies and develops the most promising and insightful research. They want their pipelines to be full of innovative and valuable research that will be well-read and cited, which will ultimately increase their journals' circulation and enhance their own careers. Reviewers want a streamlined process that economizes on the time they voluntarily provide and maximizes their reviewing talents. They want to read rigorously constructed papers containing novel ideas that may have an impact on the development of their fields. They also want to learn by reviewing. As reviewers, we yearn to receive a submission that excites us, teaches us something new, or makes us question what we know.

Authors want a fair and fast process that judges the merits of their work based on the standards the journals have established. They also want to retain control over their intellectual enterprise, and ensure that their message is well-received and that their work is appreciated and accepted for publication. In the end, all parties would like a publishable piece. This goal is rarely satisfied. Given that journal submission rates are at all-time highs, the objective rate of acceptance has dropped, causing even high quality research to be rejected. In the case of the most premier journals, acceptance rates have fallen well below 10%.

Our experience as reviewers indicates that aversion to the peer-review process could be harmful to authors. We feel that this aversion does not have to be the norm but Bedeian, Miner and Starbuck argued in chapter 7 that this aversion, and the subsequent dilemmas for the discipline, reflects the current state of affairs. Despite the shortcomings of the review process, reviewers and authors can take several steps to ensure the process is more favorable – i.e., reducing authors' anxiety, assuring reviewers have impact and voice, and increasing the likelihood of eventual acceptance. Much depends on how the parties write, view, value and respond to peer evaluations. There are a few skills and steps that authors can learn to apply, making it easier to find success in the review process. Building on our reviewing experiences, we offer a list of dos and don'ts for both reviewers and authors. Our goal is to set the stage of our discussion of the peer-review process in the following pages. Reading through our list in Table 12.1, it should become clear that authors and reviewers jointly share the responsibility for the fate of any given manuscript, and for the tone and effectiveness of the ensuing intellectual discourse.

The revision process as a social exchange

As reviewers, we have learned that the academic journal review process is one of social exchange, with all the attendant complexities, challenges and rewards. A social exchange is defined by reciprocal acts of benefit, where the parties involved offer help or advice without the prior negotiation of the terms or conditions and without knowledge of if, how, or when the other parties will reciprocate (Blau, 1964; Molm,

Table 12.1   Dos and Don'ts in the Revision Process

Focus	For Authors	For Reviewers
Dos	• Revise your paper quickly. • Begin your response with a letter to the editor, detailing the major changes you have made. • Retain control over your paper. • Consider comments carefully. • Indicate how you have addressed each comment. State what you have done, how you have done it, and where it appears in the revision. • Explain why you might have disagreed with the reviewers' comments. • Get honest feedback from experienced colleagues before resubmission. • Be thoughtful in your replies and thank reviewers for their insights. • Break reviewers' comments into three categories: 1) easy to fix; 2) fixable, but with effort; 3) unknown. Address items 1 first to provide a sense of accomplishment. These are also easier to find and execute before the paper undergoes substantial revisions.	• Provide a list of major and of minor issues needing to be rectified. • Leave the control of the paper to the authors and the editor. Clarify the comments to be taken most seriously. • For a second review – understand the author does not have to accept ALL of your comments. • Be constructive. Don't just point out shortcomings; offer actionable alternatives and solutions. See chapters 5 and 6 for more information on writing constructive reviews. • Your homework, and admit the limits of your own expertise. • Engage in an intellectual debate, but bolster your beliefs with citations, not just your own suppositions.
Don'ts	• Compromise your argument/ message. • Ignore reasonable comments as incompetent or ideological, simply because you do not like the feedback.	• Try to hijack the author's paper to push your own research agenda • Present comments that might be seen as ideological argument.

Table 12.1   Do's and Don'ts in the Revision Process – *continued*

Focus	For Authors	For Reviewers
Don'ts	• Sit on the paper for long and agonize over the review. • Assume that a rejection by one journal kills the paper; consider another outlet. • Try to figure out who the reviewers are. • Take reviewers' comments as personal insults. • Pass up on an opportunity to revise. Your chances of publication have just increased at least ten-fold. • Criticize or complain about reviewers.	• Be harsh; the idea is not "breaking the spirit of the enemy". • Give hints about who are you (e.g., do not ask to cite too much of your own work). • Make comments that might be taken personally. • TRY to figure out the author's identity. • Create false hopes. Offer your candid comments. See chapter 4 for more information on writing realistic reviews.

Takahashi, & Peterson, 2000). Throughout the review process, editors and reviewers offer their judgments and suggestions. In return, authors offer ideas and promise to be attentive to the suggestions they are presented. As with many other social processes, the parameters of this exchange are only broadly defined.

While randomness and flawed human judgment sometimes lead to the rejection of some interesting and insightful manuscripts, authors themselves frequently contribute to the failure of their own work. In this chapter, we build on our reviewing and publishing experiences, focusing on some of these failings, hoping to encourage authors to take the time and exert the effort necessary to craft their revisions in ways that engage the reviewers, excite editors, and build mutual trust. We also offer reviewers insights to help them develop a positive relationship with authors, leading to improved scholarship. We believe that successful revisions center on: (a) investing in building trust among editors, reviewers and authors; (b) identifying major themes in the reviewers' comments; (c) attacking the revision in a systematic fashion, (d) maintaining the paper's perspective while showing flexibility in addressing the recommendations offered by reviewers; (e) selling the value added of the ideas the paper contains; (f) calling upon all available resources to craft the paper; and (g) paying special attention to intangibles. In discussing these points, we highlight the social exchange nature of the review process and discuss key ways to learn from it.

Building trust among participants in the review process

We see the academic journal review process as an arena for social exchange where authors, reviewers and editors engage in a reciprocal dialogue about the worth of a paper and its potential contribution. The value of this contribution is likely to vary by time, individual and even one's perspective. Understandably, rarely is there consensus on whether a paper is a seminal piece or makes a significant contribution, leaving considerable room for judgment and debate. Evaluations are complicated by the fact that participants' assumptions, knowledge, expertise and expectations also differ. One editor likens the role of authors, who work hard to win over the minds of the reviewers, to that of the courtroom attorney who persuades a jury through evidence, credibility and trust (Ketchen, 2002).

As reviewers, authors and editors expect us to be impartial and open-minded. As we state in Table 12.1, reviewers need to carefully reflect on all the evidence and support the authors provide. But we believe that reviewers' responsibilities go beyond those of a trial jury that merely votes on guilt or innocence. Reviewers are obligated to assist the authors craft their arguments and develop their cases, as advocated in Table 12.1. They often offer authors evidence that supports their cause. Reviewers also engage in the intellectual debate to consider competing claims and make a worthwhile contribution. Some reviewers might even champion emerging perspectives, seeking their acceptance and legitimization. Consequently, good reviewers simultaneously act as members of the prosecution, the defense, and the jury.

Trust between the parties is likely to increase when both reviewers and authors are honest, responsive, thoughtful and forthcoming. Factors that affect trust in a reciprocal relationship include behavioral consistency, behavioral integrity, open communication and demonstration of concerns (Whitener, Brodt, Korsgaard, & Werner, 1998). These factors are critically important for success in the academic journal review process and reviewers and authors should work together to foster a relationship reflective of these values.

Authors can build trust with editors and reviewers in several ways. First, effective authors carefully justify the use of a particular theory, measure or empirical technique. Reviewers who challenge authors might not necessarily disagree with the tact the authors have taken. More likely, reviewers do not believe the authors have convincingly stated their case or they are confused by the way the ideas were summarized or presented. Some authors might discuss a certain construct but do not clearly explain how and why they have chosen a particular way to measure it. If authors are concerned about the reviewers understanding and appreciating their work, then they should work harder at educating the reviewers about their research and its potential contributions. Clear and straightforward communication can build this trust. Authors can also provide authoritative citations or additional evidence of the merits of their claims. We have found that in many cases, authors did not have to change anything they had done to satisfy a reviewer; they just had to do a better job of explaining what they did and why.

Second, successful authors usually describe and clearly communicate the evolution of their thought processes as they wrestled with a particular issue in the revision. By showing that they had carefully considered the alternative perspectives of the reviewers, authors can signal their good intentions, assuring reviewers their perspectives have been considered. Successful revisions, and responses to reviewers' comments, always acknowledge multiple theoretical explanations and justify the choices made. Nothing leads a reviewer to recommend a rejection of a paper faster than a dismissive author.

Third, successful authors usually concede on non-contentious issues. As our observations in Table 12.1 would suggest, responses to reviewers are not debates about who is right and who is wrong; they are more often about negotiating a balance between the interests of reviewers and authors. Demonstrating flexibility on non-essential items is the fastest, easiest way for authors to engender credibility and trust. This can create much needed social capital authors can cash in on as they debate with reviewers on more contentious issues. Flexibility, however, does not mean abandoning one's convictions or running away from a good argument. It simply means thinking creatively to find a good meeting place where the interests of the reviewers and authors converge.

Fourth, successful authors are forthcoming in acknowledging the weaknesses of their work and methodology. Rather than trying to hide the deficiencies of their research, such as common-method bias or low Cronbach's alphas, responsive authors reveal these openly, as suggested in Table 12.1. When these details are omitted, reviewers often assume the worst. Revealing and addressing such omissions helps build trust and credibility with editors and reviewers (Ketchen, 2002), who are often sympathetic to the tradeoffs necessary in conducting research and recognize that not all research is perfect.

Fifth, experienced authors view the debates and communications that occur in the review process as an opportunity to hone, sharpen or rethink their own positions. While the process can be laborious and painful, successful authors view these exchanges as a chance to learn and refine their craft and as a means to produce a manuscript whose ideas have stood up to the challenge of different points of view. The most productive approach authors can take is to engage reviewers and editors in a discussion where the latter begin to ponder their own assumptions and views. This give-and-take process fosters trust and enhances credibility, leading to the meeting of the minds in search of a common and satisfactory solution. In this case, reviewers will believe that the authors have put forth their best effort, deliberated the various issues, come to understand the limitations of each alternative, and chosen the tact they believe is truly the best.

Finally, successful authors are forthcoming with editors about similar papers currently under review and how often, if ever, any data used in the paper have been published. Editors and reviewers get leery when samples sound familiar, studies appear incremental, or data look to be thinly sliced (Feldman, 2005). Deception, idioplagiarism, and unprofessional conduct are among the surest ways to lose credibility and trust in the review process. These behaviors also hurt authors' reputations and could have dire long-term career and personal implications. Academicians need to remember the sage advice we once received: "We work for a long time in a small field."

As reviewers, we can also take steps to gain the trust of authors. For instance, we should support our criticism with valid and verifiable claims, as opposed to taking random pot-shots at the authors' work. Reviewing does not give us a "license to hunt"; it creates an opportunity for a fruitful exchange of ideas. As reviewers we should also clearly present our comments and offer potential remedies for the issues we raise, where feasible. We can also research any points of contention or acknowledge our level of confidence in our own arguments. Developmental and supportive reviewers also offer congratulations to authors for tasks done well. They are also open minded and willing to accept the authors' valid perspectives.

In any social exchange, the form of communication is as important as its content in inducing and sustaining trust. Reviewers and authors can help establish the norms of reciprocity in this exchange, and it is imperative that they establish the norm of a cordial and productive exchange. It is critical to remember that reviewers initiate the exchange. Authors' responses will most likely reflect the tone of the review and criticism offered. Effective and supportive reviewers, therefore, strive to develop a collegial atmosphere for the exchange. While authors might feel outrage when reviewers question their assumptions or argue for alternative explanations, authors need to mask their anger. Angered responses from one party might beget angered reactions, creating dysfunctional tensions.

Our experience suggests that some authors are quick to dismiss reviewers' comments, citing ideological bias. While at times this may be true, our experience suggests that this is the exception, not the rule. As we state in Table 12.1, the job of the reviewers is to question and critique the papers being evaluated and to ensure accurate findings and interpretations. Every piece of work, however, has its flaws and strengths and, as reviewers, we are expected to identify them and discuss their implications. Reviewers and authors who show mutual respect, and even thankfulness, to one another are much more likely to receive the fair hearing they seek for their ideas. We are *not* suggesting that reviewers and authors should completely agree, but we are suggesting that better papers result when the parties respond fully, thoughtfully and respectfully. In the end, offers for further revisions are often based not so much on the quality of the manuscript, but on the editors' and reviewers' belief in the authors' ability to rework the paper (Feldman, 2004). Effective authors help build confidence in their abilities through their thoughtful responses.

Identify major themes in the reviews

As noted in Table 12.1, one of the most important steps in crafting a thoughtful review is to develop a prioritized list of the major themes and comments. Reciprocity, which is critical to developing and maintaining an effective social exchange (Blau, 1964), begins with understanding the expectations of others. As reviewers, we can set the stage for a productive exchange by clearly articulating the major and minor challenges facing authors. While authors might disagree with reviewers' comments and find them difficult to accept, success in the revision process requires taking time to read and reflect on them methodically. When reading a review for the first time, the most salient comments tend to be those that authors disagree with most strongly, the ones that really get their blood boiling. Usually, those comments are not the ones that kept authors from getting their paper accepted. Reviewing essentially revolves around criticisms; it is focused on the paper's weaknesses (Harrison, 2002). Consequently, one of the most effective techniques that authors can use is to read the comments, set them aside, and then go back over them slowly and carefully a few days later.

We have found that this tactic offers two benefits. First, it helps authors evaluate the comments in a more rational, even-handed manner, permitting them to respond more constructively and respectfully. It also helps take some of the sting out of the reviews. Second, it allows authors to separate the "wheat from the chaff," revealing key ideas or re-occurring themes in the reviews. Editors often provide a synthesis of the reviewers' various comments. Once authors develop their interpretation of the major themes in the review, they can then compare them to the editors' synthesis. We believe this process can set authors on the right path, promoting their understanding of where the reviewers (and editors) are coming from and the changes necessary.

As reviewers, we believe it is legitimate to disagree with some of the comments we provide. However, in disagreeing with our comments, some authors tend to automatically assume the worst. Some may view reviewers as ideological, dogmatic or even ill-informed. There are, of course, dogmatic and ill-informed reviewers. Our experience, however, is that the vast majority of journal gatekeepers are caring professionals who search for innovative ideas that inspire and transform the field. As authors themselves, reviewers understand the unique challenges that new ideas face in their quest for acceptance. Therefore, as noted in Table 12.1, it is important for authors to take the comments they receive on face value and not assume the worst on the part of the reviewers and editors. Successful authors focus on ideas, not reviewers' motives or hidden agendas – many of which may not exist in the first place.

Editors usually select reviewers for their expertise and skill and generally value their views and recommendations. Still, some reviewers are sloppy. Others are ill-informed. Therefore, it is perfectly legitimate for authors to point out to editors where they disagree with the reviewers and why these differences matter. Editors are often sympathetic to authors, and authors of successful revisions invest in building trust with editors. One editor reminds us that authors might disagree but should never be argumentative with reviewers. He explains that, "This means they can either be argumentative or it could mean that they don't realize that what they have said isn't clear to the reviewers, who aren't really stupid." Authors also need to retain a sense of detachment from their own work, however hard this may be. They need to remember also that people see and value things differently. Reviewers and editors are no exceptions.

Identifying key themes in the reviewers' comments sets the stage for a successful revision. It also helps to ensure that the paper continues to flow well and that its key message remains intact. When authors address reviewers' and editors' individual comments in a shot gun fashion, their paper can become disjointed or fragmented. By focusing on the key themes in the review, authors can retain control over their manuscript, ensuring the clarity and coherence of their message.

Attack the revision systematically

Responding to a long series of seemingly random, conflicting comments can be a daunting task; regardless of how many times an author has revised a manuscript. The process can be confusing and burdensome, especially if authors sporadically revise the paper over several weeks or months. This condition is compounded when working with multiple co-authors with different writing and presentation styles. These different styles and even conflicting views could stand in the way of the paper's message. Consequently, it is important to attack any revision in a systematic fashion.

As we suggest in Table 12.1, after identifying the major themes in the reviews, authors should categorize each comment into one of three types: 1) easy to handle, 2) difficult, but immediately manageable, or 3) very difficult or unknown. This enables them to quickly address all the easy to handle comments first. This can give authors a sense of accomplishment as they scratch off items on their "to-do" list. These corrections are also much easier to find and identify before major revisions are made. Next, authors could divide the more challenging comments among co-authors, assigning responsibility to the individual best-suited to address the comment. Sharing the burden can help keep co-authors energized and focused and avoids duplication of effort. Authors can use the "track changes" feature available in most word-processing programs in order to find their revisions, keep track of their progress, and see what revisions co-authors have made. Alternatively, authors can simply bold the text of inserted sections. Authors using the track changes features should eliminate all evidence of changes made to the paper before re-submitting it to the journal, otherwise reviewers might be able to discover the identity of one or more of the authors.

In some cases, authors might reverse the revision process we have just described, especially when the reviewers' major concerns center on the theory or key predictions. Sometimes, a fresh perspective might be required. Once satisfied with the study's theoretical foundation, authors can move to other less challenging issues. In doing so, the authors can also revise the paper's empirical section to connect it with what they have done in their theory section. Authors can then move to the discussion section and tightly link it to their theory. In these instances, tackling the big issues first makes it easier for authors to retain the paper's continuity, integrity and central message. It also helps them avoid spinning their wheels revising parts of the paper that are dropped later.

Authors might also find it useful to write the letters responding to the reviewers and editors concurrently as their edit their manuscript. This enables them to easily inform the reviewers of the nature of the changes they have made and why they made them. Few things are worse than making dozens of changes in a manuscript and then having to face the tedious task of finding and explaining each and every change after the paper has been revised. We believe the responding letter is in many ways far more critical to successful revisions than many authors realize. Successful authors avoid being careless at the end of a grueling revision; they do not write hastily created letters based primarily on retrospective and flawed recall. These authors appreciate the importance of thoughtful and careful responses to reviewers' suggestions and queries.

Maintain the perspective of the paper

Good papers have a clear perspective and a compelling message. In revising their papers to respond to reviewers, however, some authors fail to retain control over their message. Some authors mistakenly believe that they have to forsake their ideas if they are to gain acceptance for journal publication. As reviewers, we feel quite differently about this; we search for papers that forward a unique or even controversial theoretical and empirical perspective. True, authors might frame their arguments differently to persuade the reviewers and editors. They may even collect and analyze additional data. They may also acknowledge alternative and perhaps rival explanations. Authors still need to maintain control over their papers and their central message, otherwise they risk losing the reason why they were invited to revise their manuscript in the first place. Maintaining control can be particularly important if there is a disagreement among the reviewers. All things being equal, authors need to clarify their message and use the comments of the more supportive reviewers to bolster their position. This is why comprehensive comments, even from positive reviewers, are important. In the review process, we have noticed the squeaky reviewer often gets the grease. Reviewers who think highly of a paper can help authors gain the acceptance of less supportive reviewers and editors by forcefully articulating the merits of the manuscript.

The worst thing that could possibly happen as a consequence of the review process is for the paper's argument or key message to be lost. Some authors complain that their revision often resembles a United Nations' "peace resolution;" a compilation of different and competing views that do not say anything profound. We deeply regret this feeling. But, as we stated in Table 12.1, it is the authors' responsibility to ensure that they retain control over their work and their message. Authors should search for a compromise that capitalizes on the reviewers' suggestions and their own views, but it remains their responsibility to ensure the argument is clear and competently presented. The discussion section of any manuscript is a valuable tool that often goes underutilized. Here, authors can acknowledge the alternative perspectives of reviewers, and discuss, at length, their implications. They can even thank the reviewers for their insightful suggestions. Remember, reviewers are not compensated for their time. Acknowledging the reviewers' contribution in responses or in manuscripts is sometimes the only payment most reviewers ever receive (Caelleigh, Shea, & Penn, 2001). Tucking such concessions in the discussion section allows authors to acknowledge competing views that arise during the review process, while maintaining their paper's focus and clarity.

We have observed another factor that can undermine successful revisions. Some authors believe they have to water down their argument in order to gain the journal's acceptance. As both reviewers and authors, this is the opposite experience we have witnessed. As reviewers, we have often been amazed at how easy it is for some authors to change their positions entirely to gain acceptance of their work. As authors, we have been asked (indeed, pushed) to clarify our views and articulate our positions more succinctly. As with any social exchange, there is considerable room for give-and-take in the review process. We have learned that authors can advance their views while reviewers have the opportunity to question these views and encourage authors to recognize the shortcomings of their arguments. Although Bedeian, Miner and Starbuck demonstrated in chapter 7 that there are exceptions to the rule, we feel that editors and reviewers do not expect authors' unquestioning obedience. Rather, they want authors to carefully consider and reflect on the comments offered in the review.

Selling the value-added of the paper's contribution

Retaining control over one's paper and central message requires more than giving attention to framing and marketing ideas. Some authors confuse framing their arguments with adopting or defending a particular theoretical or empirical perspective. These are two different but related things. Authors wishing to advance a given idea have multiple means to communicate it and connect it to the literature, which is an important part of the craft of scholarly writing. However, there is more at stake here. Authors should also have a clear sense of what their argument is about, what is new about it and how to best link it to the literature. Authors should spell out the distinctiveness of their work in the letters they send to editors and in their responses to the reviewers' comments. Sadly, some authors confuse this with having to abandon one's ideas in order to gain the reviewers' support, an issue we have just discussed. Reading through the best papers published in our leading academic journals, it becomes clear that they have made it to print because they say something interesting and substantive. They are also rigorous.

Graduate research and methodology courses teach students how to conduct competent research. They are attentive to the nuances of methods and interpretation of the results. Many, however, emphasize "replication" type research where incremental improvements in our understanding of issues are expected. Some programs pay far less attention to what makes for an interesting research question or paper. In fact, some doctoral and new faculty consortia reinforce a focus on extension and replication studies as a means of maximizing publications and gaining tenure. We often ask participants in these consortia to think about the papers they have read in the past five years and then identify one or two that they remember as having an impact on them or their research. After the giggling stops, there is always that empty staring in space, the wandering silence. Some participants give up in frustration, while others persist. We ask participants to write down their choices. Once they do this, we ask them: "What is it about this particular paper (or set of papers) that made such an important impression on you?" When participants share their reasons, they quickly agree that these influential papers have a distinct view point or perspective. As reviewers, we should be particularly attentive to and accepting of papers that offer such a unique perspective. An effective revision can highlight this perspective, bringing it into focus and making it accessible to readers.

Call upon all available resources

In some cases, authors find themselves confronted with comments from editors or reviewers that leave them completely perplexed. This may happen because authors are unsure of the question asked, or the point raised. On other occasions, authors clearly understand the point being addressed but have no idea how to proceed or resolve the problem. Other times, authors feel like they have addressed an issue sufficiently but for one reason or another, the reviewers did not understand their ideas. In each of these instances, authors could use the expertise and help of their colleagues.

Authors might find it especially useful to talk to co-authors and colleagues about their papers; verbalizing their thoughts can help them make their arguments sharper. Authors can also use the expertise of authorities on different topics. We have done this ourselves. In one case, after persistent disagreements with a reviewer and an editor, we contacted a leading authority on the method we used in our work. After receiving the feedback on the accuracy of our approach, we included these comments as an attachment to our responses to the reviewers. We were pleased the reviewers and editor appreciated the extra effort we took to verify the appropriateness of our empirics, which made them more comfortable with our approach.

When a major revision is too difficult to handle, authors might bring in an additional co-author for assistance. A new author can bring energy and new thinking, making the task of revising the paper easier. It can also quicken the revision process. This strategy is likely to be accepted and well-received by the editor.

When authors continue to believe that reviewers do not understand their viewpoints, they can engage the editors in the review process. Editors are rarely passive bystanders. In fact, for most journals, reviewers only make recommendations; the final publication decision lies in the hands of editor(s). Therefore, it is critical that authors give the editors' comments their serious consideration. Editors follow each step in the review process closely, making sure that papers receive timely and fair treatment. While some reviewers may focus on finding flaws in the papers they evaluate, editors are more focused on developing promising papers. As a result, authors might benefit from contacting the editor or associate editor in charge of their manuscript to seek clarification or assistance in the revision. We have done so ourselves. In one case, the editor even walked us through the empirical method he suggested we use, directing us to publications that explained the method. The editor also helped us present and interpret the results. We doubt that we would have been able to accomplish this task successfully were it not for the editor's assistance. We believe the help we received was grounded in the trust we had built in the mind of the editor in previous rounds of revisions.

Pay attention to intangibles

One simple way for authors to build trust with reviewers is to pay special attention to the intangible aspects of their manuscript. Broadly speaking, these include the look and feel of the revision and the responses to reviewers. Though no paper may be rejected solely because of poor style or an occasional grammatical error, there is clearly a cumulative effect of these intangibles that plays into the minds of reviewers. A reviewer who sits on the fence in her/his appraisal of a paper is likely to fall on the side of rejection if the manuscript is riddled with stylistic flaws. As reviewers, we have asked ourselves, "If the authors weren't careful compiling their references, then were they careful when they ran their analyses?" Authors who take time to craft their submissions in a professional way and meet the standards of the target journal are better positioned to gain trust. We are surprised to receive papers that clearly do not match the form or style of the journals for which we review. Often, these papers look like they were submitted to another journal first (and apparently rejected). Following the submission guidelines and looking at recent issues of the target journal can make a huge difference and set the stage for a productive, positive dialog between the authors and reviewers.

Getting the help of a professional editor can also improve the clarity and coherence of the presentation. Certainly, getting "friendly yet critical" peer reviews from colleagues can also help. This is particularly true of the letters responding to the editor and reviewers. Having an impartial reader review these letters can help authors remove the negative tone and make the letters more informative, user-friendly, conversational, and even cordial.

There are a few techniques authors can use to make their responding letters easier to understand and follow. First, numbering the items in the responses to reviewers could add clarity and expedite the review process. This will help all parties keep track of the discussion and changes made in the paper. It will also allow reviewers and editors to directly reply to the authors' comments in the next round of reviews. Second, in their responses to reviewers, authors can either reproduce word-for-word the reviewers' comments, or summarize their interpretation of what the reviewer suggested. As reviewers, we favor reproducing the comments fully and then adding appropriate interpretations of these comments in those cases where there might be some confusion or if the authors are not sure they completely understand the reviewer's position. Authors could do this by saying, "Based on our reading of your review, we interpret your comments to suggest...." Finally, authors should craft their response letter such that it is easy to differentiate between reviewer's comments, authors' responses, and changes made in the manuscript. Their letters might also report, verbatim, how they have addressed a given issue and refer the reviewer to the proper page and paragraph where the change has been made. For example, authors might consider the following format:

6. COMMENT: "As I read the section where you presented the descriptive statistics of your responding firms, it was difficult to understand the average age and the number of the high-tech and low-tech companies in your sample."

RESPONSE: We agree that the way we presented that information in the previous version was confusing. As a result, we have re-written this section (see page 8, third paragraph), as follows:

"One hundred and fifty-six companies responded to our survey, 96 of those respondents being in high-tech industries. The average age of the 60 low-tech respondents was 45.7 years old, while the high-tech companies averaged 39.8 years ...."

We hope that you find the revised description clearer. Thank you for pointing out this confusion.

Timeliness of your response is also important. Authors do not understand how it can take more than a couple of months to review a paper.

Reviewers do not understand how authors can take six months or two years to revise their work. Prompt responses reflect sincerity on the part of the authors. It also helps keep reviewers engaged in the process and establishes "speedy replies" as one of the norms within the social exchange.

Finally, we need to stress the necessity of a point-by-point response. While everyone shares the same mental model about what makes a good paper (i.e., interesting questions, strong theory, sound measures and rigorous analysis), there is much less agreement on what makes for ideal journal reviews and responses by authors to these reviews. Authors, of course, must meet the expectations of the journal and its editors. The editor is the coach of the review process and authors are the quarterbacks. As a result, successful authors spend time understating the game plan as established by the journal editors and respond accordingly. If a "point-by-point" response is requested, then authors should oblige. If it is unclear what the editor expects, then authors are encouraged to contact editors to clarity their expectations. Still, as reviewers, we value the authors' "point-by-point" replies. Successful authors, however, are appreciative and respectful of reviewers' time. These authors not bury reviewers in a mountain of single-spaced responses twice as long as the manuscript itself. Our advice to authors is simple: Argue your point with concise precision.

Conclusion

Revising a paper based on reviewers' feedback is a time consuming and demanding process. Of course, completing such revisions efficiently, effectively and quickly is an important part of the scholarly publication process. An effective revision starts with a genuine appreciation of the editors and reviewers' views about the manuscript. Successful authors know that without revisions, their work will not gain acceptance and recognition in the field. Building on our reviewing experience, we have outlined some viable strategies and hope they help authors and reviewers alike as they navigate the peer-review process toward a successful and well-cited publication.

References

Blau, P. M. (1964). *Exchange and power in social life*. New York: Wiley.
Caelleigh, A. S., Shea, J. A., & Penn, G. (2001). Selection and qualities of reviewers. *Academic Medicine, 76(9)*, 914–16.
Day, R. A. (1998). *How to write and publish a scientific paper*. Phoenix: Oryx Press.

Feldman, D. C. (2004). The devil is in the details: Converting good research into publishable articles. *Journal of Management, 30(1)*, 1–6.

Feldman, D. C. (2005). Writing and reviewing as sadomasochistic rituals. *Journal of Management, 31(3)*, 325–9.

Harrison, D. (2002). Obligation and obfuscations in the review process. *Academy of Management Journal, 46(6)*, 1079–84.

Ketchen, D. J., Jr. (2002). Some candid thoughts on the publication process. *Journal of Management, 28(5)*, 585–90.

Molm, L. D., Takahashi, N., & Peterson, G. (2000). Risk and trust in social exchange: An experimental test of a classical proposition. *American Journal of Sociology, 105(5)*, 1396–427.

Whitener, E. M., Brodt, S. E., Korsgaard, M. A., & Werner, J. M. (1998). Managers as initiators of trust: An exchange relationship framework for understanding managerial trustworthy behavior. *Academy of Management Review, 23(3)*, 513–30.

13
To Revise and Resubmit or Not: That is the Question

Yehuda Baruch and Yochanan Altman

What guides authors' considerations when being invited to revise and resubmit (R&R) a manuscript by a peer reviewed journal? And what would be the reviewer's impact in that context?

These were the questions we posed ourselves, as practicing editors of peer-reviewed journals, when authors failed to respond to such an invitation.

Aiming to help reviewers in this crucial stage of knowledge development, we believe that the reviewer should be aware of and acknowledge their role and the derived responsibilities within the process. The key task of the reviewer in the context of this chapter, in our opinion, is to increase the likelihood for a positive response to an R&R invitation. This is only true, of course, when the revision is merited. Otherwise, the reviewer should be fair and honest about their beliefs of the prospects of a successful revision. Should a revision be merited, then the key task of a reviewer is to be encouraging, and directive, laying down the steps for a successful revision.

Having been intrigued by the lack of response to invitations to R&R, we shared our puzzlement with eight editors of esteemed refereed journals, and were provided with ample but anecdotal evidence that the phenomenon is not uncommon (i.e., *all* the editors we consulted could identify a number of manuscripts that were invited to R&R, and had no response after 9–12 months). That was the impetus for us to conduct a study into the issue of why authors may opt for not revising and re-submitting manuscripts to the journal that invited a revision. We targeted academic scholars in the management and business area, but the outcomes are likely to be indicative to the wider academic scholarly community.

Examining the issue in question we followed Simon's (1957) bounded rationality (agents may not necessarily be opting to maximize their gains, rather reaching out for satisfactory outcomes); taking an epistemological stand following Bourdieu (1977, 1990) in evoking his key concept of *habitus*.

Defined as the "socially constituted system of cognitive and motivating structures...of durable transposable dispositions...of the generation and structuring of practices" (Bourdieu, 1977, pp. 72, 76) *habitus* articulates the idea that maximizing one's cultural capital depends on fully comprehending the attributes, constraints, antecedents and consequences of particular actions and the ways to maximize them (Gerrans, 2005). However, this takes time and practice, since central to the idea of *habitus* is its non-directive, non-conscious agency. *Habitus*, as Bourdieu puts it, is: "collectively orchestrated without being the product of the orchestrating action of a conductor" (Bourdieu, 1977: 72).

Following Bourdieu, we wanted to unearth the governing principles guiding authors' practice in responding to an invitation to revise and resubmit to a peer-reviewed journal. To do that we asked a representative sample of academic scholars within the management and behavioral sciences communities in the USA (650+) and the UK (300+) to tell us their likely response in replying to an invitation to R&R to refereed journals, and the reasons for their line of action.

This chapter focuses on a decision authors have to make when the editors invite a revision, and how the reviewing process can be an influential factor in determining the outcome of this process. The review could be instrumental in guiding the authors about the best action to take. The anticipated response of author(s) would be to R&R to the journal. However, authors have a wide choice of decisions at their disposal.

The right decision could sometimes be to bin the paper (e.g., in case of "fatal flaws"), or send it to another journal, which may better fit the issue under investigation, the methodological approach, or the readership, to mention but a few elements for consideration. As an extension of Zahra and Neubaum's advice in the previous chapter, we would argue that the worst thing a reviewer can do is encourage a revision of a seriously flawed paper. Raising false hopes and having authors jump through too many hoops is damaging, costly and unprofessional.

What authors might do?

In this chapter we first identify and explore the options available to authors when R&R is requested, explaining why authors may choose to follow each one. Later on we indicate in what way the reviewer (and editor) may help the author in making the right decision. Based on our experience as editors and writers, and having conducted four focus groups with relevant scholars, we posited the following options as covering the range of possibilities available to an author who is asked to R&R:

(1) Discard the paper
(2) Submit the paper "as it is" to a different journal
(3) Revise and submit to a different journal
(4) Revise and resubmit to the original journal
or,
(5) Challenge the decision

A number of factors may influence the preferred course of action but given the blind-review procedure, the reviewer is not in a position to learn about these either before or after the review. We may reasonably assume that personality factors may have an impact here, such as risk-taking or risk-aversion, fear of failure or achievement motivation, self-esteem and self efficacy. Career stage and career aspirations may be relevant too, as would experience in publishing. Institutional factors of relevance may be the type of Ph.D. training, the standing of the school, and available resources.

Notwithstanding the above, the communicated review is assumed to be the prime 'motivator' for a course of action.

Discarding the paper

The first option could apply to a surprisingly large spectrum of instances. Authors may be so disheartened by the decision (or its communication?) that they discard the manuscript altogether (the review might convince them that there is no chance for it to be published at all). This may be less likely if the response came from the first journal to reject the manuscript, but logically, the propensity of the manuscript finding its way to the bin increases with the same result from several journals in a row. Here, personality and culture may play a significant role. Some individuals' fear of rejection may lead them to avoid another potential disappointing experience; in certain cultures, "loss of face" may lead to a similar propensity. Experience may be highly relevant as novice authors may be more easily disheartened than veterans. Experience may also translate to a commitment to an academic career with newcomers more prone to give up in the face of rejection.

The reviewers cannot be held accountable for these background impacts, but they can and should be accountable for providing clear guidance, which Lee (1995) calls "actionable"; see Sullivan et al (chapter 4) for some examples of actionable advice.

Unless instructed otherwise, it would best be left for the editor to clarify what type of R&R it is (i.e. on the continuum of likelihood of acceptance – high vs. low risk).

In conclusion: bear in mind this default option and beware that you might inadvertently cause one to drop their paper.

Submit the paper "as it is" to a different journal

Under the second option, authors might opt to submit the paper "as it is" to another journal. The designation of the paper would indicate the level of confidence of the author(s) in their work. If they were to try a journal of similar or higher standing, that would indicate a high level of confidence; but more likely, the next step will be in decreasing order of journal standing.

Authors do that because of several possible reasons (and again, here there are implications for the reviewing process):

> Authors might construe the review a "game of luck", in which sometimes you win and at other times you lose. So they may have better luck trying elsewhere.. Unfair reviews might just be the clue authors look for to justify this worldview. Crafting a well-articulated argument in their review would reduce the prospects of such a choice, as authors will have a clear direction about where to go and how to act; reducing uncertainty (and see chapter 14 for discussion on editors'-authors' communication). In contrast, a reviewer that tries to hijack the platform of critique to push their own research agenda might increase the likelihood of submitting the paper to another journal.

On the other hand, this option and the following one can be rightly induced if the reviewer indicates that the manuscript may be more appropriate or has a better fit for an alternative journal. Again, this may well be the right and fair recommendation for the case. However, as Priem noted in chapter 2, a potential consequence of this course of action would be to have the still-unrevised, "as is" manuscript sent to the same reviewer by the different journal!

Revise and submit to a different journal

The third option is for authors to revise the paper following the advice in the reviews, but send it to a different journal. This is the most frustrating choice from the journal's point of view, and later we will try to understand why this might happen, and what can be done in the review to minimize the prospects for such an outcome.

Revise and resubmit to the original journal

The fourth option, which is the preferred one for the journal is to revise and resubmit to the original journal. As we found, it is certainly the normative option, and the one usually (but not always) taken by authors. We expect that the feedback from the reviewers will have a decisive role in effecting this option.

Challenge the decision

The last option (which may be in conjunction with some of the other mentioned above) will be taken when authors cannot undertake the required revision or do not agree with the required demands. They may therefore opt to challenge the editor. They may argue with the demands, suggestions, or recommendations. They might complain about the reviewer or the review process, or the editorial decision. Some typical statements we found in our study were: "the reviewer did not understand what I wrote"/ "the reviewer clearly has no idea whatsoever about the subject matter"/ "the reviewer made unfair comments"/ "the reviewer asked for an undoable or unreasonable revision"/...

As a reviewer you should aim to prevent that. Write the review in a way that the author(s) will not be in a position to question your understanding (better to admit lack of knowledge in specific areas). Try to be fair with your commentary and ask for doable actions. And please oh please, resist the temptation to hijack the paper to promote your own research agenda.

What authors actually do?

In the socialization process of becoming a scholar one realizes (sooner or later) what the norms are, yet we do not have explicit "rules of the game", and unless one is fortunate enough to have good mentors, there is no one there to teach us. We hope that this chapter will help in clarifying these "rules" and objectify an understanding of "the game".

To learn more about the logic underpinning authors' courses of action we asked academic scholars in the management and behavioral sciences (from both UK and the US) the following question: *"Can you indicate the main reasons for your 'most likely' options?".*

Of the large sample of respondents, 192 provided a detailed answer to the above open question. These were content analyzed to determine any order and logic in the reasoning presented. While the answers varied, we could identify two dimensions according to which the respondents based their decision. One dimension was about the "why" – what is the rationale for their decisions. Here two categories emerged: Some of the justification was relating to the instrumental reasoning, and the other to the moral or ethical aspect of the decision. The other dimension we identified was concerned with the reference entity, i.e., whether the argument was individually-oriented, or was it constructed around the whole community.

We label the dimension represented along the vertical axis (see figure 13.1) "*rationale*". This dimension distinguishes between an **instrumental** reasoning and an **ethical** one. The other dimension, represented along the horizontal axis, we label "*agency*". That dimension distinguishes between a reasoning centering on the **individual**, from one focusing on the scholarly **community** as a whole. Combined, the two-dimensional matrix of arguments generated a taxonomy comprising four quadrants, as presented in Figure 13.1.

Below we present an explanatory note for each of the four quadrants. We added certain indicative quotes for each category. Responses are given verbatim, without editing. In each category we also list indicative non-compliance statements (i.e., why people would not R&R in

AGENCY RATIONALE	Self centered	Community centered
Instrumental	Q1 *"This is the most cost-effective way to publish. I aim to maximize my research output."*	Q2 *"This is how the system works, and I have to comply. These are the 'rules of the game'* *(though I may try to beat them)"*
Ethical	Q4 *"Peer reviewing makes me a better researcher, improves the paper, and enhances scholarship."*	Q3 *"This is 'fair-play', the decent thing to do"*

Figure 13.1   A Taxonomy of "Revise & Resubmit" Reasoning

relation to this quadrant logic). In many cases respondents gave more than one account for their reasoning, which, sometimes, fell into two quadrants. The largest number of replies fell in Q1 (c. 100), followed by Q2 (c. 50), Q3 (c. 30) and just below 20 in Q4.

Quadrant 1: "what's best for me" – self-centered/instrumental argument

Responses under this label stressed practical arguments, self-centered and calculated. In terms of number of responses, this was the largest category.

Examples:

> "A bird (almost) in hand is worth two in the bush!"

> "The odds of an 'accept' after a R&R, at the original journal, are greater than sending it to a totally new journal" ... "Transaction costs are very high. If the comments are sensible, the best course is to resubmit to same journal".... "I believe the greatest probability of ultimate acceptance is with the journal that has indicated some interest in the paper"... "Probability of acceptance is higher at the original journal with the original reviewers; although it depends on how 'major' the revision is"... "Don't change horses in the middle of the stream"... "Sending it off to a different journal might raise additional objections and further delay publication"... "Advice from one journal may not transfer to views for another" ... "You publish where you do best."

A number of scholars commentated about the worth (or otherwise) of the required time investment: "R&R to original journal reduces 'time to publication'..." "why waste the time already invested in a piece..."

In contrast, among the reasons listed for opting not to R&R to original journal:

> "A major revision merely indicates a serious limitation and may be too difficult to accomplish"... "If paper needs major revision and journal is 'average' it may not be worth the time and effort to fix paper"... "Inertia – the sense that I would rather find a journal that would publish what I want to write, than publish what the journal wants me to write" ... "Given that the request for major revisions may be a polite form of refusals, I would try to take on board any criticisms and opt for a less good journal in order to have greater certainty of publication."

Quadrant 2: "Comply with the system" – community-centered/ instrumental argument

Respondents in this category emphasized the acceptance of the logic of the academic community of practice:

> *"Revise and resubmit is standard editorial response. I would expect nothing else!"*

> …*"I have normally found (R&R to original journal) to be the requirement of the review processes with which I have been concerned (i.e., they have to find something wrong!) so this is part of the rule in getting published"*…. *"this is part of the refereeing process, i.e., it is almost inbuilt that referees will ask for some changes"*…*"I feel that I have no option other than to do what the reviewers and editor request, no matter how onerous, intrusive, and at times, plain ridiculous"*… *"To resubmit as it is, even to another journal, is foolish – as the same reviewers may see it and reject outright a second time."*

Why <u>not</u> R&R:

> *"A major revision might move the paper from its original intent"*… *"A major revision merely indicates a serious limitation and may be too difficult to accomplish"*… *"The request for major revisions may be a polite form of refusal"*… *"To get a second opinion without having to do further work."* *"Some referees' views/comments are against the journal purpose, and is more his/her personal opinion."*

Many of the non-compliance comments in Quadrants 1 and 2 seem to imply that the editors were not clear in their instructions on what to focus on in the R&R and that the level of risk (acceptance chances) was too ambiguous. Common judgments such as "fatal flaw", "insufficient analysis", "sample error", "inadequate hypothesis" may be overemployed and under-specified. The common term "major revision" may itself be too vague.

Quadrant 3: "Fair Play" – community-centered/ethical argument

The stress in the following arguments is on the "common good": a community of practice perspective combined with a moral position on the mission of scholarship:

"It is fair (the decent thing to do!)"... "If it's a reputable journal I'd have confidence in the comments of the reviews and in the judgement of the editors".... "Belief that the editorial revisions improve the paper's content and quality"... "It is only fair to re-submit to the journal that has invested the time and effort..." "Where the changes required are minor, I would always comply because I think this is part of the referee process, i.e., it is almost inbuilt that referees will ask for some changes. I don't believe in being precious about minor comments or criticisms – we all have to be able to accept criticism, if not, this whole 'game' would be too depressing! Where more major changes are required, my general philosophy is one of not giving up, especially if you and possibly your co-author(s) believe in the paper. It's important to have self-belief and not to be deterred by what, after all, is a subjective judgement. That said, it is also important to listen to and to hear criticism and to learn by it – this is something we can all benefit from no matter how long we have been playing this game."

Why <u>not</u> R&R:

"This is predominantly a political game"... "We are playing and as a result I have little respect for many supposedly impartial referees"... "Major revisions required often highlight genuine improvements – but also may reflect quirky views (and vested interests) of inappropriate reviewers"... "Publication can be a 'lucky draw'."

Quadrant 4: "The developmental process improves the paper" – self-centered/ethical argument:

In this category, arguments link self-benefit with a position on the moral economy embedded in the publishing relationship.

"In my experience, reviewers usually provide valuable feedback which I take careful note of."

"Would prefer to resubmit and rework if I can appreciate the changes required: I see this as part of self development and learning". ... "No paper is perfect, so I would appreciate the referee's comments as developmental"... "By submitting to [a] journal you have entered into a relationship" ... "I feel that authors/editors have some moral obligations to each other"

Why <u>not</u> R&R:

> *"I have very little faith in the refereeing process" ... "many referees' comments clearly protect vested interests"... "Many reviewers do not fully understand the papers they are asked to review"... "There is a lot of 'back scratching' going on, despite what is said about blind refereeing."*

Many of the non-compliance comments in Quadrants 3 and 4 refer to lack of confidence in the blind-review system. This problem and possible solutions are the focus of chapter 7. As a self-governed framework based on widely assumed similarity of purpose and ethical code of practice, these comments are a warning shot at the core of the peer-review system. We may not be doing enough to sustain the confidence of the publishing community in the transparency and impartiality of the reviewing process.

Discussion

Publishing is a key element in the process of academic knowledge creation (Chia, 2003; Huff, 1999). The "sense making" (Weick, 1995; 2001) of publishing thus drives the development of a rationale that justifies R&R choices and guides respective actions. The review process is an essential part of the process, influencing not only the formal aim of knowledge creation, but also the ego of academic scholars (Miner, 1997, 2003). In relation to both the system and the individuals, the role of the reviewer may be depicted nicely by the garden metaphor (Baruch, 2004), where the reviewer, like a good gardener, helps the best plants to flourish and develop, while weeding out those with less prospects to blossom.

In this chapter we tried to sort out the cosmology of the delicate and critical stage in the publishing process, when authors face a request for R&R. Consequently the options and derived responsibilities of the reviewer were highlighted. The reviewer should be aware of and acknowledge their role within the process of knowledge creation and their derived responsibilities. The key task of the reviewer in this context is to increase the likelihood for a positive response to an R&R invitation. Would the reviewer to bear this in mind, they would take note of the following:

- Are their demands actionable (Lee, 1995), that is doable, reasonable (in terms of scope and time)?

- Are they posing a persuasive argument that will not put the author off?
- Are they not trying to push their own research agenda and other biases?
- Is the communication positive? Imagining the recipients, what should be said and in which manner, so that authors are encouraged to respond positively?

Lastly, between the reviewer and the author stands the editor. Your task is to convince the editor that the manuscript is worthwhile publishing (subject to revision), if you believe in it. How then, would you word your critique to achieve that?

- Clarify expectations with the editor – if they are clearly articulated in the guidelines to reviewers (for example, some editors prefer a decisive indication by the reviewer – accept/reject, whereas others wish to have the critical review, and make the decision themselves).
- Avoid confusion: are you recommending acceptance? Rejection? Will the editor make an informed, learned decision based on your recommendation? Is it an absolute rejection, a rejection but "leaving an open door", request for a major R&R (but generating a feeling that it would be better not to), a genuine request for a major revision, a genuine request for minor revision. The distinction might be critical for the publishability of the manuscript you were entrusted to review.

In this chapter we offered a conceptual and empirical analysis of authors' responses to a request to R&R. We found a diversity of practices, though the majority of responses almost unanimously suggested an adherence to and acceptance of the "rules of the game" of R&R, indicating a clearly consensual community of practice (*habitus*). Nevertheless, there are significant deviations from the rule, and while a quality review would reduce such threats, awareness and action are called for on the reviewer side. We offered a number of ideas and guidelines, and hope that these will contribute to the quality of the review and the legitimization of the review process, in line with the aim of this book.

References

Baruch, Y. (2004). *Managing Careers: Theory and Practice*. Harlow: FT-Prentice Hall/Pearson Education.

Bourdieu, P. (1977). *Outline of a Theory of Practice*. Cambridge: Cambridge University Press.

Bourdieu, P. (1990). *The Logic of Practice*. Cambridge: Polity Press.

Chia, R. (2003). From knowledge-creation to the perfecting of action: Tao, Basho and pure experience as the ultimate ground of knowing. *Human Relations*, 56, 953–81.

Gerrans, P. (2005). Tacit knowledge, rule following and Pierre Bourdieu's philosophy of social science. *Anthropological Theory*, 5(1), 53–74.

Huff, A. S. (1999). *Writing for Scholarly Publication*. Thousand Oak, CA: Sage.

Lee, R. M. (1995). *Doing Research on Sensitive Topics*. London: Sage.

Miner, J. B. (1997). Participating in profound change. *Academy of Management Journal*, 40, 1421–9.

Miner, J. B. (2003). Commentary on Arthur Bedeian's "The manuscript review process: The proper roles of authors, references, and editors." *Journal of Management Inquiry*, 12, 339–43.

Simon, H. A. (1957). *Models of man: Social and rational*. NY: Wiley.

Weick, K. (1995). *Sensemaking in organizations*. Thousand Oaks, CA: Sage.

Weick, K. (2001). *Making sense of the organization*. Malden, MA: Blackwell.

14

Communicating More Effectively with Editors: Strategies for Authors and Reviewers

Daniel C. Feldman

When I was a doctoral student and a young faculty member, I dreaded dealing with editors because I was afraid I would inadvertently do or say the wrong thing. And, because I attributed to editors great power over my career, I worried about the consequences of any misstep on my part. Those of us who got their doctoral degrees in the 1970s and 1980s, before e-mail communication became commonplace, will remember the "heft test" of a getting a decision letter from an editor in the mail and debating whether thick was good (like it used to be for college admissions letters) or bad (because editors needed 30 pages to convey all their criticisms to us).

Now that I am on the other side of the table as editor of *Journal of Management*, I realize that I wasted a worry. Editors are in the business of trying to publish articles, not reject them, and editors are typically more lenient than reviewers in their judgments. Perhaps more importantly, after years of being beaten up as authors themselves, editors are usually quite empathic to the unhappiness authors feel when getting negative feedback, to the frustration authors feel when getting tossed about by reviewers, and to the anxiety authors feel when important tenure and promotion decisions hang in the balance.

Over the past three years, particularly in the context of conducting doctoral student and junior faculty consortia, I've received many questions about when and how authors should communicate with editors. The frequency of such questions makes me realize that the tacit knowledge senior faculty have accumulated over the years on this topic is not as obvious to new entrants into our field, who are supposed to somehow "pick it up" through some vague socialization process along the way.

What I thought might be instructive here is providing some fairly specific recommendations about how to most effectively communicate with editors. Obviously, there will be some style differences across journals and editors in our field, but by and large I think most editors at most journals in the organizational sciences would agree with the basic principles outlined below. First, I address the communications between authors and editors; then, I address the communications between reviewers and editors. Reviewers play an integral role in editors' communications with authors and, consequently, the effectiveness of their involvement in the review process creates both opportunities and constraints on how editors converse with authors.

Authors communicating with editors

For ease of presentation, I have grouped the recommendations about author contacts with editors around the stage of the review process: the initial submission of a manuscript, after getting a letter of rejection, after getting a revise-and-resubmit letter, when submitting a revision, and bringing the process to closure.

Time of submission

1. It is perfectly reasonable to write an editor to inquire if a topic is appropriate for a journal, particularly if an author feels his/her topic somehow falls between the cracks of a couple of outlets. However, it is also a good idea to first check through the past couple of years of a journal's issues to see if a topic is one for which the journal has some affinity. If authors can't find any articles on their topic in a particular journal, then that's an early warning system that they might want to consider sending their paper elsewhere.

2. What is not so appropriate is sending editors the first five pages of a paper or an early draft of a paper for an "informal" review. The workload on editors is very high and editors realistically don't have time to pre-review papers for submission in addition to their other duties. My most bizarre experience in this regard was getting a 140-page manuscript with an author's request that I go through it and choose those parts of it which might be most appropriate for *Journal of Management*. Needless to say, I declined the opportunity.

3. One dilemma authors occasionally face is whether to communicate with editors about special requests. For example, there might be a special issue deadline and an author might want a few days' extension or a few extra pages of latitude in manuscript length. Certainly,

it's appropriate to ask; an author may not get an editor's assent, but he or she is not out of bounds for asking.

4. On the other hand, writing editors about *large* exceptions to submission guidelines is not a great strategy. If the guidelines say there is a 35 page limit and an author writes that s/he has all these special circumstances and needs 70 pages, it's not reasonable to expect an editor to make such a large exception ex ante. Remember, editors themselves have page limits with publishers. Editors almost always reject such unusual requests and by and large authors are not well-advised to ask for them. Try to stay within the +/–10% range of expectations.

5. Similarly, if a journal requests a manuscript in a specific word processing program, that request is purposeful and not ad hoc; it means that the journal's manuscript processing system (and typically the publisher's manuscript processing system, too) are built around receiving manuscripts in some standardized format. Except for faculty overseas, it is probably not appropriate to ask for exceptions to these kinds of rules.

6. When submitting an article, it is certainly reasonable to include a one-paragraph description of the paper in the cover letter that mentions the manuscript's key words and statistical techniques. Some authors, though, are now submitting two- and three-page letters of introduction to their articles. In general, those letters are overkill and just slow up the process of getting authors' articles sent out for review.

7. Depending upon an author's personal style and level of debate in the academic literature, an author can legitimately request that the editor avoid sending one or two specific people their paper to review. Fair enough. However, sending a list of a dozen who shouldn't be sent the paper is out of line because editors have a responsibility to get a wide variety of opinions on a manuscript. Even more inappropriate is sending the editor a list of the people s/he should ask to review the paper. This comes across as trying to pack the jury and should be avoided in all situations; it leaves the impression, rightly or wrongly, that the author is trying to manipulate the system. It might be worthwhile, though, providing the editor with a list of people who have previously read and commented upon the work already.

8. Particularly now with electronic mail, authors typically receive an acknowledgement of their paper within a week of submission. If, however, an author doesn't receive an acknowledgement within

three weeks of submission, it makes sense to contact the editor to see if s/he received it. If e-mails don't come back to an editorial office as undelivered, editors have no way of knowing that authors didn't get their acknowledgements. More importantly, an author might be assuming the editor received a paper when he or she has not. So, checking back after a few weeks' time if an author hasn't received an acknowledgement is an absolutely reasonable strategy.

9. Finally here, although every editor I know has pounded this point home in editorials and other venues, it bears repeating: authors must communicate honestly with the editor about other papers which have been published from the same data set, are concurrently under review, or are soon to be submitted. Invariably (not occasionally: invariably), authors cutting the salami too thinly will get caught and their professional reputation for integrity will be undermined. Authors should send the editor copies of all papers from the data set already published, currently in the review process at any stage, or currently in press. In contrast, editors do not expect authors to send earlier versions of such papers presented at conferences.

When articles are rejected after first review

1. Because reviewers are encouraged to be developmental, it sometimes happens that the reviews of a paper seem much more positive than an editor's letter suggests. If an author sees a huge (as opposed to a slight) discrepancy, it is acceptable to write the editor an affectively-neutral short letter asking for further explanation. However, please remember that editors may weigh a certain reviewer's comments more heavily because the reviewer is more technically expert on a topic or has better-reasoned arguments. And, for better or worse, the tone of the comments to the authors may be significantly more positive than the tone of the comments to the editors.

2. An author shouldn't just count up the positive and negative comments in the referee reports and assume that the net value is the way the editor's decision will fall. An author might have a great theory and be a dazzling methodologist, but the sample may be inadequate to the task at hand. So, there can be cases where the decision rests on a fatal flaw rather than on the "preponderance of evidence." In any case, an author should wait a week before writing the editor and reconsider both the reviewers' comments and the editor's letter in a more reflective state of mind.

3. In no case, though, should authors "flame out" e-mails to editors when they get rejected. It simply does no good; it doesn't change

the editorial decision and it poisons the well for authors' future dealings with the editor. I only received one major flame-out from an author during my term as editor, and I still cringe in embarrassment for the author. The author swore s/he would never submit another manuscript to me as long as we both shall live....and then six months later had to write back and say "Oops, so sorry," I want to submit again. As they say in Florida, don't insult the alligator til you've crossed the river.

4. Another issue around rejection that merits some comment is the "desk reject" phenomenon. With submissions increasing at 50%–100% every three years or so, editors of major journals have to be more selective in what they send out for review. Editors simply can't send out each and every paper they receive; there are too many submissions and too few reviewers for every paper to get a full editorial review. That means that some competent, but not acceptance-quality, papers will be desk-rejected. In these cases, it doesn't mean the editor is "dissing" an author or not "showing an author his props," nor does it warrant dueling at sunrise for casting aspersions upon or sullying an author's character. A desk reject means one thing and one thing only: the editor knows with certainty the paper will not be accepted at his or her journal. No more, no less. In the long run, authors benefit from not having their papers needlessly tied up in the review process, even if in the short run it's painful to get a quick rejection letter. So, please refrain from sending letters of righteous indignation if your paper is not sent out for full review. In the long run, you're better off sending the paper to a journal that is initially more receptive to what you're trying to achieve.

5. If an author genuinely believes that he or she has "been done wrong," the author should certainly contact the editor. In doing so, let me suggest that authors: (a) do this in writing rather than over the phone or flaming out on an e-mail; (b) wait a week before contacting the editor; and (c) pick 3–4 key issues to illustrate the case rather than providing a 25-page brief more appropriate for a death sentence appellate court. An author's odds are still low, but hostile over-kill lowers the author's chances from slim to none.

6. Here are the issues that seem to have the highest rate of success with editors (although that rate is still less than 50%): (a) arguments that the authors or editor misinterpreted data analyses or that the data analytic strategy chosen is really more appropriate than that recommended by the reviewers; and (b) instances of paradigm blocking

(reviewers trying to block publication of articles that reflect negatively on some reigning paradigm or specific article). Here are some issues that seem to have a very low rate of success: (a) an author has a higher opinion of an article's theoretical value-added than that of the reviewers and editor; and (b) the argument that a particular constellation of variables has never been studied before. As others before me have noted, not every hole has to be filled.

During the revision process

1. Most editors will specify in their letters asking for revisions when they would like to know the author's plans for revising and resubmitting a paper to their journal. In any event, the commonly accepted norm in this regard is one month. Authors have been given the courtesy of revising and resubmitting a paper by the editor; it is courtesy to accept or reject that offer in a timely fashion.

2. Journals typically ask for a revision to be turned around in 4–6 months. Editors request that time frame two reasons. First, they want to keep manuscripts flowing through the queue at a reasonable pace. Second, and perhaps more importantly, they know how hard it is to get reviewers to prepare conscientious reports on papers that have been hanging around a year or longer. (By the way, I've noticed that reviewers also seem to impose higher standards on revisions long in the incubation stage; the longer the revision time, the higher reviewers' expectations appear to be.) So, authors should take the editor's timetable seriously and only request minor extensions or, when necessary, major extensions for truly legitimate reasons (e.g., death in the family or a serious health problem). When authors write editors that they can't do revisions because they've been traveling or consulting or grading MBA cases, they convey that they don't even take their own research seriously…so why should an editor? More concretely, many decisions about a second revise-and-resubmit are based on the editor's assessment of whether an author is responsive and timely in preparing the first revision. On the margin, lateness hurts the author much more than the editor or the reviewers.

3. The revision stage is probably the most important time in the editorial review process to communicate with the editor. Most editors will try to resolve inconsistencies among reviewers in their decision letters, but occasionally that doesn't happen. It is very appropriate to write editors about how to proceed when given

totally inconsistent suggestions. In communicating with the editor at this stage, authors should go through the paper thoroughly and ask all their questions at one time. Getting 10 separate requests from a revising author over a four-month period (as I did on one paper) is pushing the envelope. Furthermore, since editors will have to go back and re-read papers with authors' specific questions in mind, it's far better to communicate in writing than over the phone so editors can have the time to give the authors' questions the careful attention they deserve. Last, to avoid duplication, it is best that all the communication on a manuscript come from one author.

4. Authors should also feel free to communicate fully and honestly with editors when given the opportunity for a high-risk revise-and-resubmit. In general, such an invitation means that the editor and the reviewers don't know if authors have the data to answer unresolved questions or don't know how the data analyses will turn out if done in different ways. Before spending months on a fool's errand, it is perfectly appropriate to look at the make-or-break points identified by editors and candidly discuss with them what can (or cannot) be done to comply with their requests before escalating commitment to a poor course of action.

5. Overall, the best strategy in these cases is to send the editor a letter or e-mail that asks if s/he can resolve apparently conflicting advice given to authors. In some cases, the authors are misperceiving the amount or level of conflict; in other cases, a conflict has gone unnoticed by the editor. So, in these cases, such requests are quite legitimate. Similarly, if the reviewer has recommended a data analytic strategy and it then becomes apparent such a strategy is incorrect or not doable with the data available, it's also reasonable to inquire of the editor how, or whether, the authors should keep on working on a revision.

6. Another frequently asked question is whether authors should tell editors of their tenure-clock problems. Such requests can be interpreted in one of two ways: as a plea for mercy or a plea to act expeditiously on the manuscript. All in all, I personally would recommend not disclosing tenure and promotion issues since doing so gives an air of desperation to the author's efforts to get published. The one exception: If you are putting your tenure packet together and have an article that is in a second revision stage or conditional acceptance stage, it's fair to ask the editor to see if he/she can bring the process to closure in a timely way.

Submitting revised manuscripts

1. By and large, editors and reviewers really want authors to provide a point-by-point response to each of the main comments made in the original feedback. Thus, general summaries or simply ignoring some reviewers' comments aren't good strategies in the revision process. The first step, then, to communicating effectively with editors (and reviewers) when resubmitting a manuscript is fully attending to the letter and the spirit of the feedback comments.

2. Having said that, most editors and reviewers don't want to plow through a 30-page response to reviewers. How can authors manage the tradeoffs between full discussion and wearing out their welcome? First, authors can briefly summarize the reviewer's or editor's comment rather than retyping it in full. However, Zahra and Neubaum argue in chapter 12 that there is value in addressing each comment separately. Second, if the same point has been made repeatedly by different reviewers, authors can easily cite "see Reviewer 2, point 3" above. Third, for typographical or grammatical errors, authors don't have to repeat the criticism as a separate line; simply write "Changed spelling of 'organization' on page 6, line 20."

3. There are occasions when a separate letter to the editor (that doesn't go out to the reviewers) is both necessary and appropriate. For example, let us say that Reviewer 2 is insistent that an author perform a certain type of data analysis. The author is an excellent methodologist and can argue with considerable expertise that Reviewer 2 is dead wrong in his/her request. However, doing so in the "Response to Reviewers" that goes to everybody will sound condescending, snide, arrogant, or rude. (Speaking as an author myself, I once had a reviewer chastise me that I "profoundly misunderstand Feldman's work.") In cases such as these, it is an excellent tactic for the author to write the editor a separate letter marked "Confidential: For Editor Only" to explain his or her reasoning. Editors are aware that these kinds of problems occasionally crop up and will respect authors' requests for confidentiality in such instances.

4. It is certainly discomfiting to receive disconfirming feedback on a paper and one's natural inclination is to reject or discount much of it. My own experiences over the years (on both sides of the table) is that about 50% of the editor's and reviewers' comments are right on the money, another 25% are "quality-neutral" (that is, they neither greatly improve or greatly detract from the original version), and that another 25% might be wrong, over-stated, or off point. If

authors find themselves discounting more than a third of the feedback they receive, they should probably wait a week before engaging the editor in a debate about the quality of the reviews.

After articles are accepted

1. If authors are fortunate enough to get their articles accepted, they should go back and make sure they conform their papers exactly to all the manuscript format requirements and submit whatever materials the editor might want (disks, CDs, electronic files, hard copies, copyright forms, etc.) as soon as possible. This will serve an author's own cause well, since manuscripts cannot be put in the publishing queue until the editor has absolutely everything s/he needs.

2. A thornier problem is dealing with page proofs and publisher's requests. I know from personal experience how frustrating it can be to have an article accepted 12 months previously and then get the page proofs from a publisher on December 23 with a do-or-die request to get them back by December 25. If an author cannot make a publisher's deadline, he or she shouldn't just blow off or ignore the publisher's request. Authors should definitely let editors know about their quandary so editors can try to intercede and negotiate a more reasonable deadline. Any given journal issue cannot go to press until everything within it is in line, so not communicating effectively with the editor about delays in the production process hurts other authors as well.

Reviewers communicating with editors

Similar to the sequence outlined above, below I discuss reviewers' conversations with editors according to the stage in the reviewing process. In particular, I address communications between reviewers and editors at the time of a review request, communications between reviewers and editors at the time of the first review, and communications between reviewers and editors during the revision process.

Time of a review request

1. Probably the most frustrating experience editors have is when reviewers hold on to a paper for over a month and then decide to contact the editors to let them know they can't do the review at all. The speed of the reviewing process is determined by the slowest reviewer on any given manuscript. The editor has a choice: either go with fewer reviewers (which cuts down on the amount of useful

feedback available to editors) or send it out to another reviewer (which delays the review process for authors). Editors know reviewers are all busy, but it is absolutely essential that reviewers get back to editors within the week if they are unable to review a paper. As Ryan pointed out, reviewers who delay making the decision to decline often end up providing only "a few cursory sentences that are of no value to the editor or the author"; for this reason they do not get invitations again.

2. The next issue is one on which there is some legitimate debate, namely, what are the professional norms for deciding to accept or reject a manuscript to review. Clearly, if a reviewer has some conflict of interest (the manuscript's author is a friend from graduate school) or somehow knows the identity of the author, then certainly those are reasonable grounds to ask an editor to assign another reviewer.

3. A more ticklish issue is whether the paper "is in my (the reviewer's) area of interest or expertise." In some cases, the journals are subfield publications and reviewers are chosen for their publication records in a specific subfield (say, technology and innovation). With these journals, it should be very rare that a manuscript would fall totally out of any board member's expertise or that a reviewer should beg off from reviewing an article.

4. Other generalist journals, such as JOM and AMJ, do not send manuscripts exclusively to reviewers in the same research cul-de-sac as the authors. Here, editors also try to get some sense of how people outside that cul-de-sac view the contribution and significance of the work. Getting a well-rounded view of the paper often requires editors to seek out a variety of opinions, particularly if a manuscript crosses several fields of interest. In these cases, it might be more appropriate for reviewers to give the editor the requested feedback but focus on those areas of expertise which are closest to the reviewer's own specialization. For example, if a reviewer is in network theory and the manuscript is on networks among mentors and protégés, it's reasonable to assume the editor wants the reviewer's feedback on the network theory parts of the paper and not on the mentoring parts of the paper per se. The editorial process depends on reviewers not all being one-trick ponies.

5. If a faculty member serves on the editorial board of a journal, he or she has an affirmative responsibility to provide professional reviews and to return those reviews in a timely manner. Editors are very clear in their expectations of board members when issuing invitations to join an editorial board (and often point out the hazards of

serving on more than one major journal's editorial board at a time). So, editorial board members, in particular, have a responsibility to ensure the review process is handled professionally and to not send back review requests with a note that you're too busy to review. For editors, that excuse will fall on very deaf ears.

6. Journals often rely heavily on ad hoc reviewers in the review process and the communication process here is somewhat harder to manage perfectly. Editors may not know ad hoc reviewers as well as their board members, either in terms of their areas of expertise or their other obligations. So, certainly ad hoc reviewers have a legitimate right to refuse to do a review as long as they do so quickly. However, once having committed to doing the review, an ad hoc reviewer has an equal responsibility for preparing a timely and professional referee's report.

7. Sometimes reviewers wonder about how much information about their own expertise they should provide to authors and editors. Here, the professional norms are quite clear: everything about your own level of expertise should be in the "Comments for Editor Only" but not in the "Comments for Authors." For example, if you're sure you know the theory is bad but are uncertain as to your assessment of the methodology, it's fine to pass that on to the editor.

8. I occasionally hear from individuals who request that they be put on the editorial board. All in all, that's not great etiquette. Editors have to balance a lot of different needs in choosing a board – topic areas, methodologies, and diversity among them – and for this reason not every talented reviewer can be put on an editorial board. Similarly, many journals like to limit the number of consecutive terms a faculty member can serve on an editorial board to increase the heterogeneity of reviewers over time; consequently, even some wonderful reviewers don't serve on an editorial board ad infinitum. What would be more appropriate is volunteering to be an ad hoc reviewer for a journal. In many cases, editors expand their boards as the volume of manuscripts expands and they often look to their best ad hoc reviewers as a source of new board members.

9. Perhaps most importantly here, faculty members should be willing to review for a journal commensurate with their own use of a journal's resources. It is galling when an author who has two or three manuscripts under review writes that s/he can't review for a journal because s/he is too busy. In chapter 2, Priem and Rasheed cite a study which documents this unfortunate phenomenon. If an author hasn't published in a journal and doesn't expect to, of course

it's reasonable to decline an editor's request if time is limited. However, if individuals have benefited from a journal's reviewing process, they have a greater responsibility to help out in reviewing other authors' work. (In fact, some journals now explicitly write authors submitting manuscripts that they will be expected to do some reviewing for them in return.) To whom much is given, then, much is expected.

Time of the first review

1. On the first page of every journal evaluation form, there is space for reviewers to provide editors with feedback that won't be sent back to the authors. There are two main issues on which editors would like reviewers' feedback here. The first is a candid assessment of the paper's likelihood of ultimately making it across the finish line. In other words, in a reviewer's opinion, can this paper be saved? Second, and perhaps more importantly, what are the critical issues on which a successful revision might rest?

2. The more specific guidance reviewers can give editors about what the major problems with a manuscript are, the more focused advice the editors can provide to authors. In practice, probably only one third of reviewers provide such comments, but they are always welcome. Also, this is a good place to point out nuances in your recommendation. For instance, you might want to convey the following sentiment where appropriate: "I can live with the authors' theoretical arguments at this point, but their refusal to add control variables continues to be a sticking point for me." Or: "At this point I don't need to see the paper again; I'm satisfied with it even if the other reviewers aren't."

3. If a reviewer feels there are plagiarism or idioplagiarism problems with a manuscript, it is also critical to communicate those concerns to the editor as soon as possible. This will give the editor more time to investigate the extent and seriousness of the problem and to devise an appropriate course of action.

4. I know from personal experience how infuriating it can be to review a paper that one frankly finds ridiculous. If a reviewer needs to vent his or her frustration, the "Comments to the Editor" space is where such sentiments should be expressed. That being said, reviewers should then refrain from telling authors they are hopeless misinformed and poorly trained in the "Comments to the Author" section.

5. Ultimately, the editor is on the front line with the author. If a reviewer writes an outlandish review (too general, too sarcastic, too demeaning), it is the editor who has to apologize for those comments. Even if a reviewer has to strain to do so, it is most helpful if a reviewer can find at least a couple of positive things to comment on in a paper, a few actionable items to improve the paper, or some alternative outlets for the manuscript. The most negative reactions from authors come when they get short, evaluative, non-specific dismissals of their research from reviewers. Reviewers can greatly help editors manage the process better by providing better raw material to the authors.

6. Last here, reviewers need to calibrate the tone of the "Comments to the Author" to the "Comments to the Editor" (minus the rants mentioned above, of course!). That is, if a reviewer writes the editor that the paper is atrocious and then writes the author that the paper was very insightful, the reviewer is sending too many mixed messages. If a reviewer believes a paper is horrible but doesn't want to bluntly say that to the authors, it's perfectly reasonable to write something like "These are my major concerns with the paper......In the event the editor decides to invite a revision, I'd like the following changes in the manuscript...."

During the revision process

1. There are numerous similarities in the types of communications between editors and reviewers when revisions have been submitted and when manuscripts are initially submitted. Here, too, editors are interested in getting reviewers' assessments of the likelihood of ultimate success and the major issues on which an acceptance decision might hang. More and more editors are trying to make the ultimate "go/no go" decision after the first revision, so reviewers should be particularly precise and specific in their comments to the editor at this point in the process.

2. Naturally, each reviewer wants to ensure that his or her concerns about a manuscript are addressed in a revision; indeed, that is why editors request authors prepare a point-by-point response for each reviewer. That being said, though, it is important that each reviewer evaluate the revision in terms of what was requested by other reviewers and the editor as well. For example, it sometimes happens that a paper is stronger theoretically than it is empirically and an editor recommends that the author resubmit the paper as a theory paper. It is then unfair to criticize authors for not revising the

empirical analyses they were told to delete. In communicating with editors about the successfulness of a revision, reviewers should try to take the full set of recommendations to an author into account.

3. Much to the surprise of some authors, there are often times when a revision is evaluated more harshly than the original submission. This can happen for at least two reasons. First, the authors may not be very diligent in preparing the revision. Second, and more likely, the clarification of the theory section now makes the holes in the logic more obvious or the results of the new data analyses are less significant or provide a less compelling story. It really helps both the editor and the authors if reviewers can explain why their opinions of the revision are lower than the first time around, what (if anything) can be done to reverse the trend, and (if this is the case) why the reviewer believes the process should now come to an end.

4. Almost always after the second revision, editors take over sole responsibility for shepherding a manuscript to the end of the process. This is not done to cut the reviewers out of the loop after all their hard work. Rather, at some point not all reviewers' requests can be accommodated by authors and editors are the people best equipped to monitor the extent of successive changes requested of authors. In addition, editors don't want final manuscripts to look like they were written by committee; sometimes there has to be unity of command at the end of the process to ensure that the final product has a coherence of argument and style. Finally, after two rounds of reviews, most reviewers have made up their minds about a manuscript and asking reviewers to keep on re-reading a paper after they have recommended acceptance or rejection is counterproductive and a waste of most reviewers' time. Believe it or not, most editors do not want to wear out the good graces of their reviewers needlessly.

Conclusion

It may be hard to believe – indeed, I probably wouldn't have believed it myself if I hadn't been an editor – but editors really want to find reasons to publish authors' work. We are not in the rejection business; we are in the publishing business. We want to publish the very best articles we can, but we are mindful that there are no perfect studies, either. In addition, there is no sense of personal satisfaction for editors that comes from rejecting manuscripts. Indeed, all the gratification of the job comes from bringing manuscripts along to successful conclusion. I hope that the guidelines suggested above help authors and reviewers work more constructively and derive more benefit from their interactions with journal editors in the future.

Bibliographic note

The ideas discussed in this paper have developed over the past three years during my term as Editor of the *Journal of Management*. They have been presented, in part, in a series of editorials about the publishing process prepared for JOM. These editorials and their original publication information are presented below.

Feldman, D. C. (2003a). Sense and sensibility: Balancing the needs of authors, reviewers, and editors. *Journal of Management, 29*, 1–4.

Feldman, D. C. (2003b). When is a new submission "new"? *Journal of Management, 29*, 139–40.

Feldman, D. C. (2004a). The devil is in the details: Converting good research into publishable manuscripts. *Journal of Management, 30*, 1–6.

Feldman, D. C. (2004b). Easier said than done: Becoming a more developmental reviewer. *Journal of Management, 30*, 161–4.

Feldman, D. C. (2004c). Negotiating the revision process. *Journal of Management, 30*, 305–8.

Feldman, D. C. (2004d). What are we talking about when we talk about theory? *Journal of Management, 30*, 565–8.

Feldman, D. C. (2005a). Writing and reviewing as sadomasochistic rituals: De-escalating the punitive cycles in publishing. *Journal of Management, 31*, 325–9.

Feldman, D. C. (2005b). Publishing from the editor's perspective. *Journal of Management, 31*, forthcoming.

Index

Abrahamson, E., 16
academics
  community, 4, 75, 76, 105, 115, 231
  competition and passion, 48
  pre-tenure, 79
  scholars, 233, *see also* scholars
  theories, 184
Academy of Management, 12, 38, 77,
  90–1, 124, 168
  division membership, 107
  three pieces of advice, 91
  William Newman Award, 128
Academy of Management Executive,
  118, 174, 184, 186
Academy of Management Journal (AMJ),
  27, 38, 67, 69, 70, 94, 104–5,
  107–8, 116–17, 121–2, 124, 168,
  175, 245
Academy of Management Review (AMR),
  67, 69, 70, 104–5, 107–8, 122,
  175, 196–7
ad hoc reviews/reviewers, 38, 41, 44,
  56, 178, 194, 246, *see also*
  reviewer(s)
Administrative Science Quarterly (ASQ),
  97, 127–9, 135, 175
alternative explanations, *see under*
  peer review process; reviewing;
  revise and resubmit (R&R)
Altman, Yochanan, xv, xix, 74, 135,
  224
American Psychological Association
  (APA), 130, 168
Anderson, M. S., 76
Arbaugh, Ben, 91, 101
Aristotle, 186
Ashford, S. J., 120
author(s), *see also* editor(s)/editorial
  build trust with editors and
    reviewers, 211
  comments for editor, 246–7
  continual development, 70
  disclosures, confidential, 49

and editor(s), 3, 5, 31, 59, 105, 130,
  188, 191, 237, 246, 249
  feedback to, 99
  "flame out" e-mails to editors, 239
  innovative ideas, 135
  intellectual integrity of, 113
  intellectual property rights of, 117
  methodology, 152
  most effective techniques, 214
  motivation and belief, 135
  proper roles of, 104
  rejection of a paper, see rejection
  reputation for integrity, 239
  response to, 185
  responsibility, 217
  retain control over their work, 217
  risk-sharers, 34
  two benefits, 214

Barnett, Mike, 136
Barrett, G. V., 7
Baruch, Yehuda, ix–x, xv, xviii, 74,
  135, 205, 224
Baugh, S. Gayle, xiv, xix, 68, 156
Beach, Dennis, 186–7
Bedeian, Arthur G., xiii–xiv, xix, 37,
  44, 52, 54, 67, 70, 74, 104,
  116–18, 120, 121, 207, 218
Beyer, J. M., 12
bias(es)
  not constructive review, 178
  criticism, 114
  ideological bias, 213
  imposing, 85
  manuscript, acceptance of, 160,
    see also manuscript/paper
  methodological, 131
  personal, 182
  understand your own, 148
Binning, J. F., 7
blind/double-blind reviews, 52, 121,
  see also review(s)
  lack of confidence in, 233

QM LIBRARY
(MILE END)